RITUALS FOR
OUR TIMES

Sara Rain—
With much love in
taking part in our
new family.

♡ LisaEve,
Jefferson,
& Logan Skye

RITUALS

FOR OUR

TIMES

*Celebrating, Healing, and
Changing Our Lives
and Our Relationships*

EVAN IMBER-BLACK, Ph.D.
JANINE ROBERTS, Ed.D.

HarperPerennial
A Division of HarperCollins*Publishers*

PEANUTS, p. 17, reprinted by permission of UFS, Inc.

Cartoon on p. 137 reproduced by special permission of *Playboy* magazine: Copyright © 1986 by *Playboy*.

Cartoon on p. 233 by M. Twohy; © 1987 The New Yorker Magazine, Inc.

A hardcover edition of this book was published in 1992 by HarperCollins Publishers.

HarperCollins books may be purchased for educational, business, or sales promotional use. For information please write: Special Markets Department, HarperCollins Publishers, Inc., 10 East 53rd Street, New York, NY 10022.

First HarperPerennial edition published 1993.

Designed by Jessica Shatan
Illustrations by Anthony Russo

The Library of Congress has catalogued the hardcover edition as follows:

Imber-Black, Evan.
    Rituals for our times: celebrating, healing, and changing our
lives and our relationships / Evan Imber-Black and Janine Roberts.—
1st ed.
      p. cm.
    Includes bibliographical references and index.
    ISBN 0-06-016714-9
    1. Habit. 2. Ritual—Psychology. 3. Rites and ceremonies—
Psychological aspects. 4. Life change events—Psychological
aspects. 5. Interpersonal relations. I. Roberts, Janine, 1947–
II. Title.
BF335.I53   1992
306—dc20   92-52589

ISBN 0-06-092210-9 (pbk.)

93 94 95 96 97 PS/RRD 10 9 8 7 6 5 4 3 2 1

This book is lovingly dedicated to:
My mother, Dena Imber,
the first ritual maker in my life.
—EI-B

and to
My mother, Phyllis Pennell,
and my sister, Tanya Roberts—
two women who have always been there for me.
—JR

Contents

Acknowledgments

OUR PROFESSIONAL WORK with rituals began with our loving and productive collaboration with Richard Whiting, Ed.D. Dick worked with us to develop many of the concepts in our first book, *Rituals in Families and Family Therapy*, which provided the basis for our current work. Dick is a creative and compassionate family therapist whose colleagueship and caring friendship infuse our present work.

We want to thank several researchers of family rituals whose work has particularly informed our ideas, including Steven J. Wolin, M.D., Linda A. Bennett, Ph.D., Jane S. Jacobs, Ed.D., Judith Davis, Ed.D., and Mary Whiteside, Ph.D.

We thank Joan Laird, M.S.W., whose thoughtful work on women and rituals has contributed to our ideas on gender and rituals.

We feel especially fortunate to have had Janet Goldstein at Harper-Collins as our editor for this book. Her excitement about our work, her generous involvement with our ideas, her belief that we could learn to translate our academic writing to a more public form, her supportive direction and feedback, and her willingness to connect our writing to her own rituals helped us bring forth this book. We also want to thank Peternelle van Arsdale of HarperCollins for helping us with all of the many details connected to organizing our manuscript.

We thank our colleagues and friends, Jo-Ann Krestan, M.A., and Claudia Bepko, M.S.W., for their willingness to share their experience and insights, and for their caring support of our publishing this book.

We give our deepest appreciation to Marie Mele, who typed and retyped this book for us, did all of the detective work necessary to locate cartoon copyright permissions, and never let Evan walk out with the only copy of a chapter! She did it all with lots of humor, hugs, Italian recipes, and personal enthusiasm for our book's ideas.

We were able to create this book because we have had generous and moving dialogues about rituals with many hundreds of individuals, couples, and families in the therapy room, the classroom, and in workshops. We have been privileged witnesses and sometimes humble guides for the courageous journeys many have taken to reclaim meaningful rituals. It is their changing, healing, and celebrating through rituals that enabled this book to come to life.

EVAN IMBER-BLACK

My own family-of-origin gave me my first love of rituals and set me on a path where rituals have often marked the way. I give deep thanks to my late father, Dr. Elmer M. Imber, for all of the years he sat with me at the Seder table and sang long into the night; to my mother, Dena Imber, who taught me by example to lovingly look after all of the necessary details of family rituals; and to my sister, Meryle Sue Mitchel, and my brother, Ariel Barak Imber, who, as children, kept the magic of rituals alive for their baby sister. The form of many of the rituals in my life looks different now, but the substance that started at home remains alive. The desire to think and write about rituals began with all of you.

Throughout the writing of this book, I have been blessed with loving friends who have supported me. I want first to thank Betty Carter, M.S.W., whose professional insight has enabled me to at once focus my work and enlarge it to encompass intergenerational and gender issues, and whose dear personal friendship, availability, and capacity to shift at a moment's notice from the personal to the professional to the political and back again have eased the writing of this book. Our two families' wonderful sharing of holiday and life-cycle rituals has expanded my definitions of meaningful rituals.

While writing this book, I have met weekly with Peggy Papp, A.C.S.W., in a clinical collaboration working with families. Peggy's own special creativity with couples and families has encouraged me to think more creatively about rituals for families in therapy. Her generous and loving friendship has offered me a special vision of rituals' continuity and change by her own example.

Just prior to starting this book, I developed a new friendship with

Rosmarie Welter-Enderlin, M.S.W. As codirector of the Aus-bildunginstitut für Systemische Therapie und Beratung in Switzer-land, Rosmarie was able to confirm many of my ideas about the power of rituals in other countries. We met at a time when both of us were preparing books, and were able to give each other support across the Atlantic through telephone calls, letters, and wonderful visits. She welcomed me into her own family's rituals as if I were her sister.

I also want to thank Monica McGoldrick, M.S.W. Monica's work on ethnicity and families has contributed in a continual way to all of my work with rituals and has enriched my own capacity to celebrate diversity. Her caring friendship and reliable support of my work have always nurtured me.

I want to give special thanks to my coauthor and dear friend, Janine Roberts. I could not ask for a more generous, balanced, open, good-hearted, caring, and collaborative partner. Janine's talents as a maker of rituals that are infused with symbolic meaning and value relationships over form have expanded my vision of what's possible. Janine and I are as different as we can be in our ethnic and religious backgrounds, in our preferences for urban or small-town life, in our desire to spend our free time sitting by the fire or cross-country skiing, in how much television we watch and in our tolerance for shopping malls. Over the years of our work together and especially during the writing of this book, I have grown increasingly thankful for the similar ways that we view the human heart and spirit, and for our capacity to make use of and celebrate our differences!

Finally, this book would not have come to be without the love, support, and encouragement of my family—my husband, Lascelles Black; my son, Jason; my daughter, Jennifer; and my stepdaughter, Naomi. Their interest in my ideas and their willingness for me to take the time to do this book have eased my way. My conversations with Lascelles about the place of healing rituals in his own work with AIDS patients and their families have expanded my thinking. His willingness to enter with me into the sometimes difficult, sometimes invigorating, always meaningful terrain of making family rituals in our multiethnic, multireligious, multiracial remarried family has affirmed my belief in rituals and my wish to write about them for others. Jason's and Jen-nifer's good-humored teasing about rituals have helped me keep per-spective. Naomi's ability to move between the rituals in her two families has underscored my belief in the integrating power of rituals. During the planning and writing of this book, Naomi graduated from junior high school, Jennifer from high school, and Jason from college, and Lascelles received his master's degree in social work. We have been blessed with many reasons to celebrate and create rituals together.

JANINE ROBERTS

As we grew up in our Lake Killarney house, our ritual life embodied what was important—creativity, making things with our hands, embracing the outdoors—and seeing ourselves as an active family that cared about the world. Thank you with all my heart to my mother and father for the vision to sustain and nurture that environment and for their ongoing support of me, and to my sister, Tanya, and my two brothers, Kabir and Mark, who gave me endless hours of magical children's ritual making as we camped out and explored the three islands and woods around us. I also deeply appreciate the Litowitz family, who took me in later as their daughter and taught me a whole new style of ritual making, allowing me to value on a daily basis differences from one family to another.

Throughout the time of the development of the ideas and writing of this book, many professional and personal relationships have sustained me. Dick Whiting, in our clinical work for over a decade, gave me unfailing support to learn with and from families about their ritual life. His attentive thoughtfulness, care, and humor deeply shaped my work. Ron Fredrickson has always been there—forthright, knowledgeable, and compassionate. I will miss him. Alisa Beaver and Gail Isenberg tracked down the most obscure references, and followed through on many tedious tasks with skill and wit.

Evan Imber-Black has been, and continues to be, the kind of collaborator one dreams of, but rarely finds. Her incisive mind, far-reaching empathy, and wise sensitivity to all the possibilities of rituals illumined the whole process of writing this book. She was always available, generous with her time, and respectful of each of our unique voices. The rich braiding of our professional and personal worlds which she offered and modeled I will carry with me for the rest of my life. I could not have asked for a better partner. My thanks to her go beyond words.

My work could not have been done without the ever-present support of the Tikos and "Mutti," our family's second mother. Arleen Thomson nourished me on many levels with our weekly rituals. Liliana Sver's forays into her past, present, and future, and her migrations between two cultures, taught me anew the power of looking at things from multiple perspectives, and how imagination is a communal experience, linking people across very diverse experiences. Being joined to Li Chieh's family both here and in China is the highest honor. Putney Road neighbors, thank you for the sharing of our daily lives.

None of this would have been possible without the invigorating experimentation with rituals that my new family has engaged in with me. My husband, David McGill, my daughter, Natalya Zoe, and my two stepchildren, Jesse and Heather, opened for me the deepest meaning-making possibilities of rituals. David's multicultural sensibilities and willingness to travel with me both literally and with questions and words have enriched this book. Jesse, Heather, and Natalya's creativity and imaginativeness continuously teach me new ways to think about and see the world. Natalya's inquisitiveness about my work and her poems and notes of encouragement those last days—found in my wallet, on the printer, and stuck onto my toothbrush—helped carry me through to the end. Our newly enlarged extended family who took us all in so graciously—especially Grandpa Don—has shown us the best of what it means to be family.

Preface

WE ARE TWO FAMILY THERAPISTS who have worked with individuals, couples, and families for over two decades. In the late 1970s many practitioners in our field became interested in rituals and we were among them. As therapists, we were amazed at the capacity of rituals to ease difficult life transitions, to provide a lens to look both at family history and current relationships, to tap wellsprings of individual and joint creativity, to heal personal pain, and to celebrate life. Our first exploration of rituals resulted in the textbook *Rituals in Families and Family Therapy*, which we coedited in 1988 with Richard Whiting.

As we continued to work with rituals in our therapy, teaching, and professional and public workshops, we noticed that we were increasingly hearing from people who were longing to revitalize the rituals in their present lives. The need to have rituals that could provide a sense of personal identity and family connection appeared to be particularly crucial for all of us living, as we do, in times of rapid and dramatic change. But where were people to find meaningful rituals? Many of the people we talked to felt alienated from the static and obligatory rituals they experienced growing up. Others were struggling with how to make rituals in an ethnic or religious intermarriage. Some had lost all of their family's rituals due to migration or assimilation. People from divorced families felt torn in their loyalties to rituals from Mom's family and rituals from Dad's family. Some came from a family where alcoholism, drug addiction, or abuse had overwhelmed family functioning, and the rituals were either abusive or had disappeared. And many of those who came from families where their memories of rituals were warm and loving were trying to figure out how to make satisfying rituals now in their own lives—lives that included two parents working outside the home, divorce or remarriage, situations that were not as common in the rituals of their childhood.

We found in our work that when people were given a framework to examine past and present rituals they often became makers of rich and significant rituals in their current lives. We found, too, that rituals provided a key to unlock confusing and painful family relationships and friendships. We saw how looking at even one ritual could speak volumes about our own beliefs and our repeated interactions with those who matter to us. And we watched, sometimes in awe, as people shaped and reshaped their rituals to make fundamental change in their lives. And so this book was born in order to offer this framework more widely.

We have attempted to show how rituals can simultaneously connect us with our common humanity and with our own unique path in life. You will learn how you can use the contributions of rituals from your family-of-origin to shape rituals for today, and how you can put painful memories of rituals to rest. Our own commitment to recognizing the richness of diversity is illustrated throughout the book with rituals drawn from a variety of ethnic and religious heritages. Our experience as family therapists tells us that rituals can work effectively with differing couple and family forms—each chapter includes special issues and possibilities for rituals with nuclear families, extended families, single-parent families, and remarried families, as well as for single adults, heterosexual couples, and homosexual couples. Each of the author's personal and work experiences have enabled us to portray rituals that span large urban, small city, town, and rural settings, as well as a variety of socioeconomic levels of family life. Throughout the book we have paid special attention to how rituals work for men and for women to shape and express gender roles. Our own commitment to gender equality had helped us to examine the ways that rituals can either work for or against such equality. This book will enable you to look at how the changing roles of men and women are affected by your rituals and how you can deliberately use rituals to alter gender roles and relationships.

With this book, you will learn to use the power of rituals to maintain and alter important relationships, to facilitate complicated life-cycle changes, to heal losses, to express your deepest beliefs, and to celebrate life. The many examples of people making rituals will encourage you to think about your own rituals. Throughout the book we have designed exercises to help you reflect on your past experiences with rituals. You may choose to do the exercises as you read the book or at a later time. You can do them alone or with someone who is close to you or with your whole family. We have constructed these exercises to open conversations about rituals and relationships and to help you with practical aspects of shaping meaningful rituals. Some of the examples and exercises may put you in touch with wonderful, exhilarating memories, while some may evoke painful parts of your life. Go slowly and use this book with others, including your spouse or partner, children, one or several close friends, a therapist or support group, and clergy.

Rituals have existed throughout time—they seem to be part of what it means to be human. We hope this book will give you a new way to know and have rituals that enrich and enliven your mind, your heart, and your spirit.

PART I

Rituals and Relationships

The Possibilities for Rituals Today

RITUALS SURROUND US and offer opportunities to make meaning from the familiar and the mysterious at the same time. Built around common symbols and symbolic actions like birthday cakes and blowing out candles, or exchanging rings and wedding vows, many parts of rituals are well-known to us. This familiarity provides anchor points to help us make transitions into the unknown such as turning a year older, or becoming a married person. Rituals bestow protected time and space to stop and reflect on life's transformations. They engage us with their unique combination of habit and intrigue. The wish has to be made before the birthday candles are all blown out with one breath, and this wish needs to be kept secret from others. As children go to sleep at night, they want a story read, or a hug and kiss given in a particular way, and then parents and children say things to each other like "Sleep tight, don't let the bed bugs bite," or "Sweet dreams." Presents are often given for certain holidays, but they are to be kept secret by wrapping them or hiding them away. All cultures mark the miracle of birth and the mysteries of death with life-cycle rituals from baby namings to funerals. Celebrations both religious and secular honor the wonders of the changing of the seasons. The known and the unknown are available to us through our rituals.

Rituals in Context

Rituals are a central part of life whether it be in how meals are shared together, or how major events are marked. They are a lens through which we can see our emotional connections to our parents, siblings, spouse, children, and dear friends. Rituals give us places to be playful, to explore the meaning of our lives, and to rework and rebuild family relationships. They connect us with our past, define our present life, and show us a path to our future as we pass on ceremonies, traditions, objects, symbols, and ways of being with each other, handed down from previous generations. These can be as simple as a ritual Eveline Miller, aged sixty-two, does when she needs to sort things through. She goes to her grandmother's rocking chair and rocks. When she was a child and needed comfort, this was where she used to go to lay her head upon her grandmother's lap. Her grandmother would stroke her hair and say, "This too will pass." Now, as Eveline rocks and thinks, she repeats the words to help calm herself and provide perspective.

Or perhaps it is a more elaborate ritual such as the gathering Celeste Jemison's music group does at Thanksgiving. Each year, people gather at a different house. Everyone brings food, always rotating which family makes the turkey and stuffing. At first, the adults created, found, or resurrected from their childhood the poems, music, and sayings to join together in giving thanks. They planned the menu and the day's activities. The children made placemats, decorations, and little favors. As the children grew older, they began to share in some of the cooking and menu planning, as well as writing blessings and songs for the dinner. The adults initiated buying them small gifts to have at the table. Each year the ritual has warm, familiar parts, and each year it changes just a bit.

Or perhaps it is a newly created, evolving ritual such as the one Jed and his wife, Isabel, designed for his brother. Several months after Isabel and Jed's wedding, Jed's mother suddenly died. As his father had already died several years earlier, Jed's younger brother, Brian, nineteen, came to live with Jed and Isabel. This couple, in their early twenties, found themselves not only just married but also new "parents" of a young adult. One day Brian said to his brother and sister-in-law, "You know, I feel like I don't have a security blanket."

"What do you mean?" asked Isabel.

"Oh, my friends at school, other people in my classes—most of them have at least one parent still alive. They can help them if they're having trouble in school, or if they need a place to stay, or can't find a job. And I don't have that security blanket at all because both of my parents are dead."

Isabel and Jed thought carefully about what Brian had said because it seemed so important to him. Jed thought about the afghan his mother had made for him when he had left home and thought maybe he should give it to Brian. But no, he didn't want to do that—he kept that afghan on his bed and it was a particularly strong connection for him to his mother. As Jed and Isabel talked further, they thought, "Why don't we make him some sort of blanket?" and they came up with the idea of making him a quilt. Later, in sharing this idea with his sister, Jed found out that she had an old nurse's uniform of their mother's.

"We can cut it up and make squares for the quilt out of her uniform," suggested his sister. An older brother had a marine camouflage shirt of their father's. They added that to the quilt as well. Some old fabric was found in their mother's things. As they began to cut squares, they realized that they needed help with actually sewing them together. Jed thought of his maternal grandmother—she had sewn a number of quilts for other family members.

The siblings and the grandmother began to gather in secret, sew, share memories of their parents and their earlier life. They decided to present the quilt to Brian at their grandmother's eightieth birthday and to make a party for all of them. Brian received the family quilt—a blanket that symbolized both the ability of Jed and Isabel to take the lead and show creative ways in which they might "parent," as well as the new networks of contact they had made between the siblings and their grandmother. They demonstrated that they all were his "security blanket."

RITUALS AS LIVING HISTORY

Rituals give individuals and families possibilities to be the makers and interpreters of their lives in a number of ways. Symbols embrace meaning that cannot always be easily expressed in words. Eveline Miller's rocking chair was much more than a place to sit. It evoked safety, reassurance, and memory of her grandmother. The blanket made for Brian was not just a cover, but represented a network of people in his life from the past and the present that he could carry with him into the future. The symbolic actions included in these three rituals helped the participants to enact their life changes. As Isabel and Jed created and presented the quilt to Brian, they both *marked* and *made* the change—acknowledging they were his symbolic new parents who could connect him to resources. The activities at Celeste Jemison's Thanksgiving ritual reflected shifting relationships as the children grew up and took on more central roles in the preparation and dinner, as well as in their families.

Symbols and symbolic actions are powerful activators of sensory memory—smells, textures, and sounds. Scenes and stories are recalled of previous times when similar rituals were enacted or some of the same people were together. The protected time and space offers a chance to stop ordinary activity and reflect and remember the uniqueness of each of our lives. Because of their action and sensory elements, rituals appeal to all ages. They create special time out of ordinary time to make meaning out of where our lives have been and where they are going. But how can rituals such as these help us with the needs of today's families?

THE CHANGING FACE OF THE FAMILY

As family therapists, we are struck by how different families look in the 1990s than they did fifty years ago, or even twenty years ago. One out of every four children in the United States is being raised by a single parent today. Two-thirds of all mothers work outside the home, including more than half of all mothers of infants. Some fathers are trying to be more intentionally involved with parenting. Many people are waiting longer to have children, and are having fewer of them than in previous generations. More gay and lesbian couples are choosing to have or adopt children.

The divorce rate continues to hover around fifty percent. Fifty percent of all marriages today are remarriages for at least one of the partners. More people are living in step-families, and more people are living longer.[1] Many extended families no longer live close to one another. Given these changes, family members often express to us that they do not feel like they have road maps for what family life should be like. As Tamara Kruger said, "My neighbors and I always talk about how we have to invent each step as we go along. When we grew up our fathers were the only ones who worked outside of the house and God forbid if you were divorced or a single parent or remarried. Who knew from that? We don't have any models for how to go through this." Rituals that both borrow from the past and are reshaped by present relationship needs can provide such road maps.

In addition, most countries of the world are more culturally diverse than ever before. Intermarriage is more common, and the likelihood of having neighbors and others in your community come from a different background than your own continues to increase. While these different ethnic and racial backgrounds can be a rich resource for ritual life because they bring a heritage of special foods, clothing, language, and activities, they may mean the presence of conflicting traditions in your life as well. Perhaps you have married someone from a different religious background, or another culture, and have struggled to create mutually satisfying rituals. Or maybe you have come from such a mixture of different backgrounds that various traditions do not come forth enough to give meaning to your rituals.

But what does this mean for adults and children in families today? Here's an example. Janine's daughter, Natalya, ten, has a Russian-Jewish background from her father's side and a Welsh, British, Scottish, French, and Irish-Protestant heritage from her mother's. She has five grandmothers (three of them are step-grandmothers) and three grandfathers (including two step-grandfathers). She has two half sisters, ages twenty-five and thirty-three, and a step-brother and step-sister, ages thirteen and ten. Her closest grandparent lives six and a half hours away by car, the other seven all live three thousand miles away.

Her great-grandmother recently died at age 101—her oldest grandparent right now is eighty-five. She started day care at age two; her mother has always worked outside the home. In her first decade, she has lived in a nuclear family, in a single-parent household, and now in a step-family.

The changes exemplified in Natalya's family life have implications for how rituals can be done today. With people holding membership in more than one family, living long distances from relatives, and both parents working outside the house, we need rituals that adapt to these new circumstances. As you will discover, rituals are a rich resource for marking family membership changes, connecting people across geographic and emotional distances, and honoring mutual and differing heritages.

Because rituals are condensed expressions of many of our relationship patterns, looking at them is a good way to understand our lives. The simple act of remembering a ritual from your childhood may put you in touch with many difficult, unresolved, or painful family issues. In this book, you will be guided, through looking at rituals, to new understandings of old family relationships. And you will discover ways to use rituals to alter relationships in the present. We will share how others in these times have adapted rituals to fit their changing lifestyles. We will also give ideas and examples of how to be more intentional with your rituals so they support you as you make and mark various shifts in your life.

We are *not* in an era of the demise of the family. Membership within a family group is still the primary way in which most people identify themselves. But the family does look different. Our ritual life is a resource that can help us to appreciate the changing shape of families because *every* family has rituals no matter what their background or where they are in the family life cycle.

Families get together to celebrate, commemorate, and remember. As a visitor from Germany said after living in the United States for six months, "I can't believe what great lengths and effort American families go to to gather and share holidays and family times."

However, this ritual life is not happening just within the family. It is greatly influenced by societal expectations. There are pressures from the media as well as religious institutions that can have important influences on how we think about our ritual lives. Differences in what we expect men and women and/or children to do in family life also have an impact on ritual practices.

MEDIA, MESSAGES, AND MEANING MAKING: THE SOCIAL CONTEXT OF RITUALS

As we have done workshops around the United States, Canada, Australia, and in Europe, many people have commented on how they are looking for ways to celebrate that are free from the intense commercial pressures that often exist for holidays: pressures on what to buy, who to send cards to, how to decorate, what to eat. They are quite aware that these expectations, of course, generate income for the billion-dollar greeting card industry, toy factories, and bridal dress manufacturers. Some families we have talked to have been able to turn to various religious traditions that often help create a more internal and meaningful experience out of various life changes. But many other people have shared how they are not truly connected to a formal religious institution, often because they feel that the religious traditions have not adjusted to encompass changing values and family relationships. They, too, are looking for ways to express their beliefs, their identity, and the story of their lives.

This is sometimes hard to do when they feel bombarded by advertising messages that insert themselves into ritual making. Tom Onoff described how his seven- and nine-year-olds were insistent that they have certain toys advertised on TV, or their Christmas would be ruined. Lucia Woodward's idea, at age four, of a special food to have at the family Sunday brunch was Pop-Tarts. Heidi Glazier felt pressured to make more money to take her family away to one of the family resorts so invitingly advertised in the magazines.

Meaning making may also be affected by traditions from the past that have not adapted to reflect current values. At weddings, it is usually the bride who is "given away" by her father. When Bob and Sara Wilson decided to marry, they described how they asked both of their parents to walk each of them down the aisle. For them, this symbolized marking a more equal relationship in which they were both leaving their original families to create a new family unit.

OTHER MESSAGES FROM THE OUTSIDE: GENDER AND CULTURE

Different families have shared how they are wrestling with what messages are embedded in their rituals about the roles men and women have inside or outside of the home. As Dagmaris Cabezas said: "Whenever we have family gatherings, all I can think of is the ads or shows that always have the men carving or barbecuing the meat, and the women shopping, preparing, and cleaning up the food. When was the last time you saw a man praising the virtues of a Purdue turkey or Joy dishwashing soap? I mean, there it is in my own family. The women do the nitty-gritty work while the men sit at the head of the table and are given the best parts of the meat. Or my father: when did he last buy me a present? He gives my mom the money and she selects it, pays for it, and then wraps it. The card always says, 'Love, Mom and Dad,' but he never even knows what it is until I open it."

Women have often traditionally taken care of more of what happens "inside" the family. This has many implications for your ritual life. Women often feel that they have more say in it, and sometimes there are more links with their extended family or friendship networks. While they may have a lot of input into rituals, they are responsible for much of the work. Many men around the country have said that they do not feel as involved in the rituals as they might like to be. Some of them wish the rituals were a little simpler, so it would be easier for them to get into them. Others have talked about how the traditions seemed to be passed on more through the women in their families.

Couples are sometimes surprised to find how gender roles are embedded in preparing for and/or doing rituals. Joanie Ross described how whenever they went on a family vacation, it was always her husband's job to service the car and then pack it just before they left. Ed drove and was usually the one who decided when it was time to stop and eat. She prepared the food, helped the children to put their clothes together, and packed Ed's clothes as well as her own. Joanie was taken aback to see the repetition of these actions year after year and how they both expressed and maintained beliefs about gender roles in the family.

As women are working outside of the home more, some men and women are trying to rethink who does what of the ongoing work of family life. Women do not necessarily want to work overtime by being responsible for planning and preparing most of the family rituals. On the other hand, men have not necessarily been supported to be attentive to ritual needs. Throughout this book, we will examine how rituals sometimes reflect gender roles as well as other societal expectations.

Other people have commented on how certain holidays seem to have been taken over by a dominant cultural or religious heritage that does not easily make space for varying interpretations of the meaning of the day. It is essential not to make assumptions about what a holiday means to an individual or family. Thanksgiving can be a very different event for a Native American family than for a family that has been here for six generations and has been accepted into the mainstream culture. And both of these will be quite different from a family who recently arrived from Cambodia! Each family will have its unique ways of incorporating meaning from the larger culture. As you read this book, you'll find ways to integrate your cultural and religious heritage into rituals that feel authentic and meaningful.

POTATO LATKES AND BACALAO

In the Lieberman-Narciso family, the husband, Raul, was from a Portuguese-Catholic background and Rachel Lieberman was raised Jewish. The couple felt that it was difficult to celebrate Hanukkah in December when it usually fell with all of the hoopla that surrounded Christmas, such as the countdown of shopping days, Santa Clauses everywhere, and Christmas music piped into stores, malls, even elevators. As she grew older, Rachel experienced Hanukkah as being more and more like Christmas, with an emphasis on things such as presents being given on each of the eight nights as a way to compete with the December 25 celebration. But Hanukkah was an important part of her childhood and Rachel wanted to pass it on to her three young children, especially her interpretation of Hanukkah's meaning, which included ideas on the significance of freedom and liberation for all peoples.

Raul Narciso experienced his Catholic upbringing as unsupportive of some of the more egalitarian ways he was trying to live his life, yet the traditions of the holiday time that included certain foods, the family getting together, and a sense of spirituality were very meaningful to him. However, in his family, it was primarily his mother who did the ritual preparing, and he remembered it as a time that seemed burdensome to her. He wanted to share the preparations more equitably than had happened in his family-of-origin. So Rachel and Raul set out to create their own Jewish/Portuguese-Catholic holiday tradition that would sidestep commercial pressures, reflect their different heritages, and communicate who they were in their current life. For Hanukkah, they downplayed present giving and highlighted different cultural aspects of their background. So they had traditional Jewish foods one night such as potato latkes, applesauce, kugel, and challah. Another night they played Hanukkah games with the grandparents. A third night was stories of freedom from Jewish history and from Portuguese history, and so on. In order to express gender equality, they alternated being in charge of setting up the activities for each night. Later, on Christmas Eve, they had a big feast with Raul's family-of-origin including traditional Portuguese foods—bacalao (salted codfish) and Portuguese bread. Doing it potluck style, everyone helped in the food preparation.

Rachel and Raul took some of the structure of Hanukkah and Christmas and used it to give shape to the holidays that fit their own values and heritage. Their children, all under the age of six when they began this, accepted it as how the holidays were done, and felt connected to each of their parents.

BRAIDING CONTINUITY AND CHANGE

Rituals embrace both constancy and transformation. At a funeral, knowing that prayers will be said for the person who has died, that his or her life will be honored in some way, and that the group has gathered to collectively express their sorrow gives people support to accept a loss in their lives. At the same time, these more structured parts of rituals need to be balanced with some open parts so the ritual reflects the unique transformations of the individual, group, or family.

When Elinor and Bill Walters celebrate their wedding anniversary, they return each year to the restaurant where they had their first date. This is an agreed-upon structured part of their anniversary ritual. They also order the same meal they ate on that first night. When they pour the same Chardonnay, they laugh, remembering how Bill pretended he knew fine wines on their first date but had actually never ordered wine before in his life. All of this repeated action connects them to the past, and to what was a very special night in their lives. And then they exchange their gifts. "Many years ago, we decided to give each other little gifts—one to express symbolically what the past year has meant, one to say what issues we need to pay attention to now, and one to say what we hope for in the new year," said Bill. This gift exchange is the open and ever-changing part of their ritual.

Idell L'Tainen had cancer for five years. When it was clear she was going to die, she designed her own funeral service, following the structured parts of any funeral while including special open parts. The music Idell chose, the people she asked to speak, the words she wrote to friends and family who had gathered there—all communicated Idell's distinct life story. The service began with an opening prayer, similar to most funerals. Then Idell's closest friend who had sat with her during her last week of life told the community of family and friends what it had been like to plan this service with Idell, and about her courage as she faced her own death. Idell's husband spoke, imparting her final message to everyone. Those who gathered felt as if Idell were with them there in the church and each had a chance to say a genuine good-bye to her. The familiar aspects of a funeral combined here with the open parts to allow what was distinctive about Idell to emerge. The funeral became a celebration of Idell's life, demonstrating in words and action that she was a woman who cared deeply about what came after her.

Symbols and symbolic actions in our rituals are also open to multiple interpretations. This allows for the braiding of continuity and change.

The seemingly simple act of decorating a Christmas tree connected Bonnie Johnson to years and years of warm and loving memories of her family. She was bewildered when her husband, Doug, left the house each year while she decorated the tree, at first alone and later with their children. Ten years into their marriage, Bonnie refused to go through this again. She demanded some explanation and Doug finally told her how each year as a child his father would talk for weeks about the fabulous Christmas tree they were going to get, and each year he would get too busy with work and would bring home a scrawny, leftover tree late on Christmas Eve. "When I watch you decorate that tree, all I can see is the disappointment on my mother's face and all I can hear is the inevitable fighting between them," Doug told Bonnie. The symbol of the Christmas tree and the symbolic action of decorating it held very different connections to the past for this couple. After Bonnie heard Doug's story, she quietly remarked, "This is a different tree, Doug— let's make this a different Christmas," letting him know that this same symbol could now hold meanings about their own family and about change.

Rituals are consistent reminders to us of life's inevitable movement through time. After Sara Marks and her husband, Joe, divorced, she did not feel like cooking as much without another adult to help, plan food shopping, and cook. Also, she and her three children found that when they sat around the dining room table they were all reminded of when Dad used to be there eating with them—it was a time when he was particularly missed. They slipped into eating more premade meals such as frozen dinners and canned or snack foods, often sitting in the other room in front of the TV—anything not to be reminded of their previous mealtime routines. Over time, Sara became uncomfortable with this and realized they needed mealtime rituals that observed who they were as a changed family unit, not one that avoided how they were organized before. So, with the help of her children, they began to change their mealtimes. First, they changed the dining area around, shifting the table and removing the extra chair. They renegotiated who would help with the cooking and cleanup so Sara had more help. They talked about how they were all particularly reminded of their father's absence at the table, and openly acknowledged the unspoken feelings of loss.

Rituals' ability to embrace both continuity and change is found in all rituals from simple daily ones such as meals and bedtimes, to family traditions such as birthdays and anniversaries, to holiday celebrations like the Fourth of July and New Year's Eve, and life-cycle rituals including baby naming, graduations, marriage, retirement, and funerals.

The Four Types of Rituals

DAY-TO-DAY ESSENTIALS:
EATING, SLEEPING, HELLO, AND GOOD-BYE

Zoe, seven, always takes fuzzy Bear-Bear to sleep with her at night. And there is the reading of a story and good-night hugs and kisses. The door has to be left open just so, and Bear-Bear is slipped under her arm and cuddled close.

When Carol, ten, and her brother, Jim, twelve, and sister, Susan, fourteen, set the table, they know that their parents want to sit next to each other. Each child generally sits in the same place, too. Eating begins when all are at the table. At special occasions blessings are given, or hands are held together around the table for a few moments.

Joseph Collins and Peter Korn make sure to protect twenty minutes every evening to talk about their day. Each work long hours and used to get disconnected from each other's life. This ritual provides a point of connection each can count on.

Daily rituals give us a sense of the rhythm of our lives, help us in making the transition from one part of the day to another, and express who we are as a family. They provide us with continuity and security over time as we know that our spouse or child will give us a hug and wish us a good day each morning as we say good-bye, or that the kitchen cleanup will be done each night by someone who did not do the cooking. We need this familiarity in order to feel connected, and so that family members are not spending a lot of time each day renegotiating interactions such as when to begin eating, or whether or not the TV can be on during dinner.

These are not just routines. They are meaningful actions, often including symbols that can express far more than words. For instance, Zoe's Bear-Bear that she sleeps with is more than just a very loved stuffed animal. He is a symbol of both generational connections and continuity. He was given to Zoe by her grandmother when she was seven weeks old. Zoe loves to hear the story of how she flailed her arms in excitement when her grandma first gave him to her. Bear-Bear also accompanies Zoe when she sleeps in her two different beds in two different homes. As a child of divorced parents, she goes back and forth between her mother's and her father's home. Bear-Bear is always with her as part of her bedtime ritual, providing a link not only with her grandparents but also between her different families. Symbols in your daily rituals may express feelings, thoughts, relationships, and values.

Where people sit at the table, when they are served, what role they take on in food preparation often tells a lot about how people are connected in a family. In the Isaacson family, the father sits at the "head" of the table, is served first so as to have his pick of foods, and does no food preparation. In the Odo family, all members serve themselves and share various parts of the work of the meal. Life and relationships are experienced quite differently in these two families.

Because daily rituals happen frequently, they offer more possibilities for spontaneity than a ritual that only occurs once or twice a year. There is also the likelihood that they will fall into set patterns over time without people becoming aware of how fixed they are. And as a family develops, daily rituals need to be adapted to different family needs. For instance, in the Jensen family, when the children were in elementary school and junior high, they often sat down and ate dinner together. This was an important time of the day to share what was happening in each of their lives, to experience a sense of family, and to coordinate family plans. As the children got older, they were off to part-time work, friend's houses, or practices, and the family sat down together for dinner less and less frequently. They found themselves without a regular time to count on to touch base with each other, and people expressed a sense of disconnection. First, the parents tried to insist that everyone be there for dinner. This did not work, so calling everyone together, they talked about what times everyone was likely to be there, and how often they might realistically gather. The Jensens initiated hot chocolate-and-cookies night (or juice and fruit in the summer) at nine-thirty on Mondays and Thursdays, and asked that all members be there at that time.

Other rituals in families do not happen as frequently, but they are sometimes more dramatic because they tell the story of unique events in a person's life or the life of the family. Let's look at another type of ritual that does this particularly well—family traditions.

FAMILY TRADITIONS: THE INSIDE CALENDAR

In family traditions, day-to-day activity is altered to celebrate special dates such as the formation of the family (anniversary), entrance into the world (birthday), family connections (reunions), or distinct family times (like vacations). They are on what we call the *inside calendar* of the family. You will not find these dates marked on any store-bought calendar as you will Halloween, Labor Day, Passover, etc., but each family will know these days on its internal calendar and will often write them in on a printed calendar. People outside of the family do not necessarily know these dates unless there is some "advertisement" from family members.

There are common symbols and symbolic actions that are found across families to celebrate traditions such as having cakes, giving presents or flowers, sharing special foods, or going to a significant location. But these customs have a lot of flexibility so they can be adapted to the unique situation of each family. You are not *expected* to dye eggs on an anniversary, or set off firecrackers for a birthday. There is also some fluidity about moving dates and times for marking these events. For instance, a child's birthday will often be moved from its actual day to a weekend to make it easier to invite others to share it, or a fiftieth-wedding-anniversary celebration will be held in the summer (even though the actual anniversary date is in March), because it is a time of year when it is easier for extended family to travel and gather. This is in contrast to outside calendar holidays like Thanksgiving or New Year's Day, which cannot be moved as easily and have more prescribed symbols and symbolic actions, such as eating turkey or making New Year's resolutions.

Family traditions often have memorable customs that have been passed down through the generations. For instance, since red represents good luck in the Chinese culture, the Jen family made up the custom of eating red foods on a person's birthday (lots of red peppers, pomegranates, tomatoes, etc.). Even birthday cakes and breads are dyed red. In this simple and playful action, the family easily connects to its history, passes on its heritage to growing children, and speaks its love without words.

Relationships are marked in many ways by who does what for whom in celebrating these dates. For instance, when children are younger, parents usually organize birthday celebrations for them. As they grow older, they want more involvement with their peers in celebrating and less with their parents. Then, as parents age, children often take on the responsibility of creating birthday celebrations for them, especially decade or three-quarters-of-a-century birthdays, etc. Couples usually celebrate anniversaries themselves until they get up in the higher numbers; then other family members often remember it in some way.

Where there have been major changes, family tradition rituals offer good opportunities to acknowledge what is different. For example, a wedding anniversary is unique for a couple and family when there is remarriage and the children have been involved in the wedding. Amira (age nine) asked her mother, Jane, and her stepfather, Ken, what kind of cake they would *all* have on their first wedding anniversary. Since she and her two brothers had been able to pick three different flavors for the three layers of the wedding cake, she felt they should have a say about the type of anniversary cake. Amira also wanted to know if the family would go back to the place where the wedding occurred. The wedding anniversary of remarried families is not just a marker of the couple coming together, but of the new family as well. This is quite different from a more couples-focused anniversary.

While family traditions dramatize memorable events in the life of individuals and the family, holiday celebrations signify important occurrences in the larger culture. The story that is being told broadens to encompass meaning making in the community. Through these rituals, individuals, families, and communities have vital possibilities to name and celebrate their connections.

HOLIDAY CELEBRATIONS: THE OUTSIDE CALENDAR

Holidays on the outside calendar provide opportunities for us to come together with our families and friends, and to be linked to the outside world with community and cultural fellowship. At the same time, people can experience these rituals as very alienating if they feel the holidays are imposed on them, are oppressive, and/or do not tell the story of their own experience. Columbus Day, for instance, celebrates Columbus's "discovery" of America, paving the way for European immigration. Meanwhile, Native Americans had been here for thousands of years.

People often come together to mark occasions held by the larger culture as somehow being important. These are often related to seasonal changes, such as the solstice; national events, such as the Fourth of July in the United States, or Bastille Day in France; or religious and cultural beliefs, such as Passover, Ramadan, Three Kings' Day, Christmas, Chinese New Year's, or St. Patrick's Day. Sometimes there are community events that are unique to just one or two communities, such as Goose Day in western Pennsylvania, or events that are only celebrated in certain parts of the country, such as Decoration Day in parts of Appalachia.

There are often more shared symbols and symbolic actions of these times. For instance, people would think it strange if a person put up an evergreen tree on the Fourth of July and decorated it with colored eggs, or if a child dressed up in a costume and went from house to house asking for candy on Thanksgiving Day. That means that there is shared meaning over time that is passed from generation to generation. There is often also protected time and space to mark these holidays. Having a day off from work or school or having holidays on weekends allows us to anticipate an exact time for these rituals. Because of these shared meanings and because these are dates that are commonly agreed upon on the outside calendar, there may be more commercial pressure to celebrate these times in certain ways.

Many families mention Christmas as being a time when they feel very pressured to celebrate in certain ways—either because of the predominance of certain religious traditions, or media bombardment about what to buy, eat, how to decorate, or when to get together. Both parents and children are subject to idealized images of what the family should look like and be doing. We have talked to many people who feel like they fall short of these "perfect" families.

There may also be ways that these celebrations on the outside calendar become very rigid and unchanging over time and do not offer a lot of meaning to the participants. Jim Taggart described how in his family of seven, even as many of the children were well into adulthood, they still had to decorate the tree with the felt and paper ornaments that had been made by them in school and in Boy Scouts. Midnight Mass was required attendance even though some of them had stopped going to church years ago. The Christmas meal was basically unchanged over the previous twenty-two years. His main job for preparation was setting up the bar. As he described it, "The bar consists of about five bottles and an ice bucket. No one even uses the bar so it's pretty pointless. My father, who doesn't even drink, insists on having the bar set up just for effect." Much of Jim's description of the holiday has an obligatory feel to it.

Kwanza, the seven-day holiday that celebrates the heritage of African-Americans, is a good example of communities evolving new celebration rituals that are more meaningful. A Swahili word, *Kwanza* means "first fruits." It was created in 1966 by Maulana Karenga, a professor at the University of California at Los Angeles. Some religious organizations have embraced it and it is celebrated by millions of families, as well as in some schools and community groups, as a way to honor the links of African-Americans to Africa. Since no American holiday enacted this link, the holiday has its roots in African harvest festivities. Each day of Kwanza emphasizes a different principle or attribute necessary for a successful harvest: unity (*umoja*) on the first day; then self-determination (*kujichagulia*); collective work and responsibility (*ujima*); cooperative economics (*ujamaa*); purpose (*nia*); creativity (*kuumba*); and finally, faith (*imani*). Since most African-Americans are not involved in a literal "harvest," the holiday offers lots of opportunities to explore the rich symbolic meanings of these values. The symbols of Kwanza are a seven-branch candelabrum with one black candle and three each of red and green, and a unity cup that is a link both to the past and among those celebrating Kwanza. We have heard people say that you cannot create new rituals. Kwanza is a wonderful example of creating a new ritual that captured the imagination and met previously unmet needs of an entire community.

Celebrations on the outside calendar offer both the continuity of known dates, symbols, symbolic actions, and repetition year after year, along with the need to keep "reinventing" them to make them meaningful. When they work for families, they offer rich possibilities to pass on the values and ethnic traditions of the larger culture. When couples have children, they often become much more involved in these holidays. The deep attraction children have to secrets, mystery, and groups of people coming together seems to invite people to think about what it is they want to pass to the next generation. Powerful memories are often evoked for the parents from their own childhood. These celebrations also provide opportunities for the adults to reexperience various holidays as they recreate aspects of them for their children.

In contrast, most life-cycle rituals happen only once. They link all peoples in their common human journey from birth to death.

LIFE-CYCLE RITUALS: FROM BIRTH TO DEATH

Life-cycle rituals are often extended family and community events where major arrivals, departures, and milestones in a family are witnessed and supported by a social network. Baby showers, adoption days, naming ceremonies, engagement parties, confirmations, Bar and Bat Mitzvahs, graduations, weddings, retirement parties, and funerals sanctify our shared humanity. As generational shifts in roles take place, life-cycle rituals are there to name them. For instance, when a child is born or adopted into a family, the mother and father (or mother and mother, father and father) become parents, their parents become grandparents, and their grandparents become great-grandparents. There is a realigning of relationships throughout the extended family. Acknowledging these times can help us to stop and understand the implications of the changes, as well as alert the larger community to the shifts and bring in their support.

At Horace Nielsen's funeral at a Quaker meetinghouse, people gathered in several tiered circles in the community room. His widow and two adult children opened the service, saying a few words about how they wanted to remember him and the importance in his life of the people gathered there. Others were then invited to share their memories, sorrow, and farewells. Some people brought music to play that Horace had especially liked; others told stories that illustrated what he had been to them in their life. Words of comfort were offered to his family. Afterwards, the group shared a potluck dinner of foods he had especially enjoyed. People organized a two-week food and support network for his widow. Each day someone brought dinner to her house and asked what other things she needed.

With this ceremony, people had protected time and space to come together and mourn with community support. They had access to each other's memories and experiences, thus creating a much fuller picture of Horace's life than any one person could do alone. Some ongoing structure was created for Horace's widow and each other to stay in contact.

As families have changed, life-cycle events have changed, too, and some life-cycle rituals have not always kept up. For instance, pregnancy loss, divorce, new stepchildren, or step-siblings are all events that are more common in families now, yet few families have a ritual life to help incorporate these shifts. Many families are becoming more intentional about their rituals and finding ways to mark these events. As you read this book, you will discover many ways to create rituals that incorporate these transitions.

Or sometimes, rituals have not shifted with changing roles. For instance, in traditional wedding ceremonies, the bride is expected to feed the groom the first piece of wedding cake. And in case you were wondering why people tie old shoes on the back of the newly married couple's car, it dates back to an old Anglo-Saxon custom in which a shoe was given by the bride's father to the groom. This signified the passing of the father's authority over the bride to her mate.[2] You may want to think twice before you consider tying those shoes onto the bumper. Because rituals are often repetitive and embedded in cultural traditions, they are sometimes difficult to change without careful reflection and planful action.

Life-cycle rituals may also not be available to people because of differences in cultural backgrounds, war, loss, or fear of marking an event openly. For instance, a Russian-Jewish family that had not been able to have a Bar Mitzvah for their child in Russia for fear of further persecution celebrated it in Israel once they immigrated there, even though the child was by then almost eighteen. Gay and lesbian couples have not traditionally had wedding or commitment ceremonies available to them. When there is a suicide, funerals are often done differently with fewer people in attendance and much secrecy.

When people participate in life-cycle rituals, not only is time and space provided to stop and think about familial changes; the transitions are also enacted. When Janine and David decided to marry, it was the second marriage for each. They decided to have a yearlong engagement to begin to prepare everyone, including themselves, their three children, grandparents, siblings, and even former spouses. Engagement is a ritual that has gone somewhat out of style, but it offers many possibilities to acknowledge that in remarriage there is both loss and connection happening at the same time.

Parents and siblings were visited first and told privately of the upcoming engagement. This enabled people to have time to rework with those close to them any residue of feeling about the two divorces that preceded the marriage. Former spouses were also told just before the children so that the children would not be caught in the middle of deciding whether they should tell their other parent or not. Engagement announcements with the names of new family members and the ages of the children were sent out to family and friends. Pictures were included of both the couple together and the children together, to signify that this engagement period included a time of realigning relationships for each generation. A family engagement party was held with rings for both adults and children, a favorite food picked by each member of the family, and T-shirts for all from where Janine and David met. Many relationship issues were incorporated in the planning and executing of this ritual. Family dynamics were considered to minimize people feeling left out, or with unfinished business, or caught in the middle. How rituals are planned and executed can be as important as the actual ritual event itself. In the planning, many relationships are defined, issues are worked through, and pieces of new roles tried on.

Rituals and Telling Our Stories

Our participation in this rich range of rituals enables us to make meaning of our ever-changing lives. As you work with this book, you will discover how ritual transmits the known and familiar through ceremonies, objects, and words passed down the generations, while magically transforming feelings, beliefs, and relationships, as the rituals are reenacted. You will see how rituals help us to recognize who we are and what we value and to come together in community to share and acknowledge both the joy and pain of our existence. In the next chapter, we will look more in depth at rituals' capabilities to address common human needs.

2

How Rituals Work for Us

THE FIVE PURPOSES OF RITUALS

Jennifer Comes of Age

Evan's daughter, Jennifer, was born with some severe disabilities that affected her capacity to read, write, and speak. During her childhood her mother watched in amazement as she took her handicap in stride, despite some very cruel teasing from other children about her differences, and despite coming from a family where high academic achievement was the norm. She willingly spent hour upon hour with tutors and speech therapists. She went to some fine schools with excellent teachers and some schools that tried to hide youngsters with disabilities, as if other children might "catch" it. Through it all she taught her family a lot about perseverance in the face of enormous struggles, and about building on strengths, rather than focusing on weaknesses, as she developed warmth, humor, compassion, and a keen sense of responsibility toward relationships and work.

When Jennifer was nineteen, it was time for her to graduate from high school. Unlike her brother, Jason, she had not had a Bat Mitzvah celebration to mark the transition from childhood to adulthood. And, because of her disabilities, she would not be going to college. Clearly, high school graduation was to be her rite of passage, and the family had lots of talks about how to mark Jennifer's "coming of age" with a ritual that would both honor all she had accomplished and send her forth into the adult world with confidence.

Jennifer wanted a party at a Chinese restaurant—her favorite festive food. Her mother and stepfather chose a restaurant and made a list of people to invite who were important to Jennifer, including extended family who lived far away, friends who had supported her from young childhood on, special teachers, and coworkers from her part-time job. Unbeknownst to Jennifer, the invitation included a secret that read "We are making a special 'becoming an adult woman' album for Jenni. If you would like, please bring anything you want to add to this album, including poems, letters, photos, stories, drawings, etc." During the weeks before the party, her mom worked secretly to construct an album that began when Jennifer joined the family as an adopted infant, and marked it with significant sections of her development, such as toddlerhood, starting school, and adolescence. Since her handicaps sometimes made it difficult for both Jennifer and those around her to notice her growth and changes, this album recorded them for all to see. When Jennifer arrived at her party, the album was waiting for her as a special symbol of her development. What she still didn't know was that the album was open-ended and that a new section, "Becoming an Adult Woman," was about to be added. After we ate Jenni's favorite foods, people were invited to give their presentations to Jennifer. A very moving and unexpected ceremony unfolded, as person after person spoke about who Jenni was to them, what she meant to them, how they experienced her, and gave her their own special brand of advice about living.

Her grandma Dena, Evan's mother, gave Jenni a photograph of her late husband, Jenni's grandfather, down on his knees proposing marriage to her, and spoke about enduring love and her wish that Jenni would have this in her life. Her aunt Meryle Sue, Evan's sister, composed an original poem, "Portrait of Jenni," and after she read it, spoke through tears about what this day would have meant to Jenni's grandfather and how proud he would have been of her. Her cousin Stacey Landsman also wrote a poem that captured who Jenni was to her and gave words to Jenni's future:

J is for Jen
Joy. Jewel. Just Jenni.
Easy to love.
Now moving forward with
Nothing to stop her.
Interesting places and people to see.
Free to keep growing with confidence and faith.
Everyday, everyway, especially now.
Rarin' to go, Jenni!

Person after person spoke with grace and love and special stories of Jennifer's strengths that they had experienced. Advice about men and what to beware of was offered by Jennifer's step-grandfather, and received with much laughter. Photographs of strong women in history were presented. Her mother watched as Jennifer took in all that she was to people, the sometimes unknown impact that her own courage had had on family and friends. And then all who gathered witnessed the emergence of Jennifer, the adult woman, as she rose from her seat and spoke unhaltingly and with no trace of her usual shyness, thanking each person in turn for what they had given her in life, talking about the loss of her grandfather and her wish that he could be with her today, and ending with all that she anticipated next in her life.

The weeks and months following this ritual were perhaps even more remarkable as her family experienced a changed Jennifer, a Jennifer who moved from adolescence to young womanhood, starting a full-time job, auditing a community college course, traveling by herself, making new friends, and relating on a level previously unseen.

This ritual contained all of the elements of how rituals work for us. Jennifer's "Coming of Age" ritual involved *relating*, the shaping, expressing, and maintaining of important relationships. People gathered who were seldom together in one place, including extended family who lived in different parts of the country. Established relationships were reaffirmed and new relationship possibilities opened. The ritual included *changing*, the making and marking of transitions for self and others. Jennifer's change from a teenager to a young woman was both marked and, in fact, made. Her mother and stepfather changed, too, from the parents of a teen to the parents of a young adult. *Healing*, the recovery from loss, occurred through the special tributes to Jennifer's grandfather, who had died four years earlier, enabling a new kind of healing. The ritual included *believing*, the voicing of beliefs and the making of meaning. Thus each person gave voice to deeply held beliefs about life and helped Jennifer to create new meaning about what she had achieved in the face of her disabilities. Finally, *celebrating*, the expression of deep joy and the honoring of life with festivity, marked this ritual as everyone celebrated Jenni's accomplishments and her very being.

As you look at rituals in your life, you will find that they function in your individual development and in your interactions with others to enable *relating, changing, healing, believing,* and *celebrating*, which are, in fact, major themes in all human existence. Any given ritual, whether it be a daily ritual, a special tradition, a holiday celebration, or a life-cycle ritual, naturally may contain one or more of these elements. A particular ritual can be shaped and reshaped to include aspects that you deem necessary.

Relating: Shaping, Expressing, and Maintaining Relationships

All human systems must deal with relating, including questions of who is in and who is out, who belongs, who decides who belongs, who is close to whom, and who is distant. Rituals can help us to *see* aspects of our relationships and enable us to rework relationship patterns, rules, roles, and opportunities. They allow us to preserve human ties, even during times of intense turmoil. The relating aspect of rituals occurs daily during meals when seating arrangements, allowable topics, and allowable emotions metaphorically define and redefine family relationships. Who gets invited, who chooses to actually attend, and who is left out of any given ritual is, of course, an implicit comment on relationships. Where a given ritual is held—for instance, at whose home Christmas dinner occurs each year—may tell you a lot about who holds power or influence in family networks.

In the 1990 film *Avalon*, changing family relationships are poignantly portrayed through three different Thanksgivings. In the first, the entire extended family, including many aunts, uncles, and cousins, is present. The oldest generation reminisces about their migration to America, telling stories about their now-dead father. The middle generation laughs and makes fun of these stories. The youngest generation simply enjoys the connections, the food, the holiday. The relationships seem warm and close, anchored in a shared sense of the past. By the time of the second Thanksgiving, part of the family has moved to the suburbs, making the major shift from working class to middle class that can powerfully affect family relationships and family rituals. At this Thanksgiving, a long-standing family rule is broken, as the turkey is cut before all of the relatives have arrived. While, at first glance, this may seem a small matter, this action is symbolic of much larger relationship changes in the extended family in which distance and misunderstanding replace the previous closeness. At the third Thanksgiving, no one from the extended family gathers, and one small nuclear family is portrayed with turkey dinner in front of the television. The erosion of the entire extended-family network of relationships is seen through its absence.

WHERE ARE THE CHILDREN?

Jonas and Ellen Korba were a remarried couple. Both had two children from a previous marriage. Jonas had two daughters and Ellen had two sons. All of the children lived with them. Each one's children fought ferociously with the stepparent, and the brothers argued constantly with the sisters. Each parent sided with his or her own children, and so fought with each other. To save their marriage, the couple was seriously considering giving up custody of all of the children. During a therapy session, Jonas and Ellen described their wedding, which had occurred three years previously. When asked "What part did the children have in the wedding?" Ellen replied, "Oh, they weren't there—they had made such a fuss about our getting married and I really didn't want to have to worry about children making noise during my wedding." So this most important life-cycle ritual had happened *without* the children. Without realizing it and without intending it, Jonas and Ellen sent their children the message that they were not expected to form good relationships in the new family. Rather than using the ritual to form the relationships of a *remarried* family, Jonas and Ellen created a ritual more appropriate to a first marriage where there are no children.

All rituals have an important relationship component. They help us to "see" what's going on in relationships, and offer a specific time and place to highlight ongoing relationships and to make relationship changes. Rituals to welcome babies may involve the creation of a grandparent generation or new sibling relationships. Children have long marked special friendships by becoming "blood brothers" or creating secret ceremonies. All of the preparation for a ritual, the drama of the ritual event itself, and the period of time following a ritual can have an enormous impact on relationships that may endure for many years.

When we choose to forgo an important ritual, usually there are troubled relationships among extended family members, and no one can figure out how to do the necessary work on the relationships to make the ritual happen. When parents have had a bitter divorce, for instance, a young adult may run off and get married because having the parents come together is just too difficult and having a wedding without one or the other is just too painful. *If you find that you are avoiding creating or attending rituals, this is an important signal that relationship issues need attention.* Preparatory work may need to be done, opening areas of tension for conversation and repairing relationship cutoffs, before a ritual occurs. If you are not on speaking terms with your brother and you simply invite him for a New Year's brunch, his likely refusal to come will solidify the cutoff even further.

Sometimes, however, the sheer act of everyone getting together at the same time and in the same place for a particular ritual can alter previous patterns of anger and distance. Sammy Cohen's parents were divorced, and the two extended families had not seen each other or spoken for seven years. All the relatives wanted to attend Sammy's Bar Mitzvah, however, and the importance of the event helped everyone to transcend their anger. A portion of this ritual included passing the Torah from one generation to the next. Maternal and paternal grandparents handed the Torah to Sammy's mother and father, and together they placed the Torah in Sammy's hands. This powerful symbolic action, handing sacred knowledge down the generations, enabled Sammy to know that family members were there for him, despite their conflicts with each other. Here the power of the ritual *per se* was able to hold and confine many smaller relationship struggles. Having participated together in the symbolic action of passing the Torah from one generation to the next, rather than remaining grouped in "sides" of the family, helped to redefine relationship possibilities in this binuclear family.

Changes in relationships may be "announced" silently when the place where a ritual is held shifts from one household to another. In Ginny Granger's family, birthdays and holidays were *always* held at her parents' home. When her father died, her oldest sister, Anna, decided on her own that making the rituals was simply too much work for their mother. When Thanksgiving approached, Anna announced that it would occur at her house. The brothers and sisters were upset with this change, but no one voiced their resentment at Anna for making this decision unilaterally. Grumbling in private twosomes, all nonetheless showed up. This was the beginning of a shift in decision-making power and influence in the entire family, as Anna became the unchallenged "boss" in all extended family matters.

As you review the rituals in your life, the relationship theme will become apparent to you. When people have painful memories of childhood rituals, it is often the aspect of troubled relationships that they are remembering. Yet as we've seen, rituals can help us change and enhance our relationships in the present. A carefully planned nightly dinner ritual can ease the tension that occurs when a stepfather joins a preexisting unit of mother and children. A weekly Sunday brunch can enable a busy two-career couple to protect special time every week to be together. Family solidarity and cohesion may be experienced as family members participate together in any given ritual. And an engagement ritual can mark the formation of a new relationship and create a boundary around a young couple.

Take some time to talk about either an ongoing daily ritual or an upcoming tradition or celebration ritual. Are you satisfied with the aspects of your relationships that are being expressed through this ritual? Are other people satisfied? If not, how might this ritual be altered? Often, some work on the relationship may need to be done first. If you and your partner go out every Friday night for dinner and don't speak through the entire meal, it probably won't change much to add a Saturday night dinner. Talking over how you would like the ritual of the Friday night dinner to be different, however, is usually a lot less threatening and more productive than complaining about the "lack of communication" in your relationship. As you begin to *do* the Friday night ritual differently, new relationship possibilities get shaped in action.

Changing: Making and Marking Transitions for Ourselves and Others

Across time and cultures, rituals have been used to make and mark transitions. The truly magical quality of rituals is embedded in their capacity not only to announce a change but to actually create the change. In Jennifer's "Coming of Age" ritual, her graduation from high school was celebrated, thus marking the transition from adolescence to young adulthood, *and* the ritual made the transition through the action of family and friends giving her the "secrets" of adult life and Jennifer receiving these in her very adult acceptance speech.

Given that volumes are written advising people how to change, and countless hours are spent in therapy, often agonizing over being unable to make needed changes, it is no wonder that rituals exist in all cultures to ease our passage from one stage of life to another. Using familiar symbols, known symbolic actions, and repeated words, rituals make change manageable and safe. Simply knowing which rituals lie ahead during a day, a year, or a lifetime stills our anxiety. Change is *enacted* through rituals and not simply talked about—couples don't change from being single to being married by talking about marriage, but rather by a ceremony; teens don't graduate from high school by a teacher saying "you're finished now," but by proms, picnics, and the graduation.

In contemporary American society, the power of rituals to make and mark transitions, to truly change our identity and alter our self-concept is sometimes lost. The "ritual as social event" can easily overwhelm the capacity of our rituals to function as agents of personal and relationship change. This capacity can be recaptured by careful thought and planning to make a given ritual truly into a "rite of passage."

The change in the status of an individual, such as going from being single to being married, is an obvious part of such rituals. Less obvious are the changes occurring simultaneously in all of the surrounding participants, which are sometimes enhanced with a symbolic action. A couple who never celebrated their wedding anniversary, because the woman was pregnant before their marriage, dance with delight when the "Anniversary Waltz" is played at their daughter's wedding, publicly confirming their joy with being together.

MAKING AND MARKING YOUR OWN CHANGES THROUGH RITUAL

While the element of change is inherent in all of our life-cycle rituals, other rituals can also facilitate change and transition. Something as simple as a daily meal can mark and make transitions in children, such as when they shift from being served by adults to helping with the preparation and cleanup. Important changes in gender-role expectations can occur when fathers genuinely share in cooking the daily dinner, rather than only doing the Sunday barbecue. Birthdays and anniversaries that mark the movement from one year to the next offer unique opportunities to announce change. Shifting from number candles on a cake, which are appropriate for a young child, to trick candles, which ten-year-olds usually adore, recognizes the fact of change and growth. If these rituals remain *exactly* the same year after year, then the change possibilities inherent in rituals are lost. Family members may let you know rather loudly that they are ready for change in their life to be recognized through ritual, such as the time Corie Spalding simply didn't show up for her fifteenth-wedding-anniversary celebration at the same restaurant she and her husband had gone to for the last fourteen years. As you see the need for particular changes, or as you anticipate particular transitions, you can design rituals that enable them to happen.

"GROWING UP" KATIE

Katie Murphy was four years old when her sister, Dawn, was born. Dawn's crib was set up in Katie's room. Katie had been a fairly easygoing baby and toddler, but when Dawn appeared on the scene she quickly developed bedtime problems, throwing tantrums and refusing to go to sleep until she and her parents were totally exhausted. Months and months of midnight bedtimes went by with no change. Katie's mom, Karen, was at her wit's end. Karen and her husband, Alan, came to dread every evening and their own relationship was suffering from lack of time together and sheer lack of sleep. When Dawn was born, Karen and Alan had planned to move Katie into a new room of her own, but now hesitated to do so because friends told them she might feel more isolated and upset. As they learned a bit about rituals from their therapy, they made a new decision. They first began talking to Katie about her new room. They told her she could pick the colors she would like, emphasizing that this is something a baby can't do. Katie began to get quite intrigued. As the day for moving Katie into her new room approached, they told her she would have a special party, marking her beginning to grow up. They said this party would occur after dinner on the night when she would sleep in her new room for the first time, and told her only bigger girls had evening parties. They also began to tell her stories about the kind of bedtime rituals they had when they were her age, and that she could begin to have, but only after she moved into her new room. All of this preparation phase went on for about a week, during which time Katie began to settle down more and more quickly each evening. They asked Katie's grandparents to attend this special ritual and to bring gifts "appropriate for the room of a bigger girl." On the evening of the party, they came with a new dollhouse with small people and furniture, and told her that this was certainly something babies couldn't play with. After a small celebration, during which Dawn was put to bed, Alan carried Katie on his shoulders to her new room. When they got to the door, Katie asked to be put down because "I am a big girl now, Daddy!" She put on her pajamas and waited for the promised bedtime ritual and then went to sleep. Her previous bedtime tantrums never recurred.

Here Karen and Alan used preparation for an unusual ritual and the ritual itself in order to give Katie a new sense of herself. They worked with the normal desires of a young child to be seen and experienced as "a bigger girl" to construct a ritual that could interrupt the nightly bedtime ordeal. You can do this with needed changes in yourself and in your relationships.

Once-familiar ethnic or religious life-cycle rituals can be revived and adapted to current circumstances. The Ghanaian community in New York City has worked to keep change-oriented rituals alive. A special coming-of-age ceremony for girls is held in which elder women talk and sing all day about a woman's responsibilities and everything she needs to know about men just as it would have been done in Ghana, but now they include large stereo speakers, a microphone, and a video camera.[1] The ritual has been further modified by allowing men to attend, which we can perhaps see as an action that announces other changes in the relationships between Ghanaian men and women now living in the United States. You may want to ask your own parents and grandparents or other elders to tell you stories about rituals that promoted change in life status or in relationships. You may want to take parts of these rituals and include them in rituals that you create to make and mark changes.

Sometimes very important changes take place, but remain unacknowledged. This may be because the changes are difficult to talk about, they bring up the pain of how things used to be, or no one has thought about how to mark the change. In our experience, recovery from medical or psychiatric illness is an aspect of change that is seldom marked by a ritual. Families, relationships, and the individual's own identity remain stuck with the illness label, and behavior among family members and friends remains as it was when the person was ill. Adolescents who have recovered from cancer or adults who are now healthy after heart surgery often maintain an "illness identity," and others treat them accordingly. A ritual can declare in action that a person has moved from illness to health. Such a ritual might include a ceremony of throwing away no-longer-needed medicines or medical equipment, burning or burying symbols of a long hospital stay, or writing a document declaring new life and health. After recovering from breast cancer, Gerry Sims had a T-shirt made that read "Healthy Woman!" She wore this T-shirt to a family dinner and announced to everyone that they were to stop treating her as a patient, and that, in particular, she wanted people to argue with her as they had before she became ill. Then she passed out T-shirts to her husband and children that read "Husband of a Healthy Woman," "Child of a Healthy Woman," and "Teenager of a Healthy Woman." Everyone put on their shirts and for the first time spontaneously began to talk about what they had been through together during Gerry's yearlong illness. They cried together and talked about how scared they all had been but could not say out loud to each other. Following this, Gerry's teenage daughter picked a fight with her, just as Gerry had hoped!

SOCIAL EXPECTATIONS

As you plan rituals to announce and enact change, think about what you really want to express about yourself and others. Unfortunately, in many communities adolescent rites of passage have come to center on drugs and alcohol, rather than on the new and exciting rights and responsibilities that can come with growing up. In contrast, many black churches have developed a new growing-up ritual, combining elements of the Bar Mitzvah and African tribal rites of passage, which involves yearlong study of African-American history and culture, culminating with a celebration witnessed by the community.

Weddings have sometimes become ostentatious material displays, rather than opportunities for family and community support of a new couple. If you are planning or participating in a wedding, think through the truly important changes you would want this ritual to express.

The change aspect of rituals is powerful and you can use it. Ask yourself and your intimates if there are changes in your relationships that should be happening but are not. Are you anticipating particular transitions in the next six months to two years? Consider whether certain changes occurred, but have gone unmarked. Whatever your circumstances, rituals are always available to make and mark development, growth, and change.

Healing: Recovering from Relationship Betrayal, Trauma, or Loss

In every human life, there are times when personal and relationship healing is needed. Significant loss, such as in death or divorce, requires a period of mourning in order to fully grieve and reengage in life. Though less recognized, relationship betrayal, such as an affair, breaking an important promise, or deceiving an intimate also needs healing if the relationship is going to be able to resume and grow. Rituals to initiate healing following a death are found in every culture and religion. Even less common are rituals to heal the trauma of violence and abuse, although many people are beginning to invent these out of a profound need for healing.

Recovery from deep personal crisis is a slow process that occurs over time, and at a person's own pace. While rituals can facilitate healing, or announce completion of a healing process, they are not quick-fix gimmicks. As you read ahead, you will likely be considering experiences of loss, betrayal, or trauma in your own life. You may want to review what healing rituals you have participated in and whether these provided genuine renewal. Rituals can provide authentic healing as they connect us with forgiveness, empathy and compassion, justice, and the ways that we are more alike than different from one another in our human longings for love, support, and understanding.

HEALING RELATIONSHIP BETRAYAL
WITH RITUALS OF RECONCILIATION

The crisis of shattered trust and broken promises can lead to genuine atonement, forgiveness, reconciliation, and relationship renewal, or, alternatively, to chronic resentment, bitterness, parting, and becoming cut off. Since rituals are able to hold and express powerful contradictory feelings, like love and hate, anger and connectedness, they enhance the possibility of relationship healing.

BURYING THE PAST

Sondra and Alex Cutter had been married for twelve years. Seven of those twelve years were spent in bitter arguments about a brief affair Alex had just before their fifth anniversary. Sondra didn't want to leave her marriage, but she felt unable to let go of the past. Alex, in turn, had become extremely defensive about his behavior. He remained unable to genuinely show Sondra that he was sorry. In couple's therapy, Sondra and Alex were asked to bring two sets of symbols of the affair. The first set of symbols was to represent what the affair meant to each of them at the time it occurred. The second set was to symbolize what the affair had come to mean in their current life together. Sondra brought a torn wedding photograph to symbolize that the affair initially meant a break in their vows. Alex's symbol surprised Sondra, as he brought an old picture of his father who had had many affairs. "I thought this was just what husbands did. I thought this was what made you a man, but I found out quickly that this didn't work for me and for what I wanted my marriage to be. Then we couldn't get past it." Sondra had never heard Alex speak about the affair in this way. Her belief that the affair meant he didn't love her and that he loved another woman began to shift for the first time in seven years.

As a symbol of what the affair meant currently, Alex brought the wheel of a hamster cage, remarking, "We just go round and round and round and get nowhere." Sondra brought a bottle of bitters, and said, "This is what I've turned into!" After a long conversation engendered by their symbols, Sondra said quietly, "This is the first time in seven

years that we've talked about this without yelling and screaming."
When the therapist asked if they were ready to let go of the past, both
agreed that they were. They decided to revisit a favorite spot from early
in their relationship and to bury these symbols there. During the
ceremony, Alex cried and for the first time asked Sondra to forgive
him, which she readily did. They followed this with a celebration of
their anniversary, which they had stopped celebrating seven years
earlier.

This healing ritual, created as part of couple's therapy, gave Sondra
and Alex a new way to talk about their chronically unhappy marriage.
Bitter recriminations were replaced with a sense of empathy for one
another from which could flow a renewed sense of what they really
wanted to be about as a couple. You don't need to be in therapy,
however, to create rituals to effect healing. Common to all healing
rituals is a dimension of time, time for holding on and time for letting
go. Selecting symbols to express painful issues generally allows for a
new kind of conversation to emerge. Taking some joint action together,
such as burying the past, can impart a new possibility of collaboration.
Creating a ritual together can help you to rediscover playful parts of
your relationship, such as the couple who "put an affair on ice," placing
symbols in their deep freezer and agreeing that they could only fight
about the affair after they had thawed these symbols out!

HEALING TRAUMA WITH RITUALS
As family therapists, we frequently work with individuals who are
recovering from physical and sexual abuse. The healing dimension of
rituals provides an important aspect of our work. Healing rituals may
also assist families who are recovering from political terror.[2]

BURNING AND PRESERVING TRAUMATIC MEMORIES
Corinne found that she was flooded with memories of the sexual abuse
that occurred in her childhood. In therapy, she began to create a healing
ritual. She selected one hour a day to write out the memories. In order
to move the memories out of her house symbolically, she went to a
nearby coffee shop to do her writing. By containing the memories to
one hour a day, she found that she could function well the rest of the
day. In therapy, she began a long process of sorting through what
happened to her as a child. With her therapist as witness and support,

she made a decision to end each therapy session by burning parts of her writing about the abuse. She also sorted out certain aspects of her writing that she wanted to keep. She carefully cut and pasted paragraphs that referred to her strength, her survivorship, while burning those that described herself as a victim. She put what she wanted to save in a safe-deposit box outside of her immediate neighborhood.

In this ritual, Corinne and her therapist worked steadily to balance holding on and letting go, a process common to all healing rituals. Corinne was totally in charge of the pace, symbols, and symbolic action in the ritual, thereby reclaiming herself as the person in charge of her movement in life. The ritual was in no way a "quick fix," but instead was respectfully embedded in a therapy focused on her recovery. If you have been abused and want to work with healing rituals, we recommend that you do so within the safety provided in a therapeutic relationship or self-help group. Do not let anyone pressure you to move quickly, since participating in an inauthentic ritual or a ritual that you do not feel you own can do more harm than good. Rituals to address the magnitude of abuse and violence develop slowly, enabling you to reclaim your own voice.

Utilizing the profound healing capacity available in rituals, the Cape Cod Women's Agenda has initiated the Clothesline Project.[3] This ongoing ritual devoted to recovery from abuse is a growing collection of T-shirts, hand-decorated by women who have been assaulted. When displayed, the T-shirts are ironically hung on a clothesline. The exhibit includes ringing gongs and bells and blowing horns to symbolize how often a woman is assaulted (every fifteen seconds), raped (every six minutes), and murdered.[4] Healing in this ritual comes from the autonomous act of painting one's own shirt and from the connected sense of community grieving and public awareness made with each showing of the clothesline. The marvelous contradiction of regaining power in the face of servitude is clearly contained in these hand-painted depictions of violence hung on a clothesline.

HEALING LOSSES WITH RITUALS

There is no life that is lived without loss. We all experience the death of people we love and care for deeply. Rituals whose central function is to address death simultaneously mark the death of a person, honor what their life was about, facilitate the expression of grief in ways that are consonant with the culture, and point out a direction for continued life. The danger of self-imposed isolation immediately following a death may be warded off by rituals of shared meals and prescribed periods of visiting the bereaved. During condolence rituals, stories of the deceased person are usually shared, since the sorting through of a life by storytelling aids the process of mourning.

Since most people now die in hospitals rather than at home, the earlier connection of death and loss as part of the ongoing cycle of life has all but disappeared, making healing more difficult to accomplish. Condolence rituals may focus less on the healing capacity of storytelling, since many people have become too uncomfortable to speak about those who have died. When Susan Jackson's father died, she felt the absence of true healing. She remarked, "After the burial, people came to our house. They hugged me. They ate and drank. But we never talked about Dad. Maybe that's why it's so hard to talk about him even now—we just never began." The extremes of superficiality and lack of human relatedness in facing death may be seen in the new American practice of "drive-through" funeral visiting in which people "pay their respects" by observing the deceased on a video screen and recording their presence on a computer. Obviously such practices do nothing to promote healing.

When healing rituals have not occurred, or have been insufficient to complete the grief processes, a person can remain stuck in the past or unable to move forward in meaningful ways. Even the unhealed losses of previous generations may emerge as debilitating symptoms in the present. When this happens, new rituals can be created to address the need for healing.

RETURNING HOME

Carolyn Bell was twenty-eight when she began to recognize herself as a woman who "never finished anything." She had dropped out of college, left several jobs, ended two important relationships with no sense of why she had done so. As she thought about her life, she began to see many "unfinished" areas, which she started to talk over in therapy.

Carolyn's mother died when she was fourteen. Since she was so upset at the sudden and unanticipated loss of her mother, her family doctor recommended that she not attend her mother's funeral. Her father agreed and she was sent to a friend's home while everyone else went to the funeral. Grieving deeply and unable to live with so many daily reminders of his wife, her father sold the family home abruptly and with no discussion. Carolyn missed her junior high school graduation, and that entire transition went unmarked. In her new school, teachers began complaining that Carolyn never finished homework or projects and that she dropped out of activities she began. During high school, she asked her father twice if they could go visit their old house, but both times he declined, saying, "That'll be too upsetting for you." As Carolyn looked over this period in her life, she could see the many disconnections.

As she thought about it, leaving her home became more and more vivid and powerful to her as a metaphor for the loss of her mother. All of her relationship connections to her mother were in this house. Slowly, Carolyn constructed a new healing ritual for herself that involved several steps. She contacted the people who lived in her old house and explained why she wanted to visit. She thanked her father for protecting her when she was younger, and then told him of her plan to visit the house, enabling them to begin to finally talk about her mother and their life together in the old house. He gave her several photographs taken in the house, which they had not looked at since her mother died. She then made what she called a "pilgrimage" to the old house. She walked through each room, revisiting both happy and painful memories. She took a new photograph of the outside of the house, and talked with her father about her visit, about what had remained the same and what had changed. Four months later, her father asked if they might go see the house together, and they made a second "pilgrimage" during which they cried together for the first time. Following this healing ritual of "returning home," Carolyn returned to college and finished.[5]

By designing this healing ritual, Carolyn was able to reflect on a pattern in her life of never finishing anything and connect this with her deep need to heal all of the losses connected to her mother's death. She recognized that simply going to the cemetery was not the healing ritual she required, and that visiting her old home was far more important. As you design new healing rituals for yourself, you will need to think carefully about what will work for you, which may well be different from what might help others.

In creating her ritual, Carolyn discovered wellsprings of her own courage, both in contacting the family who currently lived in the house and in speaking with her father about what had previously been taboo. Often, generating new healing rituals requires breaking some old rules about what can and cannot be discussed.

Carolyn did not express anger at her father for not allowing her to go to the funeral and for moving the family, which would have probably made him defensive and unavailable, for she sensed that he had done what he thought best at the time, and she told him so. In our experience, healing rituals seldom develop in an atmosphere of recrimination. If healing a death hasn't occurred, this is not because people have deliberately prevented it, but because they just didn't know what to do.

By designing and carrying out this ritual from start to finish, Carolyn not only experienced a sense of healing the wound of her mother's death that had been missing for so many years, she also challenged the myth about herself as a "person who never finishes anything" that had held her back since the loss itself.

HEALING COMMUNITY LOSSES WITH RITUALS

Communities or nations may also create rituals to deal with profound losses. One contemporary example is the Vietnam War Memorial in Washington, D.C., which provides an ongoing healing ritual. Family and friends who lost men and women in the war make trips that have been called "pilgrimages," a part of many rituals. At the wall, they search for their loved one's name and make rubbings to carry back home. This ritual, repeated over and over by thousands of individuals, is able to connect personal loss with a much larger community of mourners. Public grieving for a war that carried so much secrecy and shame has been facilitated by the Wall.

More recently in the American gay community, a healing ritual has been created called the Names Project. This ritual involves a quilt consisting of individually hand-sewn patches, each memorializing a person who has died of AIDS. The ritual has extended beyond the gay community, so that anyone who has lost a person to AIDS can design a piece of the quilt. Each patch contains personal expressions meant to capture and express some essential aspect of the person who died. Every time the quilt is shown, a ceremony is held in which all of the thousands and thousands of names are read aloud as the quilt is unfolded in preagreed-upon motions of connection and uplift. The choice of a quilt for this healing ritual is striking. Making a quilt is often a community endeavor, connecting those grieving with one another, rather than isolating them as the wider community response to AIDS has tended to do. And surely a quilt symbolizes the possibilities of warmth and care, affirming life even in the face of terrible death. The quilt is painfully unfinished, serving as a stark visual reminder to the wider community of the magnitude of loss.

Rituals to heal community losses remind us of the importance of giving witness to our losses as part of any healing process. Thus, the Wall, the Quilt, the Yad Vashem Memorial to those who died in the Holocaust, and other such memorials become healing rituals for us as we make pilgrimages to get there, experience symbols that reflect the enormity of these losses, grieve publicly what has been kept secret, and return to our own communities changed by having given witness.

HEALING THE LOSS OF A CULTURE THROUGH RITUALS

Immigrants often experience a deep sense of loss for their own homeland. Keeping some familiar rituals alive can help heal these losses, but it's not always easy to do this in an unfamiliar land. The right foods may be unavailable. People who participated in the old rituals may be nowhere around. And adolescent children who are eager to "Americanize" may balk at participating. Of some curiosity is the fact that an immigrant family can arrive in the United States on November 15, never having seen a turkey in their lives, and will be celebrating Thanksgiving with all of the trimmings a week and a half later. Eager to join their new culture, immigrant families may give little initial thought to what is being left behind, only to experience a profound sense of loss later.

A key challenge for immigrant families lies in how to stay connected to where they came from, grieve what is irreparably lost due to migration, *and* begin to connect to the new culture. Many immigrant families seem to try to cope with this challenge by unconsciously parceling out roles to various family members. In Gina Napolitano's family, her grandmother remained permanently sad about what the family had lost. Her mother tried to stay connected to the "old" country through cooking, photos, and letter-writing, and had little energy left to engage in her new life in America. Her father, her brother, and she moved exclusively into the new culture, ignoring grandmother's pain and teasing mother's "old-fashioned" cooking. Over time, such roles became more and more rigid. No real healing for what had been lost occurred, and the whole family experienced a sharp sense of discontinuity.

EL SALVADOR AND THE BRONX

The Torres family approached the need to heal losses prompted by their migration through a ritual. When they first arrived in the Bronx as political refugees from El Salvador, Mrs. Torres and her son, Manuel, thirteen, and her daughter, Maria, eleven, were coping with the death of their husband and father, and recovering from their wartime experiences. They remained very close for two years. The children quickly learned English. Mrs. Torres became worried that they would soon forget that they were Salvadoran. She spoke to them in Spanish, but the children insisted on replying in English. Soon they were struggling, as Mrs. Torres wanted to talk about "home," and her children insisted that home was in the Bronx.

In family therapy, they were all asked to bring symbols to the next session of El Salvador and the Bronx. Mrs. Torres was very surprised to find that her children brought symbols of El Salvador that showed how connected they still were to their original home. Manuel and Maria brought toys and photographs that Mrs. Torres didn't know they had kept. Their symbols from the Bronx included a rock-and-roll tape and a poster from a concert, and they were able to talk about music without the usual fights. Mrs. Torres brought food for both of her symbols. She brought Salvadoran food and a small pizza to symbolize both the Bronx and the arguments they had been having when the children wanted pizza instead of her ethnic cooking. The family sat and ate both foods together. Following this sharing and mutual acceptance of symbols, the family designed a weekly storytelling ritual, in which the children agreed to listen to their mother's stories of El Salvador and Mrs. Torres agreed to listen to her children's stories of the Bronx. Over time, this storytelling ritual enabled all three to express their deep sense of loss and sadness connected to their forced migration. At the same time that this ritual provided healing, it also anchored them in a new life that could now include elements of El Salvador and the Bronx.[6]

HEALING RITUALS AND OTHER LOSSES

Throughout our lives, we are confronted with losses for which there are no agreed-upon rituals in the culture. Loss of marriage through divorce, loss of a relationship, or loss of functioning or body parts due to illness all require healing that can be enabled through ritual. Specific rituals for divorce and relationship loss will be described in Chapter 11.

Finally, as you examine and experience all of the rituals in your life, you will find unexpected places where healing can take place, even when that is not the central purpose of a given ritual. In Jennifer's "Coming of Age" ritual, space was spontaneously made for further healing the loss of her grandfather. As holidays are celebrated, traditions are marked, and life-cycle transitions are made, many families take a bit of time to consciously commemorate the death of a family member, through a moment of silence dedicated to this person, or by playing some favorite music, or reciting a prayer, or through active storytelling that calls forth memories of previous rituals when this person was present. Such moments within larger rituals tell us that healing is an ongoing process available to us in all our rituals.

Believing: Voicing Beliefs and Making Meaning

Every time we participate in a ritual we are expressing our beliefs, either verbally or more implicitly. Families who sit down to dinner together every night are saying without words that they believe in the need for families to have shared time together. When a family eats only vegetables or survives on takeout meals, they are expressing values. Nightly bedtime rituals offer parents and children an opportunity to tell each other what they believe about all kinds of matters. The sheer act of doing the bedtime ritual expresses a belief in a certain kind of parent-child relationship where warmth and affection and safety are available. Many families use Thanksgiving as a time to really express what they are thankful for, sharing beliefs about what is most important to them in life. The fact that Thanksgiving is the most traveled of all American holidays expresses a value about connecting with each other face-to-face despite long distances that may ordinarily separate us. Birthdays and anniversaries express our ideas about the passage of time in our lives. Where people sit during a religious ritual can express beliefs about the value and position of men and women. Weddings give voice to beliefs about the nature of marriage. When couples choose to construct their own wedding ceremonies or add their own vows to the predetermined and traditional vows, it is because they have recognized the ways in which this ritual creates and expresses such beliefs. Adolescent rites of passage usually contain opportunities for the culture to impart its beliefs about adulthood. In Jennifer's "Coming of Age" ritual, family and friends offered her their deepest values. The possibilities for voicing beliefs, expressing deeply held ideas, negotiating differences, changing beliefs, and making meaning are endless in rituals.

If you have had the experience of a particular ritual becoming extremely routine, empty, meaningless, or even oppressive to you, likely this ritual no longer captures and expresses what you personally believe. Those rituals that remain alive and meaningful continue to connect with deeply held beliefs and values. Vibrant rituals have room for variations that can express changing norms and opinions while still anchoring us with a sense of shared history. The Passover Seder is a good example. This ritual has celebrated the emancipation of the Jews from slavery for centuries. During the Seder, the leader takes time to talk about the meaning of the holiday. In many families, others who are gathered also take part in this discussion, enabling beliefs to be expressed and explored. Variations in the Seder can be found in Jewish practice and in particular families. These differences also express deeply held beliefs. For instance, all Passover Seders include four cups of wine. In a recent Reform Judaism Seder service, a fifth cup of wine has been added. Called the "Cup of Redemption," this fifth cup is set aside for the future, for a time when all who still lack freedom will be free. This addition to a ritual that has existed generation after generation demonstrates in action the belief that the Seder is not simply the commemoration of a past event, but a living celebration of the present and future as well. Many people have told us about other changes they have made in the Seder while still remaining connected to its essential form. For example, during the Seder, ten plagues are recited. In Evan's family, time has been added for everyone to express their beliefs and ideas about contemporary "plagues," such as racism, sexism, poverty, and war. Feminists have designed new Seders that address issues of gender equality within the overarching framework of moving from slavery to freedom.

When beliefs are expanded, altered, or challenged, new rituals emerge to express these differences, or significant aspects of preexisting rituals undergo profound changes. If you are a Roman Catholic who grew up before Vatican II, you no doubt remember a Latin Mass. You also remember a priest who stood with his back to the congregation. Think about what it means now to participate in a Mass in your own daily language presided over by a priest who faces the congregation. The repeated ritual of the Mass can connect you to the beliefs of millions of Catholics over centuries. The change in language and in the priest's position, however, expresses a new belief about an active rather than a passive congregation.

WHAT DO WE REALLY BELIEVE?

When Shanna and Bill Watson had their first baby, they struggled long and hard to create a naming ceremony that would welcome their baby into the world in ways that would express what they believed about life, while still honoring their own parents' differing beliefs. Raised as Christians, Shanna and Bill had become agnostics in their adult lives. They felt enormous pressure from their parents all during Shanna's pregnancy to plan a christening. Having a christening no longer made sense to them, as they did not believe in the meanings expressed in this ritual. Simply to do the ritual for the sake of their parents felt empty and inauthentic. For a while they thought about having no ceremony at all, but they realized that this would deprive them of an opportunity to begin their baby's life and their new life as parents with a celebration that might express their own deeply held beliefs about the meanings of family relationships. Over time, they constructed a baby naming and welcoming ceremony that was largely nonreligious, and also included an opportunity for the grandparents to offer their own values. Shanna and Bill went separately to each of their parents, and told them how they planned to celebrate their baby's birth. In these visits, they expressed appreciation for what their parents had given them in life that they hoped to give to their baby. They took care not to argue with their parents' beliefs, but to express their own simply and calmly. Finally, they invited their parents to come to the ceremony, telling them that a special time would be given to them to speak their wishes, including their prayers, for this new grandchild. The actual baby-naming ritual was held in a community park that held meaning for Shanna and Bill. During the ceremony, they asked their friends and family to offer words to the baby and to them as new parents. This ritual was ultimately shaped to accommodate a range of differing beliefs that could fit within a commonly held belief that new life was precious and should be honored.

You may want to think through the various rituals in your life and ask yourself what beliefs are expressed in these rituals. Are these the beliefs you want to be expressing? Have your beliefs changed in ways that your rituals have not yet captured? Do you find yourself silently "going through the motions" of rituals just to please other people, yet remain alienated from what you genuinely believe?

You may want to choose one ritual in your life now and have a conversation with all of this ritual's participants about what beliefs this ritual expresses. Or you may want to look at a given ritual that repeats and repeats in your life, such as Christmas or New Year's, and ask yourself and your family what beliefs have changed through the years and what beliefs have remained the same. Finally, you may decide to change one or more aspects of a particular ritual to capture and express what you believe.

BELIEF NEGOTIATION THROUGH RITUALS

Rituals not only express beliefs. They allow us to negotiate differences in our values with one another. As family therapists, we frequently use a ritual called "Odd Days and Even Days"[7] to help couples to negotiate competing beliefs. You don't have to be in therapy to use this ritual. When you and your partner are struggling with differing beliefs, try dividing up the week into "Odd Days" and "Even Days." You will need to agree ahead of time that on Monday, Wednesday, and Friday, your partner's point of view about a given issue will prevail without argument, and that you will listen and observe carefully to see what you can learn. On Tuesday, Thursday, and Saturday, your point of view will prevail, and your partner will listen and observe to see what he or she can learn. On Sunday, spend a bit of time talking over what happened. This belief-negotiation ritual allows you to step out of your normal relationship with one another. Ferocious arguments over who is correct stop immediately during the ritual time. Opportunities to really see the other one's point of view become possible.

ODD DAYS AND EVEN DAYS IN ACTION: JANNA TAKES A BATH

Anne Wright and Susan Pollard adopted a little girl, Janna, when she was four years old. Soon after Janna joined their family, Anne and Susan found that they were arguing over the best ways to raise her. Janna was afraid to take a bath. Anne insisted that she had to take a bath every night, while Susan sided with Janna and frequently let her skip a bath. Fights between Anne and Janna quickly became fights between Susan and Anne. Bath time became more and more difficult. They decided to try the "Odd Days and Even Days" ritual in order to address this struggle. When Susan stayed out of Anne's attempts to bathe Janna, Anne became much calmer, and consequently so did Janna. When Anne stayed out of Susan's methods and simply watched, she learned some playful ways to engage Janna with water that initially didn't involve an actual bath. Janna's fears subsided, as Anne and Susan learned from each other's ways of approaching the problem. Janna talked about "Anne's Janna bath" and "Susan's Janna no-bath" and managed to get clean every night. What had initially appeared as strongly held beliefs about the required frequency of children's baths went down the drain.

While not all struggles may be resolved this easily, experimenting with the "Odd Days–Even Days" ritual will give you an opportunity to fully explore your own reasons for doing what you do without defensive escalations with your partner. You'll have a chance to really learn about another way that may differ radically from your way. If a whole day seems too enormous, you can tailor this ritual to fit your own tolerance for change by trying it for an hour a day. By jointly agreeing to try this ritual, you and your partner may discover a new belief regarding cooperation.

Rituals sometimes involve us in trying new roles, roles whose values and beliefs may be unfamiliar to us. A second ritual to negotiate differences in beliefs is called a "Conversation Ritual." Jim and Ellen Marcus were struggling daily over whether or not to have a third child. Ellen wanted another baby and Jim was adamant that he did not. This issue had come to dominate all of their interactions. They had become repetitive and stuck in their own positions. They agreed to try a conversation ritual, consisting of three conversations, and held the conversations on their screened porch, a place that symbolically held good feelings for them. In the first, each would bring up all of the good reasons to have another child. In the second, each would raise all of the good reasons to limit their family to two children. In the third, they would talk over what they had learned and explore what each currently felt and believed about the issue. In order to mark these conversations as a ritual occurring outside of regular talk and arguments, they chose the same time and place. These three conversations were to occur one week apart on Sunday at 2:00 P.M., a time when their two children were out playing with friends. No other conversations about this issue would occur outside of this special time and place. Unlocked from their usual struggle, Jim and Ellen both felt heard and understood in a new way. During their first conversation, Jim was able to express what would be wonderful about having another baby. He talked about what being a father had meant to him, which Ellen had not heard before. During their second conversation, Ellen talked about some of her fears about a third child that she had hidden because she feared Jim would use these to talk her out of having a baby. As they talked over their full beliefs about this issue, rather than the partial beliefs that usually were expressed, they felt much more connected to each other. Each began to hear the other's point of view in a novel way. They made a new decision to wait six months and to revisit this issue at that time. Their daily conversations were able to shift to other topics.

As a child you may have experienced a playful "Reversal Ritual." Many schools set aside a day each year when the children become the teachers and administrators, and the adults become the students. Such reversals are found cross-culturally in rituals where, once a year, the men dress up as women and the women dress up as men. As we step into each other's roles in a time-limited and ritualized fashion, we get an opportunity to see the other one's point of view and express beliefs that might ordinarily seem quite foreign to us. After following such reversal rituals, our own beliefs tend to have more flexibility. The next time you are locked into an argument with one of your children, you may want to try such a reversal ritual, pretending to be each other and taking the other's position on the issue for a limited period of time. Then talk over what you found out. Reversal rituals will likely clarify your own beliefs and give you more of an understanding of the other side. Couples can also do such reversals of positions, as can grown children and their parents. What is required is the genuine willingness to enter the other's point of view or belief in a nondefensive way for an agreed-upon period of time, and then to discuss what you discovered.

USING COSTUMES FOR BELIEF EXPRESSION AND NEGOTIATION IN RITUALS

Costumes are often part of rituals. How we dress for a given ritual provides a visual commentary on our beliefs. Children going to church are dressed in their "Sunday best," clothing not worn the rest of the week, to express a belief in the specialness of the event. In Judaism, men cover their heads with a skull cap or yarmulke to carry out a belief regarding reverence for God. Recently, in Reform temples, some women have begun to wear these same yarmulkes, thereby expressing a belief in gender equality in religious matters. Prior to Vatican II, women in the Catholic Church were required to cover their heads while men were not, expressing the belief of St. Paul that women were merely a reflection of male glory and were under the power of their husbands.[8]

How we dress for any given ritual can also express changing beliefs. During the 1960s, many young couples changed from traditional wedding garb, both to challenge cultural mores and to express new beliefs about the nature of marriage. In the 1980s, white wedding dresses and tuxedos made a big comeback, mirroring more conservative beliefs in the society.

T-SHIRTS—RITUAL COSTUMES FOR THE 1990S

In our work with couples who are attempting to negotiate beliefs with one another, we often suggest a playful and effective ritual using T-shirts. Since every shopping mall now has a T-shirt store where you can design your own shirt for little money, this ritual is readily available to you. When you and your partner are having difficulties making meaning with each other and negotiating differing beliefs, you can each think through what T-shirt design best symbolizes your own position. Take a special trip to the store together and get your shirts made. On the next argumentative occasion, stop for a moment and put on your shirts, symbolizing a new context for conversation. The context of your argument will immediately shift to one marked by some humor and goodwill. Or put on your shirt as a signal to your mate that it's time to discuss important matters. Talks with each other while you are wearing your shirts become the special time that marks rituals.

You can also make T-shirts to challenge outmoded or stuck beliefs. Geraldine and Willie Jackson found that they were responding to one another as if they were back arguing with their own parents. They went to the store and had two shirts made. Geraldine's shirt said "Guess What? I'm Not Your Mother!" and Willie's shirt stated "Guess What? I'm Not Your Father!" Each time they found themselves responding to each other as parent and child, one or the other would call out "Shirts!" and they would don their new costumes. Old patterns fell away quickly, laughter replaced bitter arguments, and they were able to begin to negotiate with each other. After a while, they only had to say the word "shirts" to evoke a frame of reference that would preclude arguing and lead the way to negotiation.

You can create belief-negotiation rituals among your many relationships. What is required is some joint willingness to step out of the same old boring fight into an experiment with special ritual symbols and time where new rules for interacting prevail. Choose a time when you both can really be available without interruptions. Select a place that has warm and pleasant associations for each of you. Play with novel ways to hear and be heard, such as exchanging symbols of your differing beliefs, preparing documents that express your position, or wearing unique clothing, like T-shirts. One couple we know created a board game to express and negotiate their differing beliefs. The very act of making the board game together opened space for something new to happen between them. Playing the board game as a weekly ritual allowed them to negotiate their differences.[9] The bitter polarizing that so frequently occurs when human beings express differing ideas can give way through the capacity of rituals to hold contradictions and discover new and unexpected beliefs.

Celebrating: Affirming Deep Joy and Honoring Life with Festivity

Life-cycle rituals, including weddings, baby namings, graduations and funerals, religious and cultural holiday rituals, and birthdays and anniversaries, all involve celebrating. The celebration aspect of rituals is often the most visible and dramatic marker of individual, family, and community continuity and change. As we announce who we are and who we are becoming through the joyful and celebratory moments of ritual, we also connect with a sense of humanity through time. We can celebrate the accomplishments of an individual life, the positive elements of a relationship, the warmth and caring in a family.

All cultures have celebrations. These rituals usually include certain foods and drinks, ethnic, religious, or cultural expression, unique music, gifts, and particular clothing, all of which mark the celebration as "special time." In Jennifer's "Coming of Age" ritual, the guests ate her favorite food to honor her choices. Both the Jewish-American and Jamaican aspects of her family culture were deeply present. Janine and Natalya played beautiful music. Jennifer received gifts to send her into adult life. The entire ritual celebrated her accomplishments in life, along with celebrating those who had stood by her and supported her.

Since celebrating is one of the major ways rituals work for us, it may be important to examine your own rituals to discover where you are experiencing a sense of celebration and where you are not. Rituals containing celebration express warmth, comfort, support, affirmation of life, and a sense of being connected to others. While not all rituals are intended to celebrate, if you come away from rituals where you anticipate celebration, and instead feel anxious, exhausted, hypocritical, or cut off from yourself or others, then one of rituals' key functions, celebrating, is not happening. Since rituals are a lens through which you can see developmental and relationship issues, discovering the absence of celebration in rituals where you expect it to be is a signal that work needs to be done. A genuine sense of celebration is often missing from rituals when there has been relationship cutoff, when important issues have gone underground and cannot be discussed, or when losses remain unhealed, unspoken, or unresolved.

CELEBRATING JIM'S LIFE:
AN UNEXPECTED PART OF A CHRISTMAS RITUAL

Sophie and Joel found themselves dreading yet another Christmas at Joel's mother's house. "It's like a funeral, not like Christmas," Sophie complained. "No one can talk about your brother Jim and yet he's present throughout the day!" Joel's brother Jim had died in a boating accident six years earlier. The family gathered every Christmas as they always had, but the specter of Jim's death hung over the holiday. No mention was ever made of Jim, and the family went through the motions of Christmas, with no sense of celebration.

Joel and Sophie thought long and hard about how to change Christmas. They considered not going to Joel's mother's, but didn't want to upset her. Finally, they decided that they needed to take a risk in order to open both Christmas and family relationships. They made an album that affirmed and honored who Jim was in life. The album included photographs, press clippings of his accomplishments, letters he had written. During the Christmas gift exchange, Joel announced that he and Sophie had a gift for the whole family, and he took out the album. At first, Joel's sister left the room, angry that Joel and Sophie had done this, but she returned. The whole family sat and pored over the album, with lots of tears and stories about Jim being voiced for the first time since his death. The Christmas dinner that followed was a genuine celebration. Family members laughed. Joel's mother recalled the year Jim opened all of his presents two days before Christmas and then tried to wrap them all up again, only to be caught in the act. Favorite foods were eaten with joy instead of with furtive guilt. The family reclaimed its right to celebrate.

Christmas, a ritual that is supposed to include a sense of joy and celebration, had become stagnant for this family. The taboo subject of Jim's death was on everyone's mind, but no one dared mention it. Joel and Sophie knew that if they asked permission of other family members to make and present the album, they would be told not to do it because it would be too upsetting to Joel's mother. By celebrating Jim's life openly, they were able to join with the deep pool of memories of celebration that existed in the family. Joel's mother captured the genuine celebration that had occurred when she said to Joel and Sophie as they were leaving, "You gave me back Christmas and you gave me back Jim."

CELEBRATING THE UNCELEBRATED
While the celebration theme is obvious in our accepted life-cycle, holiday, and family-tradition rituals, there are many events in life that go unmarked and uncelebrated. This lack of celebration may result from shame or guilt, from the absence of social or community support, or simply because accomplishments and changes have gone unnoticed.

Since new rituals can be created, you may want to think about parts of your own life or those close to you to determine if a new celebration is in order.

For instance, in our work we knew an intermarried couple who struggled and struggled to figure out how to celebrate Hanukkah and Christmas. The dilemma was finally resolved the year that they each made room for the other to celebrate his or her own holiday, followed by a new celebration on December 27 that they called a "Celebrating Our Differences!" day. They prepared favorite foods from their own ethnic and religious backgrounds, and told previously unheard stories from their own heritage. They ended the day with the phrase "Thank you for being different and enriching my life!"

Our own society has few established rite-of-passage rituals. Some families have taken to celebrating various rites of passage, such as first menstruation, or first shaving. Marking these passages into puberty offers an opportunity to celebrate family values regarding womanhood and manhood.

Many gay and lesbian couples, whom our society will not allow to have a legal marriage and wedding celebration, have begun to create their own public commitment ritual to celebrate their relationship with family and friends present to witness and offer them support.

A family whose son was profoundly retarded created a small family ritual to celebrate each new step he accomplished, including spaghetti for dinner (his favorite food), and a toast between the parents to each other in appreciation of what each gave to their son.

John and Sue married because Sue was pregnant. They never celebrated their anniversary or their daughter Karen's birthday, as these were connected with a deep sense of shame. Following a successful therapy, they chose a new anniversary date, one that marked their being together because they chose each other and not because their parents forced them to be married. To celebrate their daughter's third birthday and to announce their own freedom from shame, they invited family and friends to a "celebration of Karen's first, second, and third birthdays."

The celebration aspect of rituals honors life with all of its dilemmas, problems, and difficulties, and with all of its joys, successes, and accomplishments. Sometimes, just persevering in the face of enormous odds deserves a celebration. You may want to think about a small but important detail, or an enormous but unmarked happening in your own life or in the lives of people that you care about that warrants a celebration ritual. Not every ritual requires weeks and weeks of preparation. A special dinner, a brief exchange of symbols, or even a nightly cup of tea together can hold and express a celebration of life.

Making Rituals Work for You

Any particular ritual may include one or some or all of the ways that rituals work for us. As you reflect on the rituals in your life, consider how these express and address *relating*, *changing*, *healing*, *believing*, and *celebrating*. Are your rituals doing what you want them to do and what you need them to do? Does a given ritual, for instance, express certain beliefs that you hold, but do little or nothing to heal relationships? Have you been able to affirm a change in personal status through a ritual, but still feel bereft of relational support? As you think over these five ways that rituals address central human needs, consider which ones may be missing from your current ritual life. Which of rituals' purposes would you like to develop? As you will discover in Chapter 3, your own family history and a variety of current life circumstances interact in powerful ways to shape your particular ritual style.

3

Your Family Heritage

UNDERSTANDING RITUAL STYLES

EVERY FAMILY DEVELOPS its own individual style of ritual practice. Most often, the ritual styles in your current life were influenced by experiences in your family-of-origin. You may discover that your rituals are minimized, interrupted by a traumatic or life-cycle event, rigid and unchanging, obligatory, or imbalanced, or you may find that your daily rituals are shaped by one style, while your life-cycle rituals are shaped by another. Changing a ritual style will have reverberating effects on your sense of self and relationships. As you discover your own ritual styles and as you experiment with altering them, you will find that the effects on closeness, connectedness, and sense of one another through time last far longer than the ritual event itself.

Minimized Rituals

Some families have very few rituals. Birthdays, anniversaries, or holidays may go unmarked, uncelebrated, or given only a tiny amount of time and space in family life. Dinnertime may be haphazard or not occur at all. There may be almost no daily rituals to give people a sense of belonging in the family. Special accomplishments, like school graduation, may receive little or no attention. In families where rituals are minimized, other aspects of life can easily intrude on planned rituals. So, for instance, Dad's work may take precedence over a birthday party, or a telephone call may easily interrupt a family event. Time and space for rituals are not protected, and the ritual aspect of family life is less highly valued than other parts of life.

Since rituals highlight and provide both continuity and change for us, a minimized ritual style means that a family may have little sense of itself through time. Everything simply blends into everything else. Families who want to avoid continuity with the past because of painful memories often develop a minimized ritual style.

The Case of the Disappearing Rituals

Regina Jackson comes from a family where her parents were bitterly unhappy with each other. Her mother was alcoholic. On nearly every birthday and every holiday, her mother and father would have a ferocious fight, and her mother would get very drunk, which frightened Regina and her younger brother. When Regina married, she became quite depressed before any holiday, but did not understand why. Her husband, Jeff, who knew little, if anything, about his wife's childhood, thought that she was just overwhelmed with holiday preparation. At first he tried what he thought was helping out with the holidays, but he and Regina would fight, and she would end up in tears and go to her room. Gradually, Jeff suggested that they simply minimize their celebrating, although Regina still became depressed around holidays. Over a few years, this couple developed a minimized ritual style that really did not satisfy either of them.

Jeff came from a family where rituals had been rich and meaningful. His family lived across the country, and so the couple had no access to these rituals in the present. Jeff realized that he missed his family's way of making rituals, especially after the couple had children of their own. When his daughter's third birthday came and went with no party, Jeff got into an argument with Regina about an unrelated and trivial issue. Soon, he realized what was really upsetting him was the now total lack of meaningful rituals in their family. When he told this to Regina, she finally began to tell him all about the very painful rituals from her family, rituals that served as periodic dramas for so much turmoil and unhappiness. Telling these stories and having Jeff listen in a loving way was very healing for Regina, as she had been too ashamed to talk about what had happened in her family. Listening to Jeff talk about the rituals in his childhood gave Regina a whole new notion about the possibilities of rituals to enhance their life. Together, they made a decision to experiment with creating new rituals, ones that would not remind Regina of the painful rituals in her family-of-origin.

EXPLORING A MINIMIZED RITUAL STYLE

To know if your own family has developed a minimized ritual style you may want to work on some questions, either alone or with members of your family:

• Are important events, like birthdays or wedding anniversaries, marked, or do they simply slide by with little notice?

• Is time protected for family celebrations, or can other things like work or school easily intrude?

• Does the family sit down for a meal together on any kind of regular basis, or do people simply grab food as needed? Does the television *always* intrude on family dinners?

• Are key life-cycle passages, like graduation or retirement, noted in some special way, or do they just blend into the rest of life?

As you work with these questions, look for trends or tendencies. We have never met a family that has *no rituals*, but lots of families do deemphasize their rituals for many reasons. Immigrant families, and particularly the adult children of immigrants who are rushing to assimilate, may abandon earlier rituals and not replace them with new ones. Adolescents may refuse to participate or be available for family rituals for a period of time. This is usually a developmental stage, corresponding to a teen's wish to go with friends, or to separate from the ways the family does things for a while. Some families respond by joining their teenager, dropping most familiar rituals, and developing a minimized ritual style. This often occurs when family rituals have been shaped primarily for the children, and the adults have neglected their need for meaningful rituals of their own. If you are a single parent with grown children or if you are a single adult, you may find that your ritual life has become quite slighted. Discovering that your rituals have become minimized as children have grown and moved on is a useful signal that adult relationships need some attention. If this has happened in your own family, you may want to talk over ways to create rituals that focus on adult and couple concerns and life-cycle passages.

If you have determined that your ritual style is minimized, we don't suggest that you rush off and create lots of rituals. The sheer number of rituals in your life is not the issue, but rather your satisfaction with your ritual life. You might try setting aside one evening a week for a family dinner during which time the adults tell stories of rituals from their own families-of-origin. If you live alone, you may want to talk with friends about rituals in their lives, and experiment with a ritual together. As you do this, you will understand more about how you developed a minimized ritual style and decide whether or not you wish to change this.

Interrupted Rituals

Sudden, unexpected changes in life, such as illness, death, or war, or anticipated but traumatic life-cycle events, like divorce or migration, may overwhelm a family's rituals. Some or all of your family's familiar rituals may be thrown off track, and you may go for months or years without reestablishing familiar rituals or inventing new ones that capture and express the changed circumstances.

An interrupted ritual style is really a signal to you or your family that you are struggling through a crisis. If your family has always had dinner together, and is now unable to because a young child is in the hospital, or Christmas is "canceled" because a grandfather died, the very absence of these rituals becomes a sign that the family is having trouble coping. A family facing a very severe trauma will often find that its daily rituals disappear, replaced by a sense of chaos. In the Colon family, nineteen-year-old Wanda was raped. The family handled this terrible crisis by getting appropriate help for Wanda, not realizing that they might need some help themselves. After a month, Mrs. Colon, Wanda's mother, noticed that the family had totally stopped having meals together, and were simply catching food as they rushed through the kitchen, careful to avoid any conversation with each other. At this point, she called the family together and insisted that they talk about what was happening to them.

Any family may temporarily abandon its rituals because all of its energy is needed for the present crisis. Unfortunately, some families find it impossible to resume their rituals after the emergency has passed. Here a family with an interrupted ritual style becomes a family with minimized rituals, often remaining dissatisfied, but unsure how to reestablish their rituals.

NO MORE BIRTHDAY PARTIES OR "CHILI BIRTHDAY CAKE"

When Carrie Sullivan was seven years old, she developed juvenile diabetes. Her parents were extremely frightened, and they watched what she ate very carefully. Her dad felt that she shouldn't go to other children's birthday parties because she would want to eat birthday cake and candy. She became quite lonely and resentful, feeling that she was no longer like other children, and began fighting with all the little girls who had been her friends. Soon no birthday party invitations came for her. When Carrie's own birthday came, her parents downplayed the event and took her to the movies. In a misguided effort to be kind to Carrie, her older brother was also not allowed to have a birthday party with cake and ice cream. On her ninth birthday, Carrie sneaked out of the house, went to a bakery, and spent her allowance money on a cake, which she sat and ate all by herself, bringing on a diabetic crisis that resulted in her hospitalization.

In the hospital, the Sullivans joined with a group of parents who were meeting to discuss the challenges and problems of raising a child with a severe chronic illness. The birthday party issue came up, as many of the parents were struggling to help their children feel less different, but still stay healthy. The Beren family described their own solution, which involved creating a new symbol for their son Jerrold's birthday other than a cake. Jerrold's very favorite food was chili. At his eleventh birthday, which was six months after the onset of his diabetes, Jerrold had what he called his "chili birthday cake." His mom made a big pot of chili and got twelve large and long candles that were put in the chili. Jerrold's friends thought this was hilarious, and started making "chicken birthday cakes," "hamburger birthday cakes," and "spaghetti birthday cakes." The family was able to construct a birthday ritual that spoke to the ways Jerrold was still quite like other children and the one way that he was different from other children!

If you and your family have experienced divorce, then you no doubt know that rituals are often interrupted for a period of time until the new family form of either single parent and children or coparenting has the time needed to develop new and more fitting rituals. If a dad always made the bedtime ritual with children and he has moved out, there may be no bedtime ritual for a while. If a young family's home has become the location for Thanksgiving with extended family, and the couple divorce, Thanksgiving may go uncelebrated for a year until the family can sort out its relationships. Very often, children will be the voice for reestablishing interrupted rituals, usually with complaints about getting things "back to how they used to be." Corey Andrews, for instance, kept insisting to her mother that they had to have an eight-foot Christmas tree, just as they had always had, before her parents' divorce. Janice, Corey's mom, just couldn't face anything that reminded her of her former husband. The Christmas tree held all the warm memories of choosing a tree, putting it up, and decorating it together. To escape from the pain of these memories, she took Corey to Disneyland for Christmas, where she was totally bewildered by Corey's inability to have a good time. Since all rituals will, of course, be different after a divorce, a parent may be confused about how to respond to a child's wish for unchanging rituals and may simply continue with no rituals at all.

Think for a moment about the ways that significant life events may have overwhelmed and interrupted your rituals. You will know if your ritual style is an interrupted one if you have a sharp sense of rituals "before" a central event, like an illness, a divorce, a move, or a death, and the disappearance of these rituals "after" such events.

The challenge for you and for your family when rituals are interrupted can be met in stages. First, someone in the family has to recognize and give voice to the interrupted style. A conversation or two about what people feel they are missing and how things were in the family previously can help you begin to determine what you will need to do to reestablish certain rituals. Since part of the beauty of rituals is their capacity to change as the family changes, new rituals will be possible. Rituals have an amazing ability to express how we are similar to others in our common humanity, and how we are uniquely ourselves. Families who are undergoing intense relationship change following a divorce or a death, or families who are working to integrate a chronic illness into their lives, can, after an interruption in rituals, reestablish a meaningful ritual life.

Rigid Rituals

One woman told us, "I don't want any rituals in my life—rituals are like being in prison!" This woman had grown up in a family where all of the rituals were confining, constraining individual development or expression, and unchanging. This is the style of rigid rituals. When a family has a rigid ritual style, all or nearly all of the behaviors in a given ritual are highly prescribed and unvaried. The ritual must occur exactly the same way today as it did yesterday, or precisely the same way this year as it did last year. In rigid rituals, there is almost no room for anything new or novel or spontaneous to occur. Playfulness and humor, so much a part of many meaningful rituals, are totally absent. Often, very rigid rituals in a family are a metaphor for a narrow range of relationship possibilities. Roles are highly prescribed for men and women and for grandparents, parents, and children. Families whose ritual style is rigid seldom invite people outside the family or immediate community to their rituals, since to do so might threaten the established order. Children may not be allowed to attend the rituals of their friends—for instance, to go to someone's house for dinner—lest they bring home new ideas about how a family might relate.

PORRIDGE, PORRIDGE, PORRIDGE

Susan Slate, thirty-seven, told us about the morning ritual when she was growing up. "There were nine of us, and every morning my father woke us up at 5:30 A.M., although school was not until 9:00 A.M. He made us march around the house in a line, calling this our 'morning exercise.' Then we had to say prayers, with exactly the same emphasis on certain words. In order of our age, we each then took cold showers, which my father said 'built character.' Finally we sat down to breakfast, each in our assigned seats, and Father gave each of us a huge bowl of porridge, which we had to finish before we would be allowed to leave the table. No talking was allowed during breakfast. My mother was treated like one of the kids. If anyone rebelled, we were beaten. I dreaded every morning!" Susan went on to tell us that she has created a life now that is deliberately devoid of any rituals.

EXPLORING A RIGID RITUAL STYLE
To determine if your ritual pattern is rigid, ask yourself a few questions:

1. Do ritual events have to occur at exactly the same time and place every year?

2. Are all or most of your rituals highly prescribed, with little or no room for spontaneity or newness?

3. How do family members respond when someone suggests trying something different in a given ritual—are they immediately negative to the idea?

4. Are prescribed roles in rituals more important than meaning and feelings of the participants?

5. Have rituals remained the same despite obvious changes in family membership, age, or beliefs?

As you think about these questions, you may discover a predominantly rigid ritual style in your family, or you may find that a particular category, such as daily rituals, or a certain ritual, such as birthdays, has become rigid and unchanging. Imagine what would happen to family relationships if a given ritual were to change. Try a very small change, like cooking a new dish for Thanksgiving, and observe family members' feedback. You may find that what seems like a small change, for instance, sitting in a new place at dinner, provokes a huge discussion. This can serve as a springboard for examining a rigid ritual style.

As we have stated before, rituals assist us in two major dimensions of human life—continuity and change. When rituals are rigid, the family attends only to the continuity dimension and to remaining the same, despite the needs of people to change and grow. The value of rituals to facilitate and mark changes is lost to families whose rituals are required to be unchanging. Just as families whose ritual style is minimized lose the continuity dimension of rituals, families whose ritual style is rigid lose the change dimension of rituals. Often, when we grow up in a family like Susan's, we respond in the next generation by developing a minimized ritual style, in order to escape what has felt like the tyranny of rituals. When this happens, all of the positive potential of rituals is also lost.

Rigid rituals sometimes originate from a protective motive. A family may have undergone a traumatic change, like divorce or a death, and attempt to mitigate the trauma by clinging to old rituals. When Suzanne Elner's fourteen-year-old brother Keith died in a car accident, her mother insisted that they celebrate holidays "just the way we did when your brother was alive." She took special care to decorate the house exactly as she did before his tragic death. She cooked all of the same foods, including dishes that were really only liked by Keith. Suzanne said, "It was as if we were frozen in time. No one dared talk about Keith and no one dared tell Mother that we needed to change." When rigid rituals develop during or after a crisis, this is a signal to you that you and your family are having trouble coping with frightening change. As you talk openly about your rituals, you will find that this enables conversations about the changes the family is facing. Think through together what aspects of the rituals that came before a major change you might still like to maintain, and which aspects really need to change to express your changing circumstances.

Obligatory Rituals

Every Fourth of July, Paul and Linda Hoffman pack their three children and their dog into their station wagon and drive 250 miles to Paul's sister's, where all of the Hoffmans gather. The event is fairly unpleasant. All of the women spend the day cooking, which Linda resents, while the men watch sports, even though Paul doesn't care for sports. The young cousins mostly spend the day fighting with one another. In the evening, Grandpa Hoffman sets off fireworks, but no one really pays much attention. On the fifth of July, Paul and Linda drive home, weary and vowing that this is the last year they will spend their holiday in this way. The following June, however, as they begin to even *think* about doing something different, Paul's older sister calls and tells them how upset their parents will be if Paul and Linda and their children don't come this year. Alternate plans fall by the wayside, and into the car they all go on the Fourth of July. If this story sounds familiar to you, then some or all of the rituals in your life may have become obligatory rituals.

When rituals are obligatory, participants celebrate events more out of a feeling of obligation than with any sense of meaning. Both the preparation process and the ritual itself are more burden than joy. Obligatory rituals have no room for spontaneity or playfulness, and are generally experienced as quite stressful by participants. Family members may feel a sense of fear and anxiety if they consider trying to change these rituals of obligation, and much guilt if they opt out all together. Often, one family member will become the "guardian," like Paul's sister, making sure that everyone participates, and invoking "how upset" someone, usually parents, will be if there is a change.

Expectations on women in our culture to be the ritual makers, the preparers of all family celebrations, means that they must shop for food, cook, buy gifts, send cards, take children to buy special clothing, do all of the inviting, and finally make sure that everyone is having a good time. Over time, rituals become empty and burdensome for women, carried on out of a sense of obligation, but with much resentment. Such gender-bound requirements regarding women as the ritual makers in families is one of the remaining vestiges of an earlier time in our culture. In families where both the man and woman are working outside of the home, women still do ninety percent of the daily dinner preparation. Most women still buy the gifts and cards for holidays for the husband's family, leaving him with little responsibility for doing the work of family rituals. Changing a woman's sense of obligation regarding family rituals requires open discussion and very deliberate effort from all family members. Such change does *not* come easily, as it challenges many of our unspoken assumptions about men's and women's roles in families.

EXPLORING AN OBLIGATORY RITUAL STYLE

Think about the major rituals in your life over the last few years:

1. Do you look forward to them, or does their approach fill you with a sense of burden and dread?

2. After a ritual is over, do you feel some sense of satisfaction and renewal of relationships, or do you just feel relieved that this event is over for another year?

3. If you are quite dissatisfied with a given ritual, can this be discussed in the family, or will you be given the message to "get back in line"?

If you determine that some or all of the rituals in your life are obligatory, you can make good use of this as a signal that some change is needed. Often obligatory rituals are only one aspect of a family pattern that is burdensome and guilt-ridden and allows little room for difference. Changing an obligatory ritual style, however, is slow and planful work. Waiting until June 15 to alter a ten-year pattern of obligatory Fourth of July celebrations usually will not work, and more likely will lead to fights, angry cutoffs, and much unhappiness for everyone.

"DON'T CHANGE!"

Karen Sissel tried to change a family Easter ritual with little planning. Karen lived with her partner, Joe Moore. Every Easter, Karen's family expected her to spend the entire day at her parents' house. Any mention that she and Joe would like to spend part of the day with Joe's family, or that they would like to celebrate with their group of friends, was quickly dismissed by Karen's mother, who told her how this would upset her father and make him ill. Karen's mother would then remind Karen of how they had accepted Joe and their living together, rather than marrying, implying that the couple should be grateful and not rock the boat. Thus embedded in this Easter ritual of obligation were many unspoken and anxiety-provoking issues. Two days before Easter, Karen called her mother and said that they were not coming this year. This announcement was met with tears, anger, and many telephone calls all around the family, including several to Karen telling her what a bad daughter she was, and threatening to cut her off. On Easter morning, Karen called and apologized. Karen and Joe quickly canceled a dinner they had organized at their own home, and once again, she and Joe spent the day at her parents'.

Karen attempted to change an obligatory ritual without careful planning and without a clear understanding of all of the relationship issues involved in making such a change. In our experience, obligatory rituals generally occur in families where there is a high emphasis on family loyalty and on the appearance of family loyalty. Challenging the obligatory ritual style often means challenging how loyalty is expressed in relationships. If, when you think of altering a given ritual or your participation in it, you imagine that your loyalty to the family will be questioned, then likely your family ritual style is obligatory.

If you determine that a given ritual or many rituals in your life are obligatory and dissatisfying, you will need to change this carefully and with sufficient time. Choose a ritual that will occur in six months or more. Think through the kinds of changes you would like. Anticipate each family member's response to the changes you plan to make. Likely, certain family members will tell you why you should not carry out your plan, who you will be upsetting, and why you absolutely should not do what you are planning to do. Speak directly and without anger or defensiveness to each family member. You do not need to ask permission. Don't expect that everyone will be delighted with your plan. Following Karen and Joe's failed attempt to alter their participation in the Easter ritual, they made a decision to work toward a change in the Thanksgiving ritual. Joe's family was never included in any of Karen's family's rituals. In May, Karen and Joe paid a visit to her parents, and told them that it would be important to invite Joe's parents this Thanksgiving. When Karen's mother protested that this would mean more work, Karen and Joe responded that they would come early and help. When Karen's father said there wasn't enough room (indeed, a metaphor for the family's wish to keep things the same), Karen and Joe produced a table plan they had worked out. When Karen's sister called her two days later to tell her how she was upsetting her father, Karen called her father directly to tell him that there seemed to be a belief in the family that he couldn't tolerate change and to ask him if this were true. Gradually the objections dissolved. The family had a new Thanksgiving, one that spoke in action of the relationship changes that were happening and so felt alive.

Imbalanced Rituals

EVAN, THE CHRISTMAS TREE SALESWOMAN

During graduate school, Evan was a single parent of two toddlers. In order to make some needed money one year, she sold Christmas trees and watched the following scenario repeated many times: A couple would enter the Christmas tree lot and begin to browse through the trees. He: "We have to have a Scotch pine, dear, because that's what my family always had!" She: "Scotch pines are nice, honey, but we have to have a Douglas fir, because that's what my family always had!" Gradually, the "dears" and "honeys" would be dropped from a conversation that grew louder and more intense. Since Evan comes from a Jewish family with no Christmas trees, the whole scene was quite confusing, until she began to understand that all couples face a central developmental task regarding their rituals—namely, to balance each one's history, legacies, and ways of making rituals. What at first seemed to Evan to be a small matter, a Christmas tree, in fact carried huge symbolic value for these couples, including connections to family-of-origin and community.

An imbalanced ritual style can occur within a generation, as when a couple celebrates only according to the ways of the husband's family-of-origin, or between generations, as when all of the rituals are organized only for the children's needs, or only for the grandparents' requirements, rather than for all of the generations.

When rituals are imbalanced within a generation, a couple may, like Luke and Judy Spencer, spend all holidays with Judy's family, take vacations with Judy's family, eat dinner in a seating pattern that was the same in Judy's family, use symbols in their rituals that come only from Judy's family, and have little or no contact with the ritual legacy from Luke's family.

Rituals may be imbalanced within a generation for many reasons. You may have had very unhappy experiences in your family-of-origin, and so may gladly abandon all familiar rituals early in a relationship, and gravitate toward your partner's rituals, only to discover later that there are aspects of your family's rituals that you miss.

Couples who are intermarried from different ethnic or religious backgrounds often struggle over how to balance their rituals in ways that can express each one's heritage. Many couples resolve this struggle prematurely by simply adopting all of the rituals of just one spouse. Kathy experienced such imbalanced rituals in her marriage. Her husband, Michael, was Jewish, while she was raised as a Unitarian. Neither partner converted to the other's religion. Michael had lived through very painful anti-Semitism when he was growing up, which grew more intense around Christmas and Easter. For this reason, he felt he could not tolerate any Christian celebrations in the family. Kathy felt sensitive to his distress, and for ten years she agreed to give up her own holidays, including not visiting her own family at Christmas. Over time, their ritual life became quite imbalanced, and Kathy began to feel more and more lonely at holiday time. Her own family had not been particularly religious, but had done lots of fun activities, like treasure hunts, cookie baking, and going to the woods together to chop a Christmas tree, which Kathy sorely missed. Gradually, they were able to compromise on some ways that Kathy's traditions could also stay alive in their relationship, without violating Michael's feelings, including Kathy visiting her own family for Christmas while Michael remained at home. Balancing rituals from two very different traditions does not mean blending them into a meaningless blob, or forcing one partner to participate in rituals that may be uncomfortable, but instead making room for two ways to stay alive.

Sometimes couples who are from the same religious background but different ethnic backgrounds may not realize how different their ritual lives are until they begin to experience each other's rituals and try to make sense of constructing a ritual life of their own. Cara Santucci is an Italian-American woman who is married to Mickey O'Donnell, an Irish-American. Since both are Catholic, they assumed that their holiday rituals would be compatible, until they began to participate in each other's family holidays. The differences in foods, in extended family involvement, in the sound level of conversation, in children's roles, in gift giving and receiving were enormous. The holiday rituals in Cara's family were far more action-packed, while those in Mickey's family were much more subdued. Just the thought of seafood on Christmas Eve seemed quite bizarre to Mickey, while Cara could imagine no other menu. Attending each other's family rituals at first felt like landing on another planet. Each thought the other one's family was quite strange, verging on "wrong" and "bad," until they began to realize that the rituals were an expression of the family's ethnic origins. Both the strengths and the lacks of each one's rituals started to become apparent in ways that enabled Cara and Mickey to select the best of each one's heritage to preserve and honor in their own family. The Santucci-O'Donnell children now think that every family has seafood first on Christmas Eve, followed by corned beef and cabbage.

Some couples develop an unbalanced ritual style because one spouse has migrated from another country. Evan was born in Chicago, and grew up experiencing all of the American holiday rituals, like Thanksgiving and the Fourth of July and all of the Jewish holidays. Her husband, Lascelles, was born in Jamaica. Not only were the American holidays unfamiliar, but Lascelles's own family did little celebrating of other rituals, like birthdays or anniversaries, while Evan's family celebrated with great fanfare. At first, Lascelles felt like a guest in his own home, as Evan made all of the rituals that were familiar and meaningful to her and her two children. Lascelles particularly enjoyed the Jewish holidays, like the Passover Seder, but the American holidays seemed much more foreign to him. Further, Evan couldn't understand why Lascelles didn't start thinking about birthdays three months ahead of time, and Lascelles was totally bewildered by all of the fuss Evan seemed to make over an anniversary. It took many years and much discussion for them to create rituals that would have meaning for both, and that could capture and express aspects of Lascelles's Jamaican origins, Evan's Jewish-American heritage, and their unique interracial family. This included the obvious contributions of different food and symbols from both cultures, and the more subtle search for shared values that cut across both cultures, such as connections with families-of-origin, a sense of liveliness and humor, and compassion and justice in relationships.

Rituals for gay and lesbian couples can easily become imbalanced if one partner's family-of-origin accepts the couple and the other's family-of-origin refuses. Jerry Elkins and Stan Bridges had lived together for fifteen years. They celebrated all of their holidays with Stan's family, because Jerry's family refused to have anything to do with them. At first they both enjoyed these rituals with Stan's family. Jerry's hurt at his own family's rejection led him to drop all rituals from his upbringing. Over time, Jerry felt the double loss of both relationships with his family and all of the familiar rituals. He began to find the warm and accepting family rituals with Stan's parents too painful a reminder of his own family. As he and Stan talked about this, they decided that was really no reason why they couldn't celebrate with aspects of rituals from Jerry's history. Jerry's parents' refusal to accept them did not mean that they had to abandon all of Jerry's background. They began by unpacking symbols, such as Jerry's grandmother's candlesticks, which she had given him, and reclaiming these for their own ritual life. They cooked some of the foods that Jerry's family traditionally had for Christmas, and brought these to Stan's family's home. Jerry said that at first it was painful, but soon he felt that he had reclaimed what belonged to him and that no one could take away.

Rituals may become imbalanced between generations when all of the rituals are organized with only one generation's needs in mind. If your family is extremely child-focused, your rituals may become imbalanced, so that only children's concerns are considered.

WHAT HAPPENED TO MOTHER'S DAY?

Bill Goren and Angela Stewart are a remarried couple who live with Bill's three children from his first marriage. Bill's first wife died seven years ago. This is Angela's first marriage, and she tries very hard to be a good mother to Bill's children. When the couple first married, Bill made it quite clear to Angela that he was very worried about his children's well-being. He seemed to believe that he had to make up somehow for the death of their mother. Part of how he tried to do this was by making very elaborate birthday and Christmas celebrations for them. Angela watched this when they were first married, and expressed some concern to Bill that he was going overboard with gifts, but he insisted that this was how it was to be. The first year of their marriage, Mother's Day came and went with no celebration for Angela. She felt hurt, but didn't mention it. However, before the second Mother's Day, Angela told Bill that she thought they should celebrate Mother's Day, as she was now the mother. Bill immediately reminded her that she was the stepmother, but agreed that they should celebrate. On the morning of Mother's Day, Bill asked Angela where she would like to go, and she mentioned her favorite restaurant. At four o'clock, Bill called everyone together and said he would be ordering some pizza to celebrate Mother's Day for Angela, since the children needed to study for exams and dinner out would take too much time. Angela stopped asking for a Mother's Day celebration, and the family continued to have rituals only for the children. Eventually, Bill and Angela broke up.

This family's style of imbalanced rituals between the generations clearly was indicative of many problems regarding unspoken loyalties to Bill's first wife and Angela's second-class position in this remarried family. When rituals are imbalanced between generations, it is usually a sign that many issues cannot be discussed and many needs are going unmet for the members of one of the generations. If the rituals are designed only with children in mind, then likely there are couple issues that need attention. If rituals are carried out only for the grandparents' needs, then issues in the nuclear family are likely being neglected.

EXPLORING AN IMBALANCED RITUAL STYLE
To determine if your ritual style is imbalanced, ask yourself:

1. Do we almost always go to one spouse's family-of-origin for holidays?

2. Is only one ethnic tradition kept alive, even though we are a multi-ethnic family?

3. What ethnic and religious heritages are honored in the family and how was this decided?

4. Are our rituals organized almost exclusively for children's needs and wants, or for grandparents' needs and wants?

5. Have there been struggles over whose rituals to follow? How have these struggles been resolved?

An imbalanced ritual style can be rebalanced with some work. A good way to begin is to review all of the rituals in your life now, and ask yourself whose family-of-origin these most reflect, and which generation's needs are most being met. Discuss what rituals were like in each of your families as you grew up, and compare this to your current ritual life. If you discover that the rituals have become imbalanced and reflect only one partner's family-of-origin, choose one ritual to experiment with by incorporating elements from each one's background. Try to enter your partner's culture like an anthropologist who wants to learn something new and different, rather than with critical judgment. If your rituals reflect only the needs of children, try emphasizing an adult ritual like an anniversary or an outing without the children in order to discover what adult issues have gone underground. As you experiment with rebalancing your rituals, you will likely recognize ways in which family relationships have more generally become imbalanced and important issues have been silenced. As the rituals start to change, more family members will find their own voice in the family system.

Flexible Rituals

In order for rituals to stay alive and meaningful to you and your intimates, they need to be flexible as individuals and relationships change and grow. Members entering and leaving the family, work and career changes, gender role shifts, and changes in beliefs all need to be reflected in flexible rituals. Such flexible rituals can capture and express the changes, while still offering families a sense of continuity and connectedness through time.

A Flexible Christmas Ritual

Eugene Walker reflected on the Christmas ritual in his family and how it had both changed to reflect family changes and maintained certain aspects that were familiar, warm, and comforting. When his children were little, the family would go for a drive to see if they could catch Santa as he came to their house. Of course, they always just missed Santa, and when they came home, all of the presents had magically appeared under the tree, put there by the grandparents. As in all families, gradually the belief in Santa disappeared, but the children still insisted on the car ride on Christmas Eve, which came to be spent telling stories of previous Christmases, like the time "Daddy honked rudely at another car on Christmas," or "the year Mom mistook the yellow gas pumps for carolers." Eugene's children have all grown and left home, but even when they can't get together for Christmas, they go on their own car rides, and then share a telephone conference call with family members to tell old stories and add some new ones.

The Walker family has adapted their Christmas ritual to the changing beliefs and emotional needs of each member with flexibility. They have done so in a way that helps family members stay connected to what were wonderful and close times in the family, while respecting each person's development. Rituals are really quite marvelous in their capacity to both continue and change in ways that help our relationships stay vibrant and alive, mark individual and family shifts, and enable us to revisit and rework troublesome issues.

EXPLORING A FLEXIBLE RITUAL STYLE

To determine if you are satisfied with the flexibility of your rituals, think through or discuss some of these questions:

1. How have your rituals changed over the years? You may want to select one ritual, like a child's birthday, or your anniversary, or Thanksgiving, and look at it year by year to see if it has changed, and whether these changes adequately reflect individual and family relationship needs.

2. When someone has entered or left the family, have your rituals changed to reflect this shift?

3. As your beliefs have changed, have your rituals altered to express new beliefs?

4. Have you or your family created any new rituals?

5. Think ahead five or ten years. How do you imagine your rituals will be? Who will be there? What aspects of your rituals will remain the same and which ones will change? How do you imagine these changes will come about?

Reflecting on Your Ritual Style

Whether the ritual style in your life now is *minimized*, *interrupted*, *rigid*, *obligatory*, *imbalanced*, or *flexible*, or some combination of these styles across various categories of rituals, you can examine your rituals and determine if they are meeting your relationship needs, or whether you want to try changing some of the patterns. A good starting place is to reflect on the rituals in your family-of-origin, and then compare these to your current rituals.

RITUAL-REMEMBERING EXERCISE

You can do this exercise alone, with a partner, or with several people. This is a lengthy exercise, and you may want to do sections of it, and then return to it a bit later. Let yourself get comfortable and begin to think about a ritual that is very vivid in your memory from a time when you lived with your family-of-origin. You can choose a daily ritual, like a meal; a family tradition, for instance, a birthday or anniversary; a holiday celebration, either religious or secular; or a life-cycle ritual, such as a graduation or wedding. You might want to imagine yourself back in the time and space where this ritual occurred.

1. What time of year is it? What time of day?

2. What does it feel like to be in that environment? What are the textures, aromas, colors, feel of the air?

3. Who is with you? Let yourself recall what people looked like.

4. Are there different sides of the family present? Friends? People with special religious or cultural roles?

5. Who gathered people together? How did people get there? How did people greet each other? Were there differences in how men and women were greeted? In how children and adults were greeted?

6. If this ritual included people outside the immediate family, what were those relationships like?

7. How were words used? Were there toasts, or special messages, or storytelling?

8. What special symbols were there? Were these symbols that have been passed down through generations, such as china or candlesticks? Where are these symbols now?

9. Are people wearing particular clothing? What is the significance of the clothing?

10. Is there music? Movement?

11. What symbolic actions are there? Do people decorate, light candles, cut bread in certain ways? What do the symbolic actions tell you about men's and women's roles? About children and adults?

12. Are there people whose role is to witness the ritual?

13. If the ritual involves transition or change, how is this communicated?

14. Are any gifts given? What is the process of shopping, preparing, hiding, giving, and opening gifts? What gender roles are expressed?

15. How did people anticipate this ritual? Were there people who looked forward to it, or people who dreaded it? Was there worry about relationships and certain people getting together? Was there excitement?

16. Who did the planning, the preparation, the inviting, the cleanup? What gender roles are expressed?

17. Rank who enjoyed the ritual the most to who enjoyed it the least.

18. What meanings did different people derive from this ritual?

19. When the ritual was over, what was the aftermath? What feelings and issues were stirred up? How were these handled?

20. If another member of your family were to tell the story of this ritual, how would it be different from your story?

As you go through this exercise, many of the issues regarding ritual styles will no doubt be apparent to you. Seeing where elements of your current ritual style come from can give you some ideas about what you want to maintain, what you want to recoup from the past that may have been lost, and what you want to change. If you do this exercise with your spouse or other intimates, many issues regarding your ritual life will come to your attention. If you go over this exercise with your children listening, they will hear new stories about your life and their own heritage. After you have done this exercise about a ritual in your childhood, you may want to select a contemporary ritual and go through the questions again. In this way, you will be able to compare and contrast past and present rituals, and begin to think through and talk about what you want to preserve and what you want to alter in your rituals.

Now that you have started to look at the four ritual categories (daily, traditions, celebrations, and life-cycle), the five ways that rituals work for us (relating, changing, healing, believing, and celebrating), and the six ritual styles (minimized, interrupted, rigid, obligatory, imbalanced, and flexible), you can apply this to creating and participating in meaningful rituals—rituals that capture and express your own and your family's unique circumstances.

PART II

Making Meaningful Rituals

4

Planning Your Rituals

PREPARATION, PEOPLE, PLACE,
PARTICIPATION, AND PRESENTS

Good Intentions, Lingering Regrets

The twenty-first birthday of Bob Hill was coming up on May 5. His father, John, wanted to do something special. John had grown up as the oldest in a family of five boys and two girls where little was made of young-adult birthdays. He still remembered the hurt he felt on his twenty-first birthday when he didn't receive so much as a card from anyone in his family. Bob was the oldest of three children and worked as a computer technician in a town across the state from his family, several hundred miles away.

John talked with his son on the phone and thought he was coming home the weekend of his birthday, May 5–7. He began making plans for a special celebration. It turned out Bob had to work that Saturday, so at the last minute, plans were switched to the following weekend.

Bob arrived on Friday the twelfth, surprised to find out that only his family was invited for the birthday dinner planned the next night. He thought his close buddies in town, whom he seldom saw now, were invited, too. In fact, he had already mentioned the dinner to a few of them and they were planning to come.

John found himself alone Friday night wrapping twenty-one small presents. His thirteen-year-old daughter, Monica, had had the idea that the family should get little gifts that symbolized each year of Bob's life. They had had fun as a family buying them together over the last few weeks and swapping stories and adventures about Bob, but they had not planned when and how they would be wrapped. One gift was a plastic frog to represent the summer when he was into digging frog pits in the backyard to house his pet frogs. The family still remembered his frog-jumping contests. A toy saxophone symbolized his interest in music, a miniature basketball the years he was on the team. While John wrapped the gifts, Monica and her mother were out at Monica's dance recital. His other son, Joel, sixteen, was playing loud rock music in his room. Joel had just realized that he would have to miss his hockey team's award dinner the next night, because of his brother's birthday. He was mad at his father for not checking out the change of dates with him.

Saturday morning found Bob's mother, Paula, baking an extra birthday cake, throwing in more baked potatoes, and silently resenting having to try to extend the food for dinner at the last minute. She wanted Bob to help her, but John was adamant that he shouldn't have to, since it was his birthday. John didn't want to help either because he'd given up his Friday night to wrap the presents alone. Bob was up and out with friends most of the day and when he arrived that night, Elise and Lucas were with him, two more unexpected guests. The meal went off without problems, but Bob and his friends were up and out right after the cake, in order to go to a club where some friends had planned a special welcome. He never opened the twenty-one presents hidden in the living room. Joel got his brother to drop him off for the end of the hockey dinner, which left Monica home, mad, and disappointed that she was there doing dishes while her brothers were out having a good time.

The next day Bob got up around noon, thinking to himself, "What a great birthday!" He was surprised to find his generally supportive father steamed at him. "What's the matter, Dad?" he asked.

"I don't know, Bob," he said. "Somehow your birthday just didn't turn out like I planned. Seems like we didn't get to see you too much, and you know, you still haven't opened your presents from us."

Then Bob got angry: It was *his* birthday. He'd had a good time. What was going on? If his parents didn't want him there for his birthday, why did they invite him?

John, in trying to organize the birthday weekend, reacted to the minimized ritual style in his own family around birthdays by trying a bit too hard to have just what his son wanted. With the planning focused on what worked for Bob, the ritual became imbalanced, leaving other family members dissatisfied or angry. In wanting to give Bob some of the things he never had, John did not plan enough with the others to include their ideas and needs. Now he regretted it.

Preparation

Most family rituals involve some combination of preparing, inviting, and deciding upon a location and activities, as well as gift giving and receiving. The planning time that precedes a ritual can be as important as the ritual itself, for it is here that families are involved in their day-to-day roles and interactions. Looking at how decisions are made to include or exclude people from events, who is part of the preparations, and how people decide on the place they will gather will tell you a great deal about who is close and who is distant, how gender roles are expressed, and what relationships are like between generations. Likewise, gift giving and receiving and the types of activities people chose to do will demonstrate important family values and how they are expressed.

There may be some parallels between ritual styles as described in the previous chapter and how planning is done for rituals. For instance, if a family has a minimized ritual style, then planning may happen in a haphazard way at the last minute. If the ritual style feels more obligatory, then planning may be perfunctory as people go through the motions of thinking about what it is they have to do. With a more rigid ritual style, people may not want to make any changes in what is usually done to plan for a ritual and there may be little flexibility to do a variety of activities or try new things. With an imbalanced ritual style, the planning focus may get skewed, as it did for Bob's birthday, on the desires of one person. When rituals are interrupted, planning time is usually the first thing that goes as people cope with the pressures of illness, migration, or other major events. Often the first step to intervening in a ritual style is changing how you do the planning for your rituals. If you can shift the planning to ways that work well for everyone involved, you will have a better chance of impacting the actual rituals as well.

Because rituals can be a condensed expression of relationship patterns, you can expect that both what is working well and not working well within your family will emerge in them. This means that rituals give many possibilities to highlight what is positive in the family along with the chance to rework and change problematic interactions. You will probably have more success changing patterns if they are addressed at the planning stage rather than spontaneously in the middle of the ritual. This gives you time to think through what the issues are and to plan small ways to introduce something different. Think about little changes, introduce them in a spirit of experimentation—and don't forget that humor can be a key ingredient. It can lighten the mood, keep things in perspective, and relieve tension.

First, it is essential to understand what the issues are for your family. The same event can evoke very different concerns for different families.

ONE CHILD, TWO FAMILIES

While interviewing Jewish families about the Bar Mitzvah ceremony for their sons, Judy Davis found that as each family prepared for the event, different family issues emerged. The Steinbergs, a remarried family, needed to find ways to honor the fact that Micah Steinberg had two families. This issue came up early in the planning with the question, "Whose name should be on the invitation?" The mother, Stacy, was firm that the name of the new wife of her former husband *not* appear on the invitation. "Micah's my child, not hers. She didn't change his diapers or take care of him when he was sick!" However, her name could not appear without her former husband Ken's name, and Janet, his second wife, was adamant that his name should not appear without hers. "After all," said Janet, "I'm paying for part of this shindig."[1]

Finally, Micah's mother, Stacy, hit upon a compromise. As it happened, Micah's given middle name was Lerner, her maiden name (which she had never given up). His last name was Steinberg, both Ken's and Janet's surname. By beginning the invitation with "The family of Micah Lerner Steinberg fondly invites you to . . .," everyone was included. The invitation symbolically stated that both families were central to Micah's life. This set the scene for future planning among the families. For instance, a hospitality suite was set up in the hotel where members from Ken's, Janet's, and Stacy's families were staying. The suite was a place open for all to come and meet one another. These kinds of actions helped Micah to feel supported by all of his parents and extended family, rather than pulled by one side or the other.

In Sandy and Mark Goldstein's family, different issues came up. Sandy's and Mark's parents had been together only one time, at their wedding fifteen years ago. This had been a difficult meeting, and Sandy and Mark were worried about what would happen at their son Seth's Bar Mitzvah with all of them there. They needed to do careful thinking to connect people before the event. Mark went to his parents and diplomatically asked them to please go and visit Sandy's parents the next time they were in Florida. They agreed, and surprisingly, all four got along well and even planned to get together again. With this worry out of the way, Mark and Sandy were able to pay attention to other parts of the Bar Mitzvah planning.

Besides each family having different relationship issues that may emerge in the planning phase of rituals, each of the four categories of rituals may involve some typical kinds of planning concerns. Daily rituals, because they often involve the same people, places, and routine kinds of participation, may be viewed as needing little planning. Or it may be taken for granted who will do the planning for them. It might take extra effort to set aside time to organize or reorganize daily rituals. Family traditions such as birthdays, vacations, and anniversaries are more typically seen as requiring some planning time as they often involve some change of location, different foods, presents, and sometimes people other than the immediate family. However, family tradition rituals can have a lot of flexibility about when and where they take place and with what participants. Life-cycle rituals and holiday celebrations usually require the most preparation because they are more likely to involve extended family, friends, and people from the community such as religious leaders, carefully chosen locations, decorating, special clothing, and more extensive menus and gift giving.

MORE THAN TWO PEOPLE AT THE ALTAR

Michael and Mary are a young couple in their twenties. They first met on a hike in the White Mountains, sponsored by the Appalachian Mountain Club. After dating for a year, they decided to get married. They had fantasies of having their ceremony at the big rock next to the stream on the hike where they had first sat and really talked to each other. When they went to their parents and told them they were planning to marry, they realized weddings are *not* just for the couple.

In an offhand way, Mary mentioned that they might want to go back to the White Mountains for the wedding. Her father quickly reminded her that her somewhat frail seventy-five-year-old grandfather could never make it out to the woods for a ceremony. Michael's parents, who had raised him Jewish, immediately wanted to know if they had found a rabbi who would marry an interfaith couple. Mary was raised as a Methodist. Mary's mother began to write down a guest list of aunts, uncles, cousins, grandparents, great aunts, and old family friends that quickly topped the two hundred mark. Mary and Michael saw their picture of a simple, small wedding with a few friends and close family under the pine trees fade before their eyes.

They were at a choice point. They could go off and do the wedding as originally envisioned. They could let their parents take over and plan a wedding that suited them. Either of these would create an imbalanced ritual. Or they could work together with various parts of the family and create a wedding that acknowledged that it was more than just the couple who were being connected. After several days of intense discussion, Mary and Michael decided to tackle a wedding that would work for them as well as for other family members. They felt that this preparation time would be well spent, given that they planned to spend many years together. They decided on a strategy to try to facilitate what they had begun to understand would be some complicated decisions. First, they would be as clear as they could with each other about what they wanted in their wedding. Then they would listen to what their parents wanted, but without reacting initially to their requests. They would just ask questions and try to understand why particular things were important to them. Next, they would see what compromises they could make while carefully explaining to their parents what was important to them. Throughout, they would check in with each other frequently. Also, they would try to tackle one issue at a time.

First, they decided to sort out who would be invited. Michael and Mary had about twenty-five of their own friends whom they wanted at their wedding. They had originally thought about having these twenty-five along with immediate family. Michael and Mary had concerns about the number of people who would come because of the expense involved. Mary's family had considerably more money than Michael's and they did not want this to be an issue at the ceremony. As they shared this with their parents, Mary's mother, Jean, reminded Mary that her maternal grandmother had recently passed away and that no one knew how much longer her grandmother's two sisters would be alive. Mary knew that the death of her grandmother had been hard for her mom, and acknowledged that it would be important to have this part of the older generation at her wedding. So they expanded the circle of immediate family members to include extended family, especially of the older generation. While trying to work out a guest list that included about sixty people, Mary's parents kept suggesting other people. Michael and Mary felt that the people invited were starting to be skewed toward her family. Mary found it very hard to keep asking her parents, especially her mother, to limit the people. They were starting to feel boxed in until Mary's aunt suggested having some other kind of reception or party after the wedding that could be more for the parents' circle of friends.

The wedding date was in the fall. Mary's parents agreed to expand their yearly Christmas party to a reception that also welcomed Michael into the family. In this way, they could invite the large number of more distantly related family and friends that Michael and Mary did not feel they had room for at the wedding.

The location of the wedding also had to be negotiated. Michael's parents wanted them to marry in a synagogue, and Mary's parents wanted them to be married in the old stone Methodist church that the family had attended for years. Neither Mary nor Michael had envisioned a religious ceremony as being central to the wedding, and the outdoors remained an important symbol to them of their first meeting. They tried to explain this to their parents, but did not feel really heard. The more Michael and Mary talked, the more they heard comments from their parents about the importance of their own religious beliefs, and questions were raised about the faith in which Michael and Mary planned to raise their children. Finding themselves stuck, they decided to at least visit the places where their parents wanted them to marry. The rabbi at Michael's parents' synagogue did not do interfaith marriages so that meant they could not have the wedding there. Mary liked the aura of the soft light coming through the stained-glass windows of the Methodist church and had good memories of family times there. But the church had no particular significance to Michael and he thought marrying there might send a message to his parents that he was giving up his Jewish heritage—a message that he did not want to send. They talked to the minister of the church, explaining that they wanted the location of the wedding to be a place that held meaning for them, and was easy for the older generations of their families to reach. Also, they wanted a place that did not violate the religious traditions of either of their families. The minister suggested an old estate in the woods in a nearby town. There was a wildflower garden there where people often were married, and the house itself had a kitchen and large living and dining rooms for a meal or reception afterwards. She also told them that she had sometimes performed interfaith services with a rabbi from a reform congregation in that town.

Michael and Mary went on to design a ceremony that included both the rabbi and the minister, along with vows they wrote to each other and to their families. They were married under a chuppah, a canopy held up on four poles, which is an important symbol in Jewish weddings.[2] Mary and Michael chose to have a chuppah because for them it symbolized the creation of a new home. In their vows, they included appreciations of their own parents along with hopes that they had for their new son- and daughter-in-law relationships. Mary and Michael found ways to balance what they wanted in the ceremony with the needs of other family members. They arrived at a ritual that launched them with a clear sense of their abilities to work together as a couple to define what was important to them, while respecting much of their parents' desires and values. Their families-of-origin were able to come together comfortably at the ceremony because they felt they had been heard in the planning stages of the wedding. Michael and Mary also began to define a flexible ritual style for themselves in relation to each other and to their families-of-origin.

Rituals have the potential to reactivate old family interactions that are problematic. They can also highlight what is working well for families. The planning process can be central to mapping the way family dynamics will emerge. A little time spent at the planning stage can have important implications later as to how things will go. In preparing for rituals, it can be useful to think about them in three ways:

• What are the parts of the ritual that you know are meaningful to people, generally go smoothly and people enjoy doing, that you want to be sure to include?

• What are the parts of the ritual that feel obligatory, strained, or lack significance for people that you believe are possible to change?

• Are there other parts of the ritual that also feel obligatory or tedious that you think would be very difficult to change? How might you limit or minimize the impact of these more problematic parts?

Making these distinctions may help you decide where you want to focus your planning energies. It may be in any of the areas discussed in the rest of this chapter: people, place, participation, and presents.

People: The Heart of the Ritual

People are usually at the center of any ritual because it is their life transitions, celebrations, and changes that are being marked. Those that gather are also central witnesses to these changes. Family members, friends, and community people such as religious leaders and neighbors may all be a part of any ritual. How they are invited and when and by whom is often the first step in defining what the gathering will be like. If it is a celebratory event, you may want to include those who had a role in helping you to get to that place in life. If there are healing parts to the ritual, you may wish to have people there who can support and nurture you.

If a predominant ritual style from the past is a minimized one, it may be hard at first to generate a list of whom you want to invite. Think of people that you interact with in other situations whose company you enjoy, or people that you would like to know better, and add them to your list. An imbalanced style may find you with a group of people that reflect only part of the family or friendship network. Think through if participants are skewed to one side of the family or not, or to a particular age group or generation, and make some small changes to balance it. With obligatory or rigid rituals, you might feel that you must invite certain people whether you want them there or not. Think about who you really want to be there and why. Don't just assume the same crowd should always attend.

There may also be people who traditionally do not come to family events, or who are "boycotting" a particular occurrence because they disagree with how something is being done. If there are cutoffs in the family, this invitational stage can be especially tricky. Thinking about who you would like present for the occasion is a place to begin to address some of these concerns.

Once it is clear who you want to invite, think about ways to invite people so they will feel genuinely welcomed. This may mean doing things like extending personal invitations to those who do not usually come, or inviting someone who is waffling to contribute something in particular to the ritual. If there are cutoffs, you may need to strategize carefully about who should do the inviting. Think through who has the best chance of getting emotionally distant people to come.

When people still refuse to come, you can ask them if they want to send a toast or other words to be read, or if they would like pictures or a video of the event. Or you can remember them by dedicating a part of the ritual to them, or telling a story about them, or making a dish that they especially like. When the Attneave family had a vacation/reunion get-together, one uncle who was unable to come sent some of his famous home-smoked salmon for the rest of the people to share. Another aunt who refused to come because of relationship conflict was simply remembered by a few words stating that she chose not to come, and that people were sorry not to see her. This openly acknowledged that there was some tension around her not being there, but did not make a big deal out of it. This prevented her lack of attendance from being something that contributed hidden uneasiness to the gathering.

Other tense situations can arise when someone is omitted from rituals because of cutoffs and/or conflict. You may find yourself at an event very aware that your favorite nephew was not invited because of a dispute he had with his grandparents, or you may be asked year after year to attend your extended family's New Year's Day reunion, knowing your brother and his family will never be invited. This may put you in the very difficult situation of deciding whether to continue to go, or to choose not to go yourself unless others are invited as well. If you decide to participate, it's a good idea to gently acknowledge the people who are missing. When there can be no mention of what is truly happening in family relationships, rituals become rigid and obligatory.

It can also be useful to think of the different ages of people that come together for events. People of the same age group may be involved as in celebrations of work promotions or a women's group that marks the personal and professional transitions of its members with rituals. In family rituals, especially life-cycle and holiday celebrations, there are often at least three generations to consider in ritual making—parents, their elders, and the children. There are different planning issues for each of these generations that need to be considered.

PARENTAL GENERATION:
WHAT IS IT THAT MEN AND WOMEN DO?

In doing workshops in the United States, Canada, and Western Europe, we consistently hear from women that they are more of the ritual makers in their families than the men. They describe that they are often the ones to make or buy the presents, do special baking, invite others over, decorate, send cards, and clean up. In interviewing men in the 1970s and 1980s about Christmas, Janine's childhood friend Jo Robinson found a similar pattern:

> The first thing that most men learn when they examine their Christmas responsibilities is that their holiday role is much more limited than their wives. The typical husband provides emotional and financial support, helps out with errands, makes a handful of suggestions, and is responsible for a few well-defined parts of the celebration. If women are the Christmas Magicians, then men are the stagehands tugging the ropes.[3]

The Middletown surveys about family roles, kinship, neighborhoods, and holiday celebrations present similar conclusions. They describe women as the people who keep the links going among both kin and community.

> Women also maintain the relationships between the family and its friends and relations. Most festivals today are celebrated in part by gift-giving; most of the gifts are chosen and given by women. Men

have comparatively little to do with gift-giving. As we will see, gifts, especially Christmas gifts, symbolize and reinforce every social relationship; thus, the women in Middletown, more than the men, define and maintain social relationships, even those of their husbands.[4]

What implications do these findings have about the role of men in rituals? In talking with men, we often hear them voice the wish that family events were not so elaborate, that things could be simpler. As Don, a forty-five-year-old Italian-American man said, "If things were not so planned out in this way and that, then I might feel that there was more space for me to get in there and do something." Because of women's central role in ritual planning, more of the traditions from a wife's family are often followed than traditions from a husband's, creating an imbalanced ritual style. Along with the work of rituals, many men feel women get a lot of control over what happens on holidays.

For women, these findings have a different set of implications. Women often feel overburdened at ritual times. Not only are they juggling work and everyday chores but the special preparations as well that rituals often entail.

WISH ME COURAGE!

AnnaMarie, a widowed and remarried woman in her fifties of Scandinavian background, realized one Christmas that not only was she trying to make the holidays as her mother did, but she was trying to incorporate traditions from her second husband's family as well as from her first family. Her and her second husband's house was the gathering spot for her adult sons and their spouses from her first marriage, as well as her husband's siblings and her two adult stepchildren. Her fear was that "Christmas would not happen if *anything* was skipped." On December 26 she found herself collapsing for two days from exhaustion.

Not only do women feel overly responsible for many of the details of the ritual, but they often try to carry on the meaning of traditions as well. In trying to let go of some of all that she did, AnnaMarie made an outline of how she wanted the week before Christmas and Christmas Eve and Christmas Day to go. She included in it such things as asking her stepson and wife to bring two dishes to the Christmas Eve dinner; more quiet time to sit and enjoy the tree in the living room before leaving for Midnight Mass; and delegating certain clean-up chores for family members. She wrote on her outline, "Must think ahead—difficult for me to ask for help!" At the end of the list she wrote, "*If* this works this year, maybe next year I will be brave enough to have one of my son's or stepchildren's families responsible for one evening meal or for all of us to eat out. WISH ME COURAGE!!!!!".

AnnaMarie found that Christmas was a little less hectic, although it was hard for her to sit and watch others doing things like cleaning up. She felt that she should be helping, too. She collapsed from exhaustion for only one day, and had already discussed a plan for the next year with some of her children to eat out on Christmas Eve.

Arleda Olsen wanted her husband, Ralph, to help more with their elaborate Easter preparations, which included blowing out eggs and making an egg tree each year, making hot-cross and cardamom buns from scratch, along with the usual Easter egg dying and baskets for the children. Ralph offered to make the egg tree and went out and bought some plastic eggs for it. He also ordered hot-cross buns from the bakery rather than making them. At first Arleda was upset that he was not doing it in the usual way. Slowly they worked out that sharing the ritual making included sharing how decisions were made about it as well. Since women have been in charge of ritual preparation, letting go of some of this often means accepting some very different ways of preparing. If you find yourself in the new position of "ritual supervisor," not much will truly change in the gender arrangements for your rituals!

THE OLDER GENERATION

The elders of a family are often the keepers of essential ritual-making material such as recipes, stories, photos, special symbols, dishes, and other family memorabilia. Sometimes they are also the carriers of the ethnic heritage, with knowledge about the significance of particular foods, songs, dances, words, or ways of doing things. It may take some effort to bring forth what they have to offer. Sometimes what they have to say is taken for granted—they assume others know about it. Or it is presented in such a rigid way that the younger generations resist participating. Both the older and younger generations may need some structure or prompting to help them put together things in a different way.

In our experience, one of the best ways to ease ordinary tensions and conflicts between the middle and older generations is to ask grand-parents and elderly aunts and uncles for specific input in ritual planning. Sandy Dowling found that the repeated struggles with her mother at holiday times disappeared when she solicited her mother's advice for ways to make the table beautiful.

As family members grow older, generations coming up from behind need to find ways to help with the work of ritual preparations without the elders feeling displaced or unable to contribute. Control over a ritual event may hold deep meaning for an elder. It may signify that they are still a strong member of the family and community that has a lot to offer. It may help them to remember and hold important memories about their life. It may enable them to connect to key traditions. When the planning of rituals passes on to younger generations, elders may feel as if they are losing some of the control over their life. Yet the work of rituals can become burdensome for them. Younger generations may also want more say in how things are done. Shifting the ritual work between the generations can be tricky. There can be tension in planning rituals precisely because people are in the middle of this kind of shift. Naming what is happening can often help people sort it out.

As Idelia Abrahms's parents moved into their seventies, she made the Passover meal at her house and took it over to their house, arriving with both the grandchildren and the meal in the car. Her parents were still able to use their special china and be surrounded by family in their home, but much of the work was done by the next generation. After the meal, the grandsons made a game of getting into the kitchen to wash the dishes, teasing their grandmother about which ones they might break in their clumsiness.

There is also the need to conserve information that will be lost when grandparents die and save it for generations coming up. Some families tape-record the stories of elders, or get copies of old pictures and make sure to get names of who is in them and when they were taken. Other people videotape family get-togethers, or ask people to gather and talk about particular family memories. Still others apprentice themselves to learn old recipes.

GETTING CHILDREN INVOLVED:
THE TOOTH FAIRY RATONCITO PEREZ

When Janine's daughter, Natalya, was eight, she fell on a stone table in Spain and cracked off a large piece of her front tooth. There was a lot of blood and they were far from any dentists and doctors. People held Natalya, cleaned the blood away, put ice on the cut on her lip, looked for the broken-off piece of tooth. But nothing soothed Natalya until Ramon began to tell her about Ratoncito Perez, a little mouse that visited any child in Spain when a tooth came out. And he made special trips particularly when they lost or broke part of a tooth. He looked for the tooth under the child's pillow and money or little gifts would be left by him for the child. Natalya immediately wanted to know whether Janine knew about Ratoncito Perez and if she thought he would leave her Spanish pesetas, American money, or a gift. She asked Ramon if Ratoncito Perez would leave something if they couldn't find the piece of tooth. Ramon assured her that he would. Natalya had long since stopped crying. Her imagination became engaged in thinking about this "tooth fairy" and how it was the same or different than the tooth fairy she knew in the United States. She was learning about a new ritual.

Children are naturally drawn to rituals. The magical qualities of symbols, the stories that are told, the secretive aspects, all pull them into ritual. The action orientation of rituals with activities, special foods and clothing, and the gathering together of people also fits with the active life-style of young ones. Sharing the wonderment and joy of children at rituals can provide sheer enjoyment for the adults involved. One Easter, a group of families gathered in a large field for an outdoor potluck lunch and egg hunt. Brian Fujita, some fifteen years later, still remembers the cries of delight of his two daughters aged three and five when the Easter bunny appeared over the hill—a man dressed in rabbit skins. He then talked to the children about new life and spring, and how important it is to welcome it each year both in the earth and in ourselves. Then the children clustered in a circle on the other side of the hill while the Easter bunny hid treasures for them. He released them to find the special gifts, asking the older children to help the younger. Brian's daughters did not understand all of the Easter bunny's words, but they understood the uniqueness of this man/animal magically appearing over the hill carrying treasures for them.

WHAT CHILDREN CAN DO

Children want to be able to contribute to rituals, not just be recipients. From the youngest age, you can find ways to include them. All those paintings and drawings that come home from nursery school can be pressed into service as special wrapping paper. Children are great card designers and makers. When they get a little older, the job of present wrapping is an easy one for them to take over. They are always able to give suggestions for foods they would like and can be good helpers as you make special things for the event. They will learn from your modeling and a little structure from you. As you show through your actions that ritual preparing is fun and important, they will incorporate that feeling.

As children grow up, you will need to continue to find ways to be flexible and include their interests. Rituals need to be open enough to allow and invite their participation. People feel more connected and involved with the ritual when there is some role for them to play, or special part that they can do. Actively including them in the planning will ensure that they have a chance to add what is meaningful for them. For instance, in some families adolescents are allowed to invite a friend to be a part of family events. In other families, rock Christmas music replaces the traditional Christmas carols when they are trimming the tree. There may be times when adolescents or young adults do not need to participate with the family and can be given permission to be absent or to go with a friend to another family's house. If you find your older children questioning the ritual, they may be feeling that it is obligatory or rigid in some way. This can further tell you that it is time to talk with them about the meaning of these traditions. Look again at some of the questions in Chapter 3 for ways to help you begin the discussion of how the rituals do or do not work for them.

Over time, you can guide children on how to be ritual initiators. Besides just getting a wish list from their children about possible birthday presents, some parents make up a wish list of their own that they give to the children before the parents' birthday. This serves as a gentle reminder to the children of the upcoming date and is also a way to communicate what present giving means. For instance, David's father, Andreas, wrote on his list things like "Coupons for car washing, dishwashing, and other jobs around the house," and "Coupons for hugs and appreciations." He let his children know that these kinds of actions were more appreciated for his birthday presents than material things.

One year when her children were seven and nine, Samira Nassif found that for the first time they had picked out little presents to go in the stockings of the parents at Christmas. Up to this point, the parents had only put things in for each other. Samira and her husband showed enthusiasm for their presents: lipstick and a little mini-flashlight. Their children were finding ways to be active contributors to the ritual.

CHILDREN AS RITUAL MAKERS

Two four-year-old boys are talking about bedtime:

Ezra: "Sometimes I dream I'm gonna die. I don't like to go to sleep . . ."

Benjy (heartfelt): "Yeah." Then, "You know what I do, Ezra?"

Ezra (intently): "What?"

Benjy: "I keep my milk right here [he indicates his bedside table] and I always drink it down just halfway, right to here."

Ezra (thunderstruck, after a pause): "I do, too! Just halfway. Then if I wake up . . ."

Benjy (intensely finishing Ezra's thought): ". . . it's right there!"[5]

These two boys on their own each constructed a bedtime ritual that would assure them that they were not going to die during their sleep. And what a deep reassurance it must have been to find a friend doing the same thing. Children are ritual makers at a very young age. If they want to do something in a particular way, or choose certain clothing or toys for important events, they are initiating their own ritual. Parents should be sensitive to children doing this. You may need to ask a few questions before you understand the meaning the children are creating. If they don't want to talk about it, simply accept its significance to them. Take a few moments and think back to your own childhood. What were any small rituals that you created? Did they involve special blankets or stuffed animals or secret places in the apartment or house where you lived or outdoors? Did your siblings or cousins have certain rituals? What did these rituals mean? How do you think you learned to make them?

Considering and coordinating different generational needs is often a part of ritual making. Being attentive to what will work for elders, the middle generation, and children will lay a foundation for the personal connections at the heart of rituals. Mix and match different events among the generations. This will prevent the ritual from becoming imbalanced or rigidly focusing on the needs of primarily one generation. Have elders recall and tell stories about what they did at similar ritual times as children. Help the middle generation to see themselves as conduits that pass on from elders to children and children to elders essential parts of their experience. Think of ways the children can honor and remember the older generation. Look at your expectations about what it is men and women are to do in ritual making, as well as what you expect from children. In doing these things, you will be helping the generations to hear and be with each other.

There will be times, too, when it is appropriate to have just one generation or only two generations in your ritual making. Or you may want to have just the immediate family or only friends attend. The wedding anniversary couple may want to go away together themselves. The retirement party may be primarily coworkers. An adult child might take vacation time to see parents alone. Teenagers may want to have a birthday party without adults always present. Being clear about what generations, friends, and associates will or will not be included and why can help people not feel excluded or in some way left out.

Place

The location of a ritual can have significance on a number of levels. In terms of *practicality*, is it a place that people can get to easily? Is the space laid out well for the kinds of activities you want to do? Is it a place that is comfortable for the ages of people that will be there? After their baby daughter's christening, the Nelson family wanted to have a reception. They were first going to hold it in the parish hall next to the church. Then, they started to think through how this would work for them. They were going to have as guests a number of families with young children. There were no separate rooms at the parish hall that could be used to put them down for naps. Also, there was no kitchen. To have all of the food catered would be very expensive. They decided to move the reception to their home and a neighbor's house next door.

That way they would have yard space for the children to play and bedrooms for babies to sleep in, and they could prepare much of the food ahead of time in their own kitchen.

There may also be *historic* significance to a place. A war memorial may be where a group of veterans gather. A school reunion might be held at an old stomping ground. Distinct meanings may be attached to a location because people have lived there, or it was a place a family visited that holds particular memories. A healing ritual may be located near where a person's ashes are scattered or in a cemetery. You might want to highlight or remember the meanings of the place in order to make links to past feelings and memories. For instance, the Heaton family, after finding out that one of their great-great-great-grandfathers fought at the Battle of Ticonderoga in New York, decided to have their family reunion there.

Finally, you need to think about *location and family dynamics*. Is the place one that everyone feels good about coming to or is it seen as a location for only certain factions of the family? Is it much more convenient for one part of the family to get to than others? Or do people feel that there has not been a fair shift of locations? Has there been a chance to celebrate different heritages or histories of the family through shifting locations? The Wilson family usually had a Fourth of July get-together at their Great Aunt Sophronia and Uncle Bill's home. Over time, as their aunt and uncle aged and the younger generation started having children, the long commute to their lakefront home became difficult for the families to make. The house itself was full of knick-knacks and other things collected over the years, and the children had to be watched carefully to see that they did not break anything. With the changing needs of the families, the location needed to be changed for the Fourth of July.

TRYING TO FIND "NEUTRAL" TURF

Sheila Alson describes trying to work out a location for the birthday party for her two children, Alex, five, and Amy, ten, both born on the same day. Steve, the children's father, and Sheila were divorced and the children lived half-time with each of them. The children wanted Steve; his new woman friend, Joanne; her daughter, Susan; and Sheila all to be together for the party. Sheila had never even been inside the house where Steve and Joanne lived. So Sheila and Steve had agreed that the party should be held at a neutral place like a roller rink or restaurant. But the children did not accept this decision, especially Amy. On the phone, Amy's mother proposed, "I will meet you and Daddy and everyone else in the restaurant at five, and we'll all eat together. Then I will leave for my class."

Amy responded, "But I don't want to open my presents in the restaurant. I want you to come over to Daddy and Joanne's house before the restaurant so I can open all the presents at the same time."

"Don't push it, Amy! I said what I would do. I won't do any more." They hung up, furious at each other.

The next morning Amy called with another proposal. "Daddy suggested that Alex and I go over to your house after school and we'll open presents from you there. Then you, Alex, and I will meet Daddy with Joanne and Susan in the restaurant at five. We can all eat, then you can leave."

"Okay."[6]

Amy and her mother negotiated until they found a way to have locations that were comfortable for two different configurations of people and two different types of birthday activities. It is common for rituals to occur in several places when children live in two or more households.

When you think about the location of rituals, it can be useful to think about it on three levels:

• First, does the place work for what you want to do?

• Second, is there such special meaning attached to a location that you should seriously consider holding the ritual there?

• Third, what relationship dynamics will be evoked by the choice of one place versus another?

Participation

Rituals seem to work best when there are different levels of participation that are possible so that people have some choice to do what is meaningful and comfortable for them. When people contribute something, they usually feel more involved. The invitation for a baby shower for Liliana and Julio asked people to bring something to share for the potluck dinner, as well as any words or symbols they wanted to present to the couple to make a new parent's ritual. For food, some people brought elaborate cakes and main dishes that they had made; others just bought drinks and fruit. For the ritual, some people prepared a special toast on the joys and challenges of being parents, some spoke spontaneously at the time, and others brought "found" items such as a spider plant grown from the "babies" of a spider plant given to them when they were first parents years ago. The hope was expressed that Liliana and Julio, who would be returning back to their native Chile in another six months, would take one of the babies from this plant back to Chile to keep the plant growing with their baby. These words and symbols for the new parents set the stage for lots of conversation about parenting, and the upcoming birth. The levels of participation in the shower were open enough so that people could contribute by spontaneously doing something at the time, preparing something ahead of time, or just picking up something to bring.

If there are a lot of different ages involved in the event, you may want to think carefully about activities that mix ages easily, like treasure hunts or storytelling, or make sure you have a balance of different kinds of activities. Think, too, about the rhythm of the day. Will you want to intersperse quiet activities with more active ones? Do you have room for things to be happening simultaneously or will that make too much hubbub?

BEGINNINGS, MIDDLES, AND ENDINGS

In order to facilitate participation, it can also be important to think about beginnings and endings, as well as any special setting of perhaps more ceremonial parts. At beginnings, people need to feel welcome, and the tone is first set for how people will spend time together. At some rituals, people will immediately offer things like finger foods, drinks, and/or party favors such as hats and blowers as a way to mark entrance into an event. People will also show off special clothing or costumes and present any gifts they have brought. This begins to mark the ritual as special time outside of regular time. The scene is starting to be created for what is going to be done, and the parts people will play, but in an open enough manner that allows people to connect with each other as they ease into the new situation.

Middle parts of rituals often have some more structured aspects such as words or symbols exchanged, or sitting down more formally to share food. These closed parts announce that it is time for people to focus on the special purposes of the ritual. If there are ceremonial aspects, they may need to be set off with time and space. A procession or blessing sometimes starts a service, or a gong or music gathers people. Candles or incense may be lit. Ribbons, flowers, or a special cloth can set off special space.

Endings of ritual events usually provide some closure and winding down. Often the group comes together in a less formal way to begin to move back into less structured activities and day-to-day life. This may be as simple as leaving the dining table after a large sit-down dinner to go out onto the porch and have tea and coffee. If it has been a transition ritual of some sort, the new status of people may be marked at this time as well. For instance, at Mildred Lancaster's retirement party, after the speeches, presents, and presentation of two plaques commemorating her work, she led off the dancing with her husband. After the first dance, others joined in with them.

If you think about the beginning, middle, and end at a wedding ceremony, background music is usually playing as people arrive, and there is time for people to congregate, leave presents, and greet each other. Different music often announces the middle part—the wedding ceremony. After people have gathered, the music continues for a few minutes as people make the transition into this special time and space. Words of welcome and/or blessings then usually open the ceremony, with a formal structuring of vows and readings led by a clergy person or justice of the peace. The ceremony usually closes with some celebratory actions such as kisses, hugs, a recessional with lively music, and standing together of the congregation as the bride and groom come down the aisle. A receiving line provides opportunities for each individual to offer their congratulations and good wishes. People then often go to another location for a reception.

To conclude the event, the wedding couple may change out of their wedding clothes and into more regular clothes and go off on their honeymoon with people throwing rice or birdseed. Their car has often been painted with "Just Married"—thus announcing their new status to everyone.

FOOD AND RITUALS

Food is often a central part of rituals. As Alan Alda said, "Eating is one of the few sensuous things people can do together that doesn't lead to divorce." Eating together is also a way to express nurturance and caretaking, and many foods have symbolic meanings that are an essential part of the ritual. For instance, eggs included in both Easter and Passover celebrations stand for new life and fecundity. Heart-shaped cakes and cookies at Valentine's Day signify love. In Nigeria, a gathering of the clan does not start without the breaking of the kola nut that welcomes everyone, invokes the presence of both the living and the dead, and brings blessings to all who are there. In Polish families, oplatek is shared at Christmas. This thin breadlike white wafer has a religious scene imprinted on it. People face each other and break off a piece of the oplatek, then wish each other "health, wealth, happiness, and good years to come."

Family recipes that are passed down signify what is unique to each family and foods eaten year after year are anticipated, relished, and remembered afterwards. Ethnic heritage is carried from generation to generation with noodle kugel, pierogis, pemmican, empanadas, shortbread, or tortellini. As you walk in the door and smell the holiday cookies baking, you remember previous ritual events, and other times and places you have made the cookies. As you taste the chestnut stuffing, you are connected to the generations that made and ate the same food before you.

Mixed messages about food are also a part of many rituals. They can be a time of overeating, of guilt about the superabundance of food we have, of worry over weight gain and health problems. Yet people are expected to eat heartily as a way to appreciate the hospitality and work of the hosts. You may need to make a conscious effort to have different types of food available, less food, or perhaps even to downplay the focus of ritual times on food. You may choose to have some ritual times without food. After she found out she had a high cholesterol level, Margaret Norton, who came to Iowa from England, chose to have her daily teatime with all kinds of fancy teas, and to do away with the biscuits and cookies altogether.

NO LEFTOVERS

Valerie Harris-Greene typically found herself cooking a big ham at Easter (even though her present family almost never ate red meat), baking egg bread for breakfast from scratch, angel food cake for dessert, and passing around lots of chocolates and jelly beans. She nibbled as she cooked, and other family members helped themselves to foods that were not ordinarily in the house. Valerie did not feel well because of the changes in her diet, while others worried about their weight. Valerie began to wonder about what role she really wanted food to have at Easter. How could she both keep traditional family foods and the meaning and memories they evoked, as well as respect changing eating patterns? Valerie talked to her husband, Ethan. With heart trouble aggravated by weight problems, he agreed with her that the quantity and types of food were overwhelming. "You know," he said, "my parents always made a big deal out of eating rabbit food at Easter—meaning salads. Then the rest of the year they would say things like 'Eat your yummy lettuce so you can grow up strong like the Easter bunny.' It wouldn't hurt our kids to be eating more vegetables. Besides, you do more recipes from your side of the family anyway. Maybe you could add different kinds of salads and cut down on other things."

"That's a thought," said Valerie. "I keep buying this giant ham because my dad always made a big thing about having plenty for everyone as well as leftovers. We don't *like* having ham for a week afterwards. I'll buy a smaller ham and I'll serve lots of 'rabbit food.' And no chocolates and jelly beans out until Easter morning."

Valerie and Ethan found a way to both honor and evolve food traditions. When there are remarried families with multiple family food histories to incorporate, or a family member dramatically changes diet, there are other issues to consider. Changing food preferences can be especially difficult in families where the ritual style is rigid and difference is seen as disloyalty.

In the Sorcanelli family, when their son, Anthony, was fifteen, he decided that he wanted to be a vegetarian. When they were eating at the family home, this was not particularly a problem. They kept tofu, cheeses, beans, and other alternative protein foods available for him. But when they wanted to extend family gatherings for holidays and other family times, it was more difficult. Grandparents and aunts and uncles thought he was just "going through a phase." They belittled his vegetarian food and wanted him to appreciate the special dishes they made. They felt it wouldn't make that much difference if he had meat for one meal. So when the lasagna was served, the whole dish had meat in it even though it would have been relatively easy to make a small dish of it that was meatless. Over time, Anthony and his family educated them about simple things that could be done to respect his food preferences. They brought tofu pups to cookouts and taught them how to grill tofu. When antipasto salad was made, they set aside a portion with no ham or salami in it. Over time, the extended family incorporated both vegetarian and nonvegetarian foods. Some of Anthony's cousins even began snitching his grilled tofu because they liked it so much.

Food can be central to a ritual because of its symbolic meaning, and its historical and ethnic significance. Preparing food for one another, breaking bread, and eating together provide powerful links for people to feel connected. Think about the place of food at your rituals:

• Does it fit with your current life-style?

• Does it honor past family traditions? Does it reflect some balance of the various backgrounds of family members?

• Can people express differences with food preferences, or must everyone want the same food?

• How does the use of food enhance or detract from your ritual?

ALCOHOL AND RITUALS

Alcohol is also often found at rituals. There is a history of its use in many religious and secular events from wine at Mass or the Jewish Kiddush to the widespread use of champagne for toasts at dinners and receptions. However, historically alcohol was carefully controlled and defined in its use with clear limits set. For instance at Passover, four cups of wine are poured at the dinner but it is not expected that all of it will be drunk. The emphasis is on the symbolic pouring of wine each time. For Communion, one symbolic sip of wine is taken. Purim is the one Jewish holiday when, within the ritual, people can drink to excess. It is a time to break the rules. The "rule" of drinking to excess once a year, in fact announces that one must *not* do so at other times.

This controlled use of alcohol has broken down in many families.

Based on numerous studies, it is estimated that ten to fourteen percent of the population is alcoholic (ten to twelve percent of men and two to three percent of women). Because most of these people are in some familial relationships, 50 million people in the United States are directly affected by alcoholism. Looking at alcohol use and ritual life where alcoholism exists, Peter Steinglass and his colleagues have found three distinct patterns.[7] In some families, rituals do not change because the alcoholic in the family does not drink at ritual times or behavioral changes when they drink are such that ritual is not affected. Some families adapt and change their rituals. They accommodate to the needs of the alcoholic. As the father in the Lawton family drank more heavily, they gave up their week's vacation at a lakeside cottage. It was a full day's drive from their home and they could no longer count on Alan Lawton as a reliable driver. Also, the kinds of activities they did there such as boating, swimming, and fishing were no longer safe for their dad to do. So they decided to go to a local seaside hotel close to their home. It had bars and restaurants that Mr. Lawton could walk to and the rest of the family could spend their time on the beach. Needless to say, it was not their best vacation.

In other families, a clear limit is put on alcohol use at holiday times. As Fred Fain said, "I never got smashed on a holiday. I never screwed up on a holiday."

His wife, Claudine, added with steely but unmistakable anger, "I would have killed him if he did." This family managed to put a boundary at ritual times around the problem drinking that was not crossed. However, this is usually very difficult to do.

Some rituals get disrupted altogether by alcoholism. Often they are the daily rituals or family traditions that have less time and protected space from the outside calendar. In the Jarrell family, dinnertime changed greatly when the father, Ed, began to have problems with alcohol. Ed's two boys were sixteen and eleven. Here is what one of the sons had to say about it:

> *Don*: If Father didn't come [for a dinner], we'd spend the night looking for him. . . . When drinking started, dinnertimes weren't, they stopped. Mother would have dinner for my brother and whoever was there to eat. Just a matter of eating, not a time to look forward to. . . . Very little conversation, not a joyous occasion.

In regard to your own family, you might want to think about the use of alcohol in day-to-day rituals, family traditions, family holidays and celebrations, or life-cycle events:

• Is the place of alcohol problematic in any of these rituals? If so, how is it an issue?

• What was the place of alcohol in rituals in your family-of-origin?

• How does this influence how you think alcohol should be used in your current ritual life?

• Has alcohol caused you to interrupt or minimize your rituals?

If there is problem drinking by a member of the family, having alcohol at a ritual gathering cannot be taken for granted. People need to think carefully and supportively with one another about whether to have only nonalcoholic drinks, or a limited amount of alcohol. Nonalcoholic wines, beers, and sparkling ciders and other carbonated drinks are all readily available. These kinds of drinks are different enough from day-to-day drinks that are served and can help to mark the special occasion. And they are often a lot less expensive as well.

The fascinating thing is that ritual life itself seems to provide some protection against the passing of alcoholism from one generation to another. If rituals are *not* heavily disrupted by parental drinking, then the *occurrence of alcohol problems in the next generation is lessened*. Rituals have a protective function. If they remain intact, the family has a place to come together and support each other, express their identity, and honor their members despite parental alcoholism. This cohesion protects people against drinking problems because they are connected and involved with others and with meaningful traditions.[8]

Are you and other family members comfortable with the place of alcohol in your rituals now? If you are not, what changes would you like to make and how might you begin to make them? Changing long-standing patterns of alcohol use, especially when they are so much a part of the larger culture, may not be an easy thing to do. Gather as much support as you can from other ritual participants. Make it clear in the planning stages what changes you plan to make.

RECORDING THE RITUAL

A good way to invite people to participate is by asking them to help with documenting the ritual in some way. They can take photos, audiotape certain sections, collect memorabilia or stories. If you have access to a video recorder (they can often be rented inexpensively), people can take turns making a video of the whole event. Having a specific job to do can help someone who hangs back on the periphery. Others may interact with them more and they may feel more of a part of what is happening.

Making a record of the ritual is also a way to increase participation by sharing the ritual with those unable to come because of illness, cutoffs, distance, or conflicts in their schedule. In future years, this record can be a resource to look at when planning for future rituals. By looking at pictures, home movies, or copies of programs or stories written about it, you can think about what went well and what might need to change.

Make sure you have the necessary supplies on hand and that whoever is operating any cameras, tape recorders, tripods, and lights knows well in advance how to use them. Lots of good moments have been lost to jammed cameras and recorders with no more blank tapes.

Presents: The Metaphor for Giving and Receiving in Our Relationships

Giving and receiving presents is an integral part of many rituals. Some rituals, like weddings, baby showers, graduations, or birthdays, involve family members and friends giving gifts to one or more people. Other rituals, like Christmas, Hanukkah, Three Kings' Day, or anniversaries, generally include an exchange of presents among significant people. Presents may be a small portion of a much larger ritual, or they may be the central element, sometimes overwhelming all other aspects of a ritual. As you read ahead, think about the place of presents in all of your rituals, and whether this fits what you and your family really want gift giving and receiving to mean.

A BIT OF GIFT-GIVING HISTORY

While gift giving exists in all cultures and stretches back through history, buying presents in a store is a relatively recent phenomenon. Originally, gifts were grown, such as fruits or vegetables, or were handmade. In Roman times, for instance, honey, fruits, and lamps were given at the winter solstice, in a foreshadowing of what has become Christmas gifts. Values were embedded in Roman gift giving, as wealthy Romans were required to give gifts to those who were poor.[9] In the 1800s, Christmas gifts were primarily for children, and were usually special foods, such as oranges or nuts, or a handmade toy or item of clothing. Gifts between adults were practical and simple, such as fountain pens or handkerchiefs, and were called "holiday notions."[10] Birthday presents were expected to be useful items, like mittens or a slate, and anniversary gifts were given only on major anniversaries, such as the tenth or twenty-fifth. Presents were given unwrapped and without special cards. Clearly, such gift giving stands in major contrast to the place of gifts in our ritual lives today.

With industrialization in the late nineteenth century came manufactured goods and an increase in commercialization. As society became more affluent, the rise of store-bought gifts began. Since purchased presents were seen as less personal than handmade items, gift wrapping was invented in order to communicate that the gift had still been personally handled and "created" for the recipient.[11]

Advertisements encouraged the new gift-buying activity. A December 15, 1919, ad in *The New York Times* read: "Don't give your family and friends frivolous gifts that are sure to disappoint. Buy them worthy gifts that will let them know how much you care." The notion that a more expensive, store-bought gift demonstrated more caring was emerging and beginning to replace the idea that making a present was the way to give gifts.

PRESENTS AND PRESENCE

"My dad likes to collect pewter. He is also a connoisseur of different kinds of beer. For my mother's birthday, he gave her three pewter beer mugs. She doesn't drink."   —Joy, age 25

"My husband had seen me eyeing this orange silk blouse in the store. I didn't get it for myself because it was too much money. Then it showed up in a fancy box for our anniversary."   —Maria, age 52

When presents are given and received in rituals they symbolically express relationships between people. Gift giving and receiving speak volumes about how we see and know one another, and what we value. Hidden messages are often embedded in gifts. Two examples from popular television may illustrate, each showing the gift giving and receiving at an eighteenth-birthday party.

On "Cagney and Lacey," Harv Lacey, Jr.'s, eighteenth birthday is marked with a number of gifts whose unspoken message is "You're going to college!" His baby sister gives him a mug, no doubt bought by his mother, "for all those late-night cram sessions at the dormitory." His brother gives him pens. And his parents present him with a gift certificate for a computer, "compatible with the ones in major colleges." As the gift giving and receiving unfold, Harv Jr. becomes more and more uncomfortable, while the other family members become more and more excited, not noticing his obvious discomfort. Finally, he announces that he is not going to college and has, that very day, joined the Marine Corps. In this very moving segment, gift giving and receiving at an important rite-of-passage birthday party stand as a metaphor for all that is known and not known between family members. The gifts proclaimed, "This is what we want you to be," rather than affirming, "This is who you are."

This segment stands in sharp contrast to the gift giving and receiving at another eighteenth birthday party, this one on "The Wonder Years." It is Karen's eighteenth birthday. She and her father have become angrier and angrier with each other in recent weeks, in fairly typical intergenerational struggles. He is an ex-marine and she has joined the peace movement. Father is so angry with Karen that he tells the family that he will not give her a birthday gift. Then, during the birthday ritual, which Karen cannot wait to escape, her father hands her a gift that transcends all of the conflict and bitterness that has arisen between them. She opens the package to find his old, worn kit bag from the Marine Corps. In one sentence, giving her his blessing and permission to grow up, Father says, "It's for college or if you go somewhere—either way you have to have something to put your stuff in and this one got me through some pretty rough times." With tears in her eyes, Karen says, "I love it!" In one small act of gift giving and receiving, both the giver and the receiver were able to feel known, appreciated, and deeply connected despite their differences.

As you think about gifts you may have received for birthdays or anniversaries or holidays, think about whether you felt unknown and alienated, whether you felt known for who you are, or whether you saw an exciting new glimpse of yourself through someone else's eyes.

A TONI DOLL FOR AMY

Amy Sullivan was forty-three when she recalled the best birthday gift she ever received. Just before her sixth birthday, Amy was diagnosed with nephritis. She had to be hospitalized and was going to remain in the hospital over her birthday. On the way to the hospital, Amy's grandmother said she needed Amy's help with an important decision. Her grandmother owned a gift shop and she told Amy she needed her advice about which doll to stock in the store. Having her grandmother ask her opinion made Amy feel very important. She took Amy to the wholesale market and showed her a baby doll and a Toni doll. The Toni doll was new on the market and could be given a home permanent with sugar water. Amy didn't hesitate for a second when her grandmother asked her which doll she thought most girls would prefer—"The Toni doll, for sure!" Three days later, when Amy was in the hospital on her sixth birthday, she unwrapped a box to find the Toni doll. In her reminiscence, Amy remarked, "I felt known. I felt cared for. I was only six, but my opinion mattered. My grandmother made a special effort to surprise me with just the right present. I'll never forget the thoughtfulness of that gift!"

WHEN PRESENTS ARE PAINFUL

We've all grown up hearing "It's not the gift, it's the thought that counts." Sometimes, however, the "thought" that is being communicated in a gift is thoughtless, selfish, angry, or downright hostile. When Peter Harley began living with Janice Corrette, her family was very angry and disappointed in her choice. They let Peter know that he was not welcome in their family at Christmas by giving Janice several very elaborate gifts and giving him two or three dime-store items. As these were opened in front of everyone in the extended family, Peter felt quite ashamed and Janice felt embarrassed. No one commented on the gifts, but the entire Christmas celebration was tense and unhappy. This Christmas present pattern continued for three years, until finally Janice spoke directly to her parents and told them they must stop this. Her parents insisted it was all a joke and that she and Peter were just too sensitive. Nonetheless, the Christmas present giving changed that year, and Peter was given a gift that resembled what other family members received.

While presents are often not so openly hostile, they many times miss the mark and can affect the feeling of an entire anniversary, birthday, or holiday. Just as a gift can communicate a deep sense of being known or seen, a gift can also announce that one is not understood. Cara Janoff's father always brought her a gift when he returned from a trip. This little reentry ritual generally helped them to reconnect. When Cara became a young teenager, however, her father stopped noticing her development. He returned from a trip with a little girl's purse, appropriate for someone about eight years old. "He couldn't understand my disappointment, and my mother made excuses for him. This was the beginning of our not knowing each other."

When a present is painful or disappointing, an entire ritual may be remembered this way. Married twenty-two years, Sara Jackson bitterly recalled the first Christmas with her husband when he gave her a model airplane kit as her only gift. She could recollect no other elements of that holiday. "After that, I told him to just give me money and I would pick my own present, and that's what we've done ever since." The possibility of her husband changing, learning more about her, and showing this through gift giving disappeared from all of their subsequent rituals.

In contrast, Kelly Aptos took the risk to teach her husband a bit about gift giving. On a Valentine's Day early in their marriage, Jerry Aptos gave his wife a waffle iron. "I really wanted to just throw it at him!" Instead, she explained that the waffle iron represented more work for her to do, when what she really wanted was to spend some romantic time with him. Jerry left and returned home with a bottle of Kelly's favorite perfume and told her he would fix dinner that night. Their Valentine meal consisted of waffles à la Jerry and champagne. This meal became a humorous part of their Valentine's Day ritual, and Jerry learned to become a more sensitive chooser of gifts.

Most of us learn about giving and receiving presents during rituals as children in our families-of-origin. We may learn to give and receive gracefully, thoughtfully, artfully. We may learn that gifts are primarily for children, or that only mothers shop for presents. We may watch as our father is obviously disappointed by a present from our mother but remains grudgingly silent, or we may hear over and over that what we picked was the wrong thing and feel rejected. You may want to think about what you have learned about relationships through the metaphor of giving and receiving in the family that you come from:

• During what rituals were gifts given? Birthdays, anniversaries, holidays?

• How did gifts for children differ from gifts for adults?

• Who had responsibility for selecting the presents? Was there one person, or did everyone participate? If your mother did all of the present shopping, who bought her gifts?

• How were you expected to respond to gifts given by your mother? Your father? Your siblings? Your extended family? Were you allowed to say if you didn't like a present? Were you allowed to differentiate which gift you liked better or were you expected to receive all gifts the same way?

• What was the worst gift you ever received? What were the relationship elements that made it so painful?

• What was the best gift you ever received? What were the relationship elements that made it so special?

GIFTS AND GENDER ROLES

Just as women have borne the major responsibility for ritual preparation overall, so they have often been in charge of selecting and wrapping gifts for all family members. As children, many of us received presents with cards signed "Love, Mom and Dad," only to hear Dad say "Oh, let me see what I got you!" Often, a wife will take responsibility for buying birthday and holiday presents for her husband, their children, children's gifts to father, her extended family, and *his* extended family. In turn, a husband may ask his secretary or his sister to select his wife's present. This sort of arrangement speaks volumes about traditional gender arrangements, in which women are expected to be sensitive to all of the relationship and personal needs of everyone in the entire family, and to demonstrate this through choosing just the right gifts, while men are regarded as incapable of this task. Such an arrangement overloads women and robs men of the opportunity to tune into all of the personal needs and differences that can be expressed through gift giving. Take some time to talk with your partner about the gender patterns that have taken hold in your gift giving and receiving. Are these satisfactory to both of you? Are they indicative of an old arrangement that you may have witnessed in your family-of-origin, or have they changed along with other gender changes in your ritual life?

Presents and Values: What's Being Expressed and Passed Along?

The gift giving and receiving dimension of rituals says a lot about our values. Between a couple, such values may differ profoundly. William and Patrice Appleton came from families where the value and meaning of presents were quite different. William grew up in a poor family, and presents were regarded as unaffordable luxuries. Consequently, no one really expected birthday or Christmas gifts, even when they could afford them as adults. Patrice grew up in an upper-middle-class family, where presents were a big part of most rituals and were regarded as aspects of relationship reciprocity. This difference became a major source of conflict for this couple. On Christmas and birthdays, William would either phone his family or send a card. To Patrice, this seemed cheap and uncaring. She, in turn, bought and sent presents to all of her family, which William regarded as extravagant and a waste of their money. The conflict between them especially escalated regarding gifts for each other, as William bought small, inexpensive items for Patrice's birthday and Christmas, while she purchased very elaborate gifts for him. Clearly, this couple had learned very different values regarding presents, which were overwhelming their ability to create meaningful and enjoyable rituals with each other. It was not until they began to examine where their ideas about presents came from and ask themselves what they truly wanted to express now through gift giving and receiving that they were able to develop a new pattern.

Gift giving and receiving can be an opportunity to teach values to our children. In the Cowan family, the father went shopping alone and bought all of the Mother's Day presents for his children to give their mother. "It's just easier that way. I can do it more quickly and hand them each a box to give her. They don't mind." In the Kurlin family, the father takes his children to the store and talks with them about what they think their mother would most like for Mother's Day. "It takes awhile. Usually we spend the whole afternoon. I get to hear what's on their minds and what they think their mother really wants. They get quite excited about picking just the right thing for her." Different values about giving and receiving, about the importance of devoting time to think about another person versus simply doing what's convenient are being imparted to the children in these two families.

Children learn family values through the repeated present-giving and receiving aspect of rituals. Sarabeth Owens was astounded to discover the values her eight-year-old daughter, Eileen, had learned about giving and receiving at Christmas as she watched her daughter "playing Christmas" with her dolls. A mother, father, and two baby dolls sat in a circle around a little decorated pine branch. With fabric scraps and yarn, Eileen carefully wrapped some small items, and her mother overheard, "Here are three presents for you, and three for you. Everyone has three, a present from the mommy, the daddy, and the sister. The baby gets to open one first. Say thank you. Now the big sister gets to open one— Mommy, you be the Santa and bring the present to her." This play-acting exactly mirrored the present-giving and receiving part of the Christmas ritual in the family, incorporating the family's values of fairness, the order of gift giving from youngest to oldest, and family members watching while one person opened his or her gift.

People who you are close to may or may not have similar values to your own about presents. You may want to consider such values and make them more explicit among your intimate relationships. As you look at the following list, think about which values you agree with or disagree with, and how this compares to the values of those who are close to you.

• In order for gifts to be meaningful, they need to be hand-made or unique in some way.

• Having limits on what you spend on gifts is a good idea.

• I would never give a present without wrapping it.

• A lot of thought should go into gift selection.

• It's okay to give a card sometimes instead of a gift.

• Presents exchanged among family members or friends need to be of roughly equal value.

• Children should give presents to parents.

• Children should not be expected to know what to choose for parents. Parents should do the shopping for them.

• Adults should give presents to each other.

• Everyone should receive the exact same number of gifts on a holiday.

• Presents are mainly for children.

• A gift should always be a surprise.

• It's okay to give money and let the person choose his or her own gift.

• Extended family members should receive gifts on a regular basis.

Once family members have a clearer idea about their values regarding gift giving and receiving, all sorts of creative approaches become possible. The Chapman family has agreed that it is okay to buy presents at tag sales and thrift shops, and that what is most important is choosing a gift that the person really wants. In the McNamara family, children truly being responsible for giving gifts is important, and so the family developed a method of the children creating coupons that are good for car washes, snow shoveling, or cooking dinner. The Rosses have seven children and limited resources. They draw names out of a hat so that people buy presents only for certain other people at Hanukkah, and yet all are able to experience the act of giving and receiving. The Banners have agreed that saving the environment is the uppermost value in their family and that all birthday gifts should be contributions to environmental organizations in honor of the person's birthday. In the White family, a chart is updated every October listing each person's gift-wish list for that year's Christmas. The Ellises decided that saving money for a trip was more important than Christmas gifts on Christmas, and so did all of their shopping after the holiday in order to take advantage of sales. The Penders realized that they had developed a competition with one another for the most expensive gift, and experimented one year with giving personally written stories. The possibilities are endless, providing you take some time to talk about what you really want to be communicating with presents.

DIVORCE AND REMARRIAGE GIFT DILEMMAS

Presents for birthdays and holidays can become even more complicated when there has been a divorce or remarriage. In separation and divorce, gifts for children often become metaphors for relationship struggles between the divorcing parents. Each parent may try to outdo the other with elaborate birthday gifts in a silent competition for the child's love and loyalty. Sammy Whelan recalled his childhood birthday parties with sadness and anger. "My parents competed for me with bigger and better presents. I knew these presents were not really about me. I hated it. I never played with any of the things they gave me because whichever toy I played with meant I didn't love the parent who gave me the other toy!"

The value of one parent's gift can be discredited by the other parent. Elias Korn's father lived across the country. For Elias's seventh birthday, his father sent him a gift certificate from a catalogue Elias had admired when he had visited. Mr. Korn asked his ex-wife to help Elias use the gift certificate. A year later the gift certificate still had not been used, and Elias told his father that his mother said this was not a good gift.

When divorced parents are furious with each other, they may show this by "forgetting" presents for their children's birthdays or holidays. Here, the absence of gifts for children becomes part of the parents' war with each other. Doug Serlin was six when his parents divorced, and his father moved away. Doug never knew if he was going to receive a birthday or Christmas gift from his father. Often, this depended on the state of his parents' relationship with one another. For two years he received no presents, and his mother dealt with his sadness and disappointment. The third year, he received a large box full of toys, candy, and a hunting knife, and he couldn't understand why his mother was so angry when he was happy.

While divorce is certainly complex, it is crucial not to play out adult relationship issues through gift giving to children. Birthday and holiday rituals can become filled with all of the unfinished divorce business if parents use gifts to children as a way to speak to each other. If you are divorced, you will want to think carefully about what you are communicating to your children as you give them presents.

Gifts from children to parents are also complicated by divorce. Very young children are often unable to shop by themselves or mail gifts to parents who live away. Custodial parents may find there is no one to encourage their children to get presents for them. A custodial mother may feel resentful that she helps her children get birthday gifts for their father, but that this gesture is not reciprocated. It's important to talk with your children about this aspect of rituals when there has been a divorce. Let them know that gifts can express many things, especially including how people are thinking about one another. You may need to enlist the help of another adult, such as an uncle or a friend, who will help children choose presents, both for you and for their noncustodial parent.

If you are able to comfortably coparent following a divorce, you may want to consider talking about presents for children with your former spouse, in order to avoid subtle competition, and to coordinate gift giving so that children do not receive duplicate gifts or a grossly unbalanced number of gifts from one side of the family or the other.

When there has been a remarriage, presents and cards can often mark the beginning of new relationships. Step-children and step-grandparents will need to learn the dates of new family members' birthdays and anniversaries. Early in a remarriage, gift giving may be uncomfortable between step-parents and step-children, but sometimes a present can begin to open a relationship. When Anita Jeffers remarried, her daughter, Celie, ten, did not want to accept her new stepfather. On their first Christmas together, Celie became very angry when her mother said the presents to Celie were from her and her new husband. "I don't want presents from both of you. I just want *your* presents!" Clearly, Anita was moving too fast, trying to get Celie to accept her new husband. When Celie's birthday arrived in May, Anita and her husband tried something different. Anita gave Celie a gift just from her, as she had done for the past six years. Celie's stepfather then asked her if she would like to go shopping with him. At the store, he told her "I want to get you a birthday present, but I don't really know you that well yet. I don't really know what you like. How about if you choose some new clothes so I can begin to find out about your favorite colors." This way of giving Celie a birthday present captured the actual stage of this remarried family's relationships, and marked the opening of Celie's acceptance of her stepfather. In later years, Celie and her stepfather chose to mark her birthday by a special shopping trip, while her mother continued to give her a gift just from her.

Giving and receiving presents is an intricate part of our rituals. Often, families do not pay enough conscious attention to the ways relationships are being expressed and negotiated through gifts. You may want to talk over the patterns of giving and receiving in your current rituals, and consider what changes, if any, you want to make:

• How are the gifts you give received by others? How do you feel about how gifts are received?

• Can family members give an honest response to gifts?

• What is the best gift you've given in your current primary relationship? What made it so special?

• What is the worst gift-giving experience you've had? What happened in the relationship?

• What difficulties are you encountering in your gift giving and receiving currently? Who do you need to talk this over with?

• What do presents currently express in all of your important relationships? Do you want to change this?

• What present for what ritual would you most like to give and to whom?

• What present for what ritual would you most like to receive and from whom?

Questions to Help with Planning

As we've seen, the planning process in rituals is as important as the actual event and is often the crucial ingredient in people's sense of involvement in the actual ritual. Planning needs to be open enough to pull people in on a number of different levels at the same time that there is enough structure to share the actual work of ritual making. It is important that people not feel overworked or so exhausted that they cannot enjoy the event itself. If people can share the work in ways that are experienced by all as being fair and supportive, a tone is set for the whole ritual. Talk through ahead of time how others can be involved with their ideas, help, and cleanup skills. Plan what you want to do, and then do *half* of it and congratulate yourself on a job well done. You may want to experiment with simplifying food preparation and cleanup by serving fewer dishes, using paper plates, eating out, and having fresh fruit for dessert. You may want to try a potluck where friends and family bring foods that are unique to their own ritual heritage. Perhaps alternate years when you do special baking. If you usually don't do much cooking, you may find the special preparation of food for rituals to be a new adventure. Think about your gift giving. You might want to try putting a limit on the amount of money to be spent, doing joint gifts, drawing names out of a hat. Or you might want to experiment with giving only found or symbolic gifts, or asking people for a list of gifts they truly want. Find what works for you and for those close to you. What you do one time is not necessarily what you will want to do the next time.

Planning involves a range of variables from people to place and time, to presents, and food and drink. Each of these seemingly mundane areas has the potential to communicate what is important because the symbols and symbolic actions that they involve express the history, beliefs, values, and relationships of the participants. Making Great-grandma's shortbread recipe on Grandparents' Day in her old cast-iron shortbread mold links members of the family to her memory, communicates the importance of the generations, and teaches something about her Scottish heritage. Take time to think through what your choices are communicating.

Who gets together and plans and prepares for the rituals can be just as important as who comes to the ritual. This is where the foundation is built for how people feel connected and involved with creating meaning for the event. Extra time spent at the planning phase, not just on the details of how food will be cooked and how it will look but on the interpersonal aspects, will be time very well spent. Planning will be easier if people feel their input is important and if they think their ideas are being heard. If there have been past difficulties in planning rituals, these may need to be aired. One good way to do this is to focus on how to do the planning this time in a way that works for everyone, rather than rehashing old history about what did not work. Listen carefully to others about what might work better for them and take responsibility for what you can do differently. Keep your discussion focused on solutions. If you can start your ritual planning with a more or less clean slate, then it will not become a place to indirectly work out past slights and hurts.

Finally, have reasonable expectations for rituals, which are, after all, only one part of your life. Remember, a little humor can go a long way when things don't turn out quite as planned. The funny stories that are told ten years later about our rituals often come from things that people were pretty upset about at the time. And don't forget the story of how Erma Bombeck coped with overly high expectations. One December, she was in the bookstore looking at Martha Stewart's Christmas book for holiday entertaining. It was full of extravagant ideas on how to make the perfect holiday. Erma simply moved the book from the shelves marked "Entertaining" to the "Fiction" section.

Here are some questions that you can use as a quick check-in to think about upcoming rituals. You may want to return to these questions three to six months before any particular ritual.

Outside Pressures
• How is the ritual influenced by expectations present in the larger culture? Do these expectations support or hinder what you want to have happen?

• Are the outside pressures stronger for some people in the family than others? Who? In what ways?

• Do outside influences hinder or help how you want your rituals to provide continuity and change?

Preparation
• Who is involved in the process of planning? What is important about their involvement?

• Who is not included and why? How would things go differently if they were included?

• How can you include ideas from many of the people who will participate?

• In what ways are playfulness and humor a part of the preparations?

• In what ways are gender roles enacted in the planning? Do you want to change any of them? If so, how?

• What will make the planning easier?

People

• Who is important to invite and why? How will they be invited?

• How might you include someone who sometimes does not participate?

• How are relationship cutoffs affecting who is invited?

• Is there anything significant about who is *not* invited?

• Will different generations be there? If so, how will the generations have chances to get together?

• Will children be involved? How?

Place

• What is significant about the place where you have this event? Who feels most comfortable having it there? Least comfortable?

• How is the location chosen?

• Is there any particular meaning attached to the location?

• What can you do to help those who feel least comfortable in this location (like alternating places in different years, picking a more "neutral" place)?

• What travel considerations need to be taken into account (e.g., time, expense, distance traveled in previous years)?

Participation

• What are important activities? How are they decided upon?

• How are they influenced by gender? By ethnicity?

• Are there special symbols or symbolic items that you will use?

• What is the role of food, music, special clothing?

Planning Your Rituals

	POSITIVE—Aspects that are working well and should be maintained	PROBLEMATIC—Aspects that are not working well and need to be changed	WAYS OUR RITUALS COULD BE DIFFERENT
Preparation In the process of preparing for the ritual, what special activities are involved (like travel, getting gifts, food)? How do gender, age, culture, amd family-of-origin experiences influence this process?	1. 2. 3.	1. 2. 3.	1. 2. 3.
People Who is the occasion shared with and what family dynamics are involved in deciding who does or does not participate?			
Place Is there anything special about where the ritual occurs that influences the meaning of the experience? What are the family rules regarding the choice of location?			
Participation What activities are part of the ritual and how are they influenced by gender, culture, age, and family-of-orgin experiences?			
Presents What parts do gift-giving and receiving play in the ritual?			

- What is the role of alcohol? What would you like the role of alcohol to be?

- Who will record the ritual and in what way?

- How will you close or end the time together?

Presents
- What is the role of gift giving?

- How are gifts received?

- What changes would you like to make in what happens with gifts?

You might want to choose a family ritual that you can look at carefully. Pick an event or holiday that is coming up fairly soon, or one that has just ended. Use the chart, Planning Your Rituals, to help organize your thinking about this ritual. It can be filled out by one person alone, or by several members. If you like, photocopy the grid (or make an enlarged version of your own) and put it up on your refrigerator or some other prominent place with your comments so family members can read what you are thinking and/or add their own ideas. The grid is organized to include both the positive aspects of such times as well as more difficult parts, with a final column focusing on possible changes.[12]

If you are thinking about changes, think small, exploratory, experimental, and fun. Include input from others. Play around with some outlandish ideas. Enjoy!

5

How Rituals Make Meaning

SYMBOLS AND SYMBOLIC ACTIONS

New Beginnings

When Norm and Elinor Korner decided to reconcile after an eighteen-month separation, their children, Billy, twelve, and Sally, ten, were frightened that their parents would get back together and then separate again. Sally said, "We've gotten used to living with our mom—what if this doesn't work?" Billy agreed, adding, "What if we have to go through this all over again?" Both to calm their children and to assure them that this was, indeed, a new beginning, the Korners planned a ritual that would include the children in a special way. Billy and Sally were asked to plan a surprise for their parents to mark the father's moving back home and the family's reunification. The parents, in turn, promised to make a surprise for the children.

As the day for the family's reuniting approached, there was much playful secrecy and laughter. Billy and Sally insisted that their parents leave the house for several hours. During this time, the children made their own version of a wedding cake. Billy and Sally worked frantically to bake four angel food cakes, each layer representing a member of the family. Since they were not seasoned bakers, they didn't clean the pan between each baking, but simply baked a cake and scraped it out and piled it on the previous cake. Elinor said it was the most beautiful wedding cake she had ever seen. And Norm, who in their previous family life would have been critical of the enormous mess the children made, laughed warmly about the frosting left all over the kitchen.

For their surprise for the children, Norm and Elinor rented two adjoining rooms at a hotel and took them out for a very special night. When they arrived in their room, the children found four small gold-colored glasses. Each glass had a different family member's name engraved on it, and all four glasses had the date of the family reunification, which the parent's had decided would be "their new anniversary." Norm, who had previously been very uninvolved in family activities, had made all of the reservations, and had the special glasses made. A full-sized bottle of champagne for the parents and a tiny bottle of champagne for the children marked the occasion as especially festive.

At dinner, Norm and Elinor exchanged new wedding rings. At the moment of this exchange, they spontaneously decided to include the children in the ring ceremony. Elinor handed Norm's ring to Billy and asked him to give it to his father. Norm, in turn, handed Elinor's ring to Sally, requesting that she place it on her mother's finger.

Let's look at what happened here. With nothing other than an agreement to "make a surprise," this family drew upon *symbols* and *symbolic actions* to create a ritual and make new meaning with each other. While the parents had not spoken of this ritual as a "wedding," Billy and Sally understood that this was a whole new beginning for the family, and so chose to make a symbol of such new beginnings, a wedding cake. In choosing to make a four-layered cake, "one for each member of the family," the children were able to express that this was a different sort of wedding, a "wedding" of the entire family. Norm's tender appreciation of his children's efforts, despite the mess in the kitchen, demonstrated in action that this was, indeed, a new beginning.

Earlier in the family's life, all family activities were initiated and planned by Elinor. This time, she and Norm talked over what they wanted and Norm took responsibility for implementing their plan. The idea for the gold glasses was Norm's. "I felt I wanted something that would stay in the family after this event. I wanted some item that could both tie us all together and respect that we are separate people. These glasses, with each one's name on a particular glass, showed that we are a unit composed of individual parts. The date marked our new beginning as a whole family." The glasses were used subsequently on holidays and birthdays, and became a visual reminder of this earlier ritual.

Norm came from a family where both of his parents were alcoholics. Motivated by fear and a wish to protect, he had forbidden alcohol, even for moderate social and festive drinking. He and Elinor talked this over and decided that champagne was an appropriate symbol of celebration that they could safely incorporate into their ritual. As Elinor remarked, "I think this put to rest the fear that we would turn into Norm's parents—having a bit of champagne together lifted a cloud that had been over our earlier relationship."

Norm and Elinor chose to buy new wedding rings in order to symbolize that this was, indeed, a whole new marriage. At the moment of exchanging the rings, they included the children in a way that expressed new relationship possibilities. Billy and his dad had previously had a conflicted relationship, while Sally and her mom had been quite distant. In a very moving and spontaneous ceremony, Elinor asked Billy to give Norm the new ring, while Norm asked Sally to give Elinor her new ring. In this brief exchange, new connections were enacted and blessed.

Prior to this ritual, the family had lived a very minimized ritual style. Norm's memories of childhood rituals were extremely painful due to his parents' alcoholism, while Elinor sorely missed the lovely rituals from her own family-of-origin. Wanting to be understanding, she had agreed to Norm's insistence that they not have celebrations, but she found over time that this agreement robbed the family of any possibility of warm gatherings and marking the passage of time together. Thus the entire ritual in which Norm participated enthusiastically and creatively indeed symbolized a new beginning!

In creating this ritual, the Korners chose some symbols that defined them as being just like other families—for instance, a wedding cake and wedding rings. They chose other symbols, like the gold glasses, that spoke to the uniqueness of their circumstances as a reunited family. The choice of four cakes and four glasses highlighted each individual member. The fact that all of the cakes were angel food, forming one whole cake, and all of the glasses were gold-colored symbolized family connection. Champagne marked their passage from a family who was fearful of repeating the past to a family who was confident about the present and future. A larger champagne bottle for the parents and a smaller one for the children symbolically expressed that there are differences in what is right for adults and what is right for young children, while also marking the marriage relationship and the sibling relationship.

Symbols

The profound capacity of symbols to create meaning in our rituals is evident in the story of the Korners. Symbols speak to us without words. They enable us to create and express many different meanings with a single object. They allow diversity to flourish in families and relationships, as a given symbol will mean one thing to one person and something entirely different to another person. A single symbol in a ritual may capture and synthesize contradictions and polarities. Symbols give voice to beliefs, inner feelings, relationships, and spirituality. They are the building blocks in our rituals, providing the richness of meaning that distinguishes rituals from mere routine.

When you recall rituals from your childhood, symbols often stand out in bold relief. Indeed, a particular symbol can imply an entire ritual. Few of us can recollect childhood birthday parties without imagining a birthday cake and presents. Pumpkins and ghosts say Halloween, not Easter, and rabbits and eggs say Easter, not Halloween. Symbols are embedded in and give shape to our rituals.

Food can also serve as a symbol, evoking our memory of a given ritual. Try to imagine making a big turkey dinner on the Fourth of July and a barbecue on Thanksgiving! Think now for a moment about particular foods that are part of your rituals. What meanings do they carry and how would your rituals change if you were to change one of these *symbolic* foods?

Symbols are an obvious part of traditions, holiday celebrations, and life-cycle rituals. Less obvious, perhaps because we see them every day, are the symbols embedded in our daily rituals.

THE MANY MEANINGS OF A MICROWAVE OVEN

When Jim Hart married Alicia Povens, it was the second marriage for each. Jim moved into Alicia's house, and she blithely told him he should give away his microwave oven since she already had one. Days and weeks went by, and Jim still had his microwave. One day, Alicia came home to find the microwave set up in the kitchen. "I can't give it away. It's the first thing I bought for myself after my divorce. It probably sounds silly to you, but it represents my carrying on alone, it symbolizes my autonomy. I'll still want to use it from time to time." Their daily dinner ritual soon involved two microwaves. "I actually like it," Alicia said. "It's come to mean we can be together and still be two separate people. I know that's not what it meant to Jim, but that's what it means to me!"

CONTINUITY: SYMBOLS THAT CONNECT US TO THE PAST

In addition to culturally shared symbols in our rituals, most of us have unique symbols that are rich with meaning and connect us to family history and the past. The connotations of such symbols may change or become more complex over time, as each generation adds its own sense of meaning. When Sara Weinstein lights candles on Friday evening to mark the start of the Jewish Sabbath, she uses silver candlesticks that belonged to her grandmother. These candlesticks were the only item Sara's grandmother managed to hide and find again after the Holocaust. She brought them with her to the United States, and gave them to Sara's mother at her wedding. When Sara married, her mother gave the candlesticks to her. "These candlesticks are not just something pretty that I put candles in every Friday night. I look at them and I see the survival of my family and of the Jewish people. Sometimes I look at them and I think about the generations of women that these candlesticks symbolize and that someday they'll belong to my little girl."

Symbols may provide a sense of continuity, even when the performance of the ritual *per se* may have changed. Christopher Allenby places a ceramic angel on the top of his Christmas tree every year. "I took that angel after my mother died. It belonged to her—my dad gave it to her their first Christmas. They always put it on the tree after Midnight Mass. It meant Christmas had come. I haven't gone to

Midnight Mass myself for years, but every December 24 at midnight, I put that angel on the tree, and I think of my parents, and just that angel brings back all the Christmases in my mind."

A BIRTHDAY CAKE CONFLICT

Symbols can also find their place in family struggles and conflicts. Karen Singleton's mother always made a German chocolate cake for each family member's birthday. Over the years this cake took on many special meanings—caring, devoting time to one family member, honoring, carrying on a tradition, and a mother's love for her children. When Karen's mother died, as the oldest child she took over making this cake for her sister, June, and brother, Peter. On June's thirty-second birthday, she came to Karen's house to celebrate. Karen now had a new baby and a full-time job. When the family sat down for birthday cake, Karen brought out a cake she had bought at the grocery store. June was furious and stormed out of the house. "I saw Karen make our family cake two weeks ago for her girlfriend!" At first Karen was appalled by June's behavior, feeling it was much ado about nothing. As she began to think it through, however, she realized it wasn't just her busyness that stopped her from making the cake for June—she was also angry with June for not showing much interest in her baby and disappointed that no one in the family ever made the German chocolate cake for her birthday.

In order to begin to open the relationship with June, Karen invited her over "for cake and coffee." For this occasion, Karen made a cake she had never made before and explained to June that she wanted to change some things, and that this new cake was a symbol of that wish. The sisters talked about the German chocolate cake. They discovered that neither of them really liked German chocolate cake, but they longed for and missed what that cake had meant—their mother, her tenderness and caring for each family member. Karen had tried to replace that, but, of course, could not become the family's mother, and had ended up resentful. Without fully realizing it, changing the cake for her sister's birthday was her way to express what she was feeling. Karen and June ended up talking about what needed to change in their relationship to put it on a more equal footing.

Healing may be facilitated by special symbols that carry on through time. When Angela and Nestor Lopez lost their first child due to a miscarriage in the sixth month, they both grieved deeply. Several months later, in the spring, they decided to plant a flowering plum tree together in memory of this hoped-for child. They created their own special ritual, making this tree the symbol of both their loss and ongoing life. Over the next several years they had three healthy children. "You never fully get over that loss," Angela said, "but that tree, it put the pain in one place for us. Every spring, I see that tree bloom, and Nestor and I cry a bit even now. It's good, though—I think of who *that* child might have been, and I don't mix it up with my other children. As they got older, I told them about the tree, what it means to me. Last year, my children planted flowers all around it to surprise me. Now the tree's not alone—they're all connected."

In order to appreciate the rich diversity of meaning that is possible in any particular symbol, think about a symbol that you know is important to your family. Imagine what this symbol means to each person and then ask each person to talk about what the symbol means to him or her. You may be surprised to discover the various meanings attached to one symbol.

You might want to explore the special symbols that are unique in your own or your family's rituals:

• What are these symbols? You may want to choose one in particular to think about.

• Where did the symbol come from?

• How did it get passed on?

• What was this symbol originally used for? What were its original meanings?

• What meanings does this symbol have for you now? For others?

NEW SYMBOLS, NEW RITUALS

As you work with the ideas in this book, you may decide to change a particular ritual in your life, or to create a whole new ritual. As you do so, finding the symbols that express the multiple meanings that are possible in any ritual becomes an important step.

Changing a symbol in an ongoing or repeated ritual can herald new relationship possibilities, as we saw with Karen and June. When new symbols first appear they may quickly take on the meanings of struggle between the way things "have always been" and the way they may be changing. In an episode of the television program "The Wonder Years," the mother, Norma, starts to take a pottery class, unbeknownst to her husband, Jack, and children. A homemaker, she is making her first foray into the outside world. As her pottery starts to appear at nightly dinners and morning breakfasts, it quickly comes to symbolize (1) exciting new possibilities to her, (2) threats to her husband that she is changing and that their relationship is changing, and (3) fears to their son, Kevin, that his parents are mysteriously mad at each other. When she makes a new coffee mug for her husband, he whines that he wants his old mug, and through the symbolism of old and new pottery, we are able to see the struggle over old and new ways of relating. And when he "accidently" breaks the new mug, we know in the ensuing silence that he has made his statement regarding the symbols of change that have been entering their daily rituals.

You may want to review the major symbols in your daily, traditional, and celebration rituals to see what these symbols mean, and whether they are expressing what you and your intimates want to express. You can do the same with anticipated life-cycle rituals. You may want to do a bit of research in order to discover the original meanings of certain symbols, both in your family and in the culture. Did you know, for instance, that throwing rice after a wedding ceremony is a symbol of fertility? When Kevin and Jane Whitby were married, they already knew that they would be unable to have children. When they re-searched the meanings of various symbols connected to weddings, they decided they didn't want people to throw rice at them. Knowing, however, that their guests would want to throw something, they asked their best man to pass out bags of birdseed. "Having our guests 'feed the birds' became our own private symbol of caretaking and nurtur-ance," Jane explained. It's important to think through whether the symbols in your rituals are expressing your values or someone else's. Then you can determine what you want to do in subsequent rituals.

Since symbols are the carriers of meaning in our rituals, changing them or adding new ones is not a cavalier act. If you determine that particular symbols are no longer meaningful, or are, in fact, representa-tive of oppressive relationships, you may want to experiment with new symbols.

You can also search for appropriate symbols in order to create special rituals. Symbols created by a client working with Evan were used to make a ritual to heal a painful relationship breakup.

SETTING FIRE TO THE PAST

Alice Jeffers came to therapy two years after the end of a very stormy eight-year relationship with a man. When the relationship was going on, Alice's family had not approved. They were relieved when it ended, but seemed unable to extend any support to Alice for the pain she felt. Her friends told her she was well rid of him, since he had lied and cheated many times. Since neither her family or friends could understand her sadness, Alice withdrew from them, and over the two years became increasingly isolated. She went home from work every evening, closed herself in her apartment, and spent all of her free time thinking about her former boyfriend. She even dreamed about him at night. Formerly quite athletic, she had stopped all of her sports activities and gained a lot of weight. At the point where she found herself thinking about him at her work as a veterinarian, she came to therapy, as she was frightened that she would soon be unable to function. Her family and friends' inability to confirm her sadness and sense of loss seemed to contribute to her own need to do nothing else but think of her boyfriend.

When therapy began, Evan talked about the fact that there were no rituals to mark the end of a nonmarried relationship. Alice agreed and said that when her sister divorced, her family had supported her "just as if there had been a death," but virtually ignored Alice's situation. Evan suggested that they organize their work together to enable her to truly grieve and move on with her life. Evan asked Alice if she would be willing to take one hour every evening to review memories of the relationship in any way she wanted. "You can look at photos, take out mementos, write—bring whatever you have done to our next session and we'll look over these together." In this way, Alice could begin to create the social context that is needed for genuine mourning and letting go.

When Alice returned the following week, she brought a stack of index cards that she had made during the hour a day. She had chosen to write her memories, and had creatively color-coded the cards—"purple for mellow memories, green for jealous memories, blue for sad ones, and red for anger." She was startled to discover that her stack of "anger" cards was a lot bigger than she thought it would be. Freed from defending her boyfriend to family and friends, she was able to explore what she really felt.

As Alice sorted through the cards, she told Evan she had had a much better week, as she thought about her boyfriend only during the agreed-upon hour, and had slept free of dreams about him. Evan asked her to consider if there were cards, *which had immediately come to symbolize the relationship*, that she felt ready to let go of versus ones she wanted to hold on to. She agreed to think about this until the next session.

When Alice arrived two weeks later, she was dressed more brightly than previously and was eager to talk. She had gone out with friends and signed up for an aerobics class. She took out two stacks of cards. "I want to keep the purple ones—these memories are a part of me, things that changed me in a good way. I want to hold on to most of the red ones for now—sometimes it's hard to remember that he treated me poorly, and these keep me from romanticizing the past." She felt quite ready, however, to let go of the "green" jealous memories, which often made her feel bad about herself. She also wanted to let go of the "blue" sad memories, saying, "I've been sad long enough!" In a symbolic gesture of letting go, Alice handed these cards to Evan. With humor, she measured the ones she was still holding with the stack of cards she had given Evan, and declared, "Your pile is bigger!" Evan told her she certainly didn't want them either, and briefly left the room.

Evan returned with a ceramic bowl and a book of matches. Before her therapist could even make a suggestion, Alice broke into a big smile and said, "Oh, we should burn them!" Evan handed the cards back to her. She put them in the bowl and very carefully lit them. She used several matches in order to get a good fire going and the two women sat silently for a while and watched the flames together. During this ritual of setting fire to the past, Alice went through many moods. At first she turned to Evan and said, "It's so final, but it's good." A few minutes later she began to laugh and said, "We should roast warm marshmallows—that would be the final irony," referring to the fact that her boyfriend used to criticize her body and her weight and then bring her bakery treats. When the fire had nearly died down and they sat together looking at the glowing ashes, she quietly remarked, "This is good—my final memory is still a certain warmth."[1]

Following this ritual, Alice reconnected with her family and friends. She started scuba diving, and when therapy ended, she was beginning flying lessons. While this particular ritual occurred in the context of therapy, you may want to be thinking about aspects of your own life for which you would like to make rituals. The starting place, as with Alice, is to create or find the appropriate symbols that can capture and express many layers of emotions and thoughts. Alice's color-coded index cards temporarily *became* the relationship. Take a moment now to think about a major issue in your own life. It may be something you're struggling with, or it may be something joyous like an upcoming life-cycle event. What symbol or symbols might hold the multiple meanings connected to this issue? Take some time to talk this over with others who are important to you. Likely you'll find that the symbol you've chosen has still more meanings to them, or that they would choose different symbols.

Symbolic Actions

After Alice brought the index cards, symbolizing the relationship with her boyfriend and all of her feelings attached to it, she and Evan entered into three symbolic actions. First, she gave her therapist a large portion of the cards, thereby symbolizing in action her willingness to give up some of what she had been holding on to for two years. When Evan received the cards, this symbolized in action that another person would stand by her in her pain and that she could begin to end her isolation. Finally, Alice burned the cards, participating in an action that symbolized letting go of the past in a final way. All of our rituals contain *symbolic actions*. Just as particular objects in our rituals become symbols capable of carrying many meanings, so our actions, our behavior in rituals have symbolic value.

When we exchange rings at a wedding, when we give gifts out in a particular order at a holiday, when we sit in certain seats at a nightly dinner, when graduates march in a processional, or throw their caps in the air at the end of the graduation ceremony, when a Bar Mitzvah boy chants before the entire congregation, when holy water is placed on a baby at a christening, when we carefully place an evergreen blanket on a grave—all these and many more behaviors during rituals are symbolic actions, larger than themselves and deep with meaning.[2] Since some symbolic actions, such as processions, chanting, lighting fires, gathering for a meal, or burying have occurred in many cultures across hundreds of generations, participating in any given symbolic action connects us to our common humanity.

Many symbolic actions in rituals also carry cultural or religious meanings that may be generations or even centuries old. For instance, when Jews blow the shofar or ram's horn on the Jewish New Year, this symbolic action connects five thousand years of history with the present. When children hunt for Easter eggs, they are participating in a symbolic action that stretches back to the ancient Persian custom of giving eggs as gifts each spring to symbolize fertility and rebirth.

When the Korner family created their "New Beginnings" ritual, along with the symbols discussed earlier they used many symbolic actions. The children *baked* a wedding cake. This action involved more than simply two children baking a cake. It held the meaning of welcoming their father back into the family. Norm Korner *took responsibility* for carrying out all of the decisions he and Elinor had made regarding their surprise for the children. He demonstrated in action his new reliability and involvement with the family. The symbolic action of the ring exchange showed without words that many new relationships were now possible and welcome. Remember that the Korner children had been quite scared about their father and mother reconciling. Words alone had not allayed their fears. Acting together in ways that symbolized many of the facets of a wedding while also expressing the meanings of altering the past and creating a different future carried the family through this transition.

Like symbols, the symbolic actions in our rituals are open to multiple interpretations and levels of meaning. In a humorous scene in the film *Betsy's Wedding*, the rabbi attempts to explain the meanings attached to breaking the glass in the Jewish wedding ceremony. When he tells the young couple it refers to the destruction of the Temple in ancient times, they tell him they are not religious and don't want anything with a religious connotation at their ceremony. Next he tells them it symbolizes the breaking of the hymen, and they silently shake their heads. Finally, he says it means that they no longer belong to the past or to their families, but to each other and to the present and future. With this explanation, they agree to break the glass. Of some interest also is the fact that Betsy's fiancé is from a Christian family, and Betsy is from a family in which only her mother is Jewish. It is Betsy's mother who wants them to break the glass, not for any of the meanings described above, but because of the connection to extended family that this symbolic action implies, giving this behavior yet another meaning.

Symbolic actions may be playful or they may be profound. In our therapy, for instance, we may ask a highly conflicted couple to put symbols of their conflict into their freezer and agree to fight only after they have thawed these out. The symbolic action involved in a cooperative ritual of freezing and thawing can speak volumes about a relationship without engaging in the same old boring fight. Alternatively, symbolic actions such as "burying the past," which a couple may want

*"Before I carve the turkey, I believe Grandma
has a list of things we can be thankful for and
Grandpa has a list of things that piss him off."*

to use in a ritual of reconciliation, connect us to the finality involved in actual burials. Handing down a piece of jewelry from grandmother to mother to daughter in honor of high school graduation can infuse the entire ceremony with meanings about the value of education and the connectedness among women in a family. It is in the *doing* rather than simply the talking about that makes symbolic action such a powerful aspect of all rituals. Try to imagine that next December 25 you sit down with your family and have a discussion *about* Christmas, rather than celebrate Christmas, or that you and your partner talk about your anniversary, but do nothing to mark it together.

REMEMBRANCE DAY

Whether you are altering existing rituals or creating new rituals, it is important to know that you can reach outside of the usual symbols and symbolic actions in order to convey special meanings. When Rachel Nobell wanted to create a new ritual to mourn her mother's death, she and her family selected unusual symbols and symbolic actions to address many important issues. Just before Rachel's mother, Jackie, died, she requested that only immediate family gather to say good-bye. Since Rachel's children and husband were not present at this final moment, they wanted to create a ritual that would include action symbolic of saying good-bye. Since Jackie had loved the woods, they chose to float twigs and leaves down a nearby stream, symbolizing both that Jackie was gone and that she had an abiding presence in their lives. Since the grandchildren's last memory was one of blowing bubbles with their grandmother, they wanted to include bubble blowing as a central symbolic action in the ritual.

On the day of the ritual, the family walked together in a procession through the woods, reminiscent of many walks they had taken with Jackie. When they got to the stream, they honored her memory by telling many jokes, since Jackie was a master joke teller. Together, they floated the twigs and leaves, and then the children blew bubbles over the stream. They finished this ritual with a meal consisting of foods that Jackie had frequently cooked.

When the Nobells first created this ritual, they had intended it as a one-time event. Since Jackie had died just before Thanksgiving, the family had experienced several years of being unable to truly enjoy the holiday. When they participated together in the ritual, and allowed themselves to join in grieving and remembering and honoring *before* Thanksgiving, they discovered that Thanksgiving returned as a fun holiday. Together, they decided to make "Remembrance Day" a yearly ritual, one that included a repetition of the symbolic actions they had especially created—floating twigs, blowing bubbles, telling jokes, and eating foods cooked with Jackie's favorite recipes.

SELECTING SYMBOLIC ACTIONS

Just as you want to think about whether particular symbols carry the meanings you want to express in your rituals, so you will want to review and consider the symbolic actions. Does Mother do all of the food shopping, preparation, and cleanup for a holiday, while Father stands at the "head" of the table and carves the turkey? What is the meaning of this symbolic action? Does it express the gender relationships you want? What does it mean for a bride to be "given away" by her father to her husband? Many couples have begun to question and alter this symbolic action, creating a wedding ceremony where both sets of parents escort their offspring to the altar, symbolizing the profound change in family relationships that is about to take place. Some couples who have lived together decide to walk down the aisle together, feeling that this more appropriately captures the meaning of their relationship, while other couples each walk separately and alone to the altar, symbolizing autonomy within a relationship. It is crucial to review what symbolic actions we are participating in if we are to shape rituals that are truly expressive of our values.

You may want to take some time now to review the symbolic actions involved in a particular ritual:

- What are the symbolic actions in this ritual?

- What are the meanings of these symbolic actions to you?

- Ask other people who participate in this ritual what the meanings are to them.

- Is there a symbolic action that you would like to change?

- How might you change it so that it better expresses what you want and need this ritual to express?

All rituals have symbols and symbolic actions. They are what give our rituals depth, meaning, and values. They express what words alone cannot. Simply seeing or remembering a symbol can evoke all of the memories and feelings attached to a childhood ritual. The symbols in our rituals can connect us to shared family and cultural or religious history. Bringing an old symbol back to life and investing it with new meaning can provide both a sense of heritage and movement through time, continuity, and change. Altering a symbol or changing a symbolic action in a ritual can open many new possibilities for relationships and sense of self. In order for our rituals to remain alive for us and not simply become obligatory events, we need to consider our symbols and symbolic actions with care.

As you read Part III, "Rituals Throughout Our Lives," you will discover new ways to create and use symbols and symbolic actions in your daily rituals, family traditions, holiday celebrations, and life-cycle rituals.

PART III

*Rituals Throughout
Our Lives*

6

Daily Rituals

SHAPING RELATIONSHIPS DAY BY DAY

TAKE A MOMENT and review a typical day in your life or your family's life. As you go hour by hour, you will discover special times within each day that are your or your family's daily rituals. They may include meals, bedtime, leaving the home and coming back to the home, and leisure activities in the evening or on weekends. Differing from daily routines, such as brushing your teeth, daily rituals shape, capture, and express relationships. They announce in action who we are as individuals and what we mean to each other. Unlike holiday celebrations, traditions, such as birthdays or anniversaries, and major life-cycle rituals, such as weddings or graduations, all of which require conscious planning and preparation ahead of time, our daily rituals continue quite automatically. The seemingly involuntary nature of daily rituals means that they may continue without needed changes, even when you or your family are changing in ways that require important shifts in these rituals.

What Our Daily Rituals Tell Us About Our Family: Relating, Changing, Believing

Participating in daily rituals tells us over and over again about how we relate to each other. Daily rituals define the boundary between the family and the outside world. For instance, when your family sits down together for a meal, or gets in the car for a weekly outing, a sense of the family's own special organization is created. Through the repetition of familiar daily rituals, family membership is continually evoked without words. Who you are close to, who you are distant from, who is "in" and who is "out" all become clear when you look at your daily rituals.

Every new couple must coordinate patterns of daily rituals that each partner learned in his or her family-of-origin, or in other settings in which he or she lived. Often the arguments of new couples can be seen as an effort to shape satisfying daily rituals, such as when a young wife wants dinner at the same time every day because that is what she experienced in her own family, while a young husband prefers a changing dinner hour because that was how his family operated. Painful memories from the families we grew up in can also affect our current daily rituals.

In the Kan family, there were many fights regarding whether or not to sit down together for dinner. Mary Kan wanted a leisurely evening meal with her husband, Jim, while he wanted dinner in front of the TV, with no conversation. This couple struggled for over a year, and both were unsatisfied every night. Finally, one night after one of their now-familiar battles over dinner, Jim blurted out, "We're fighting every night just the way my mom and dad did when he would get drunk and ruin dinner!" Jim's reluctance to have a family dinner time suddenly became clear to both of them. Sitting down at a table for dinner evoked too many painful memories for him. Mary told Jim about a very different kind of dinner ritual in her family, one where people enjoyed each other, shared their day, and made plans together—a possibility

Jim never knew existed. Seeing where their struggle had come from, Jim and Mary began experimenting with a daily dinner time. He was able to embrace what Mary's tradition offered, and not be frightened that they would repeat the painful experience of his childhood.

Daily rituals are important for single adults, too, but are often overlooked. Cathy Jensen remarked that she once believed that daily rituals like mealtime were only for families. She found that her life as a busy attorney left her little room to focus on what was truly meaningful to her. "I started a nightly dinner ritual—I set the table, instead of eating in front of the television. I stopped answering the phone while I ate. I deliberately slowed myself down and made a special place for myself every evening."

Once you can discover some of the roots of your own ritual life, you can begin experimenting with changes. It is important that such changes be talked about and considered as "experimental" in order to promote open reflection and fine tuning until all participants feel satisfied.

In our daily rituals, we discover our roles and responsibilities in a group or family. The gradual shifting of roles and responsibilities as children change and grow can be seen through the lens of daily rituals. For example, when children are quite young, family activities are planned by parents, who simply take the children along. As children get older, they may begin to be invited to share in the decision-making regarding an outing. Finally, as children become adolescents or young adults, they may decide whether or not to participate in a leisure-time activity, thereby marking a change in family relationships that can be made visible through the ritual. When Evan's son, Jason, turned fourteen, he took a Saturday job. This meant he could no longer go on many weekend outings. Family leisure rituals changed, as the rest of the family went places without him, *and* needed to find new ways for all to be together. Daily and weekly rituals reflected and enacted these developmental changes.

Many issues of family identity and family and individual members' beliefs are expressed through daily rituals. Looking at our daily rituals may tell us about who we feel warmly toward and who we feel shut off from in the family. Family "rules" about allowable topics, emotions that may get expressed, conflict and its resolution are all shown through daily rituals.

Saying Good-bye and Saying Hello: Rituals of Leaving and Returning

Family members develop ritualized ways of saying good-bye when they leave each other to go to work or school, and of saying hello when they greet each other again after being apart. Such rituals of leaving and returning mark the boundary between home and the outside world, provide a bridge between life inside the family and life outside the family, and work to tell family members who they are to each other.

Such rituals of leaving and returning may be very satisfying to family members, providing a sense of care and concern. Often such rituals are very short and simple—a hug good-bye, an after-school snack, a repeated phrase with special meaning only within the family. For instance, in Evan's family, her husband, Lascelles, always parts from her by saying, "Walk good" and in that unique and repeated phrase captures all of his wishes for her to have a good day, to be careful, to stay well.

Some families may have difficulty creating rituals of leaving and returning that are comfortable. A common argument between partners frequently focuses on different ideas of how to reenter at the end of a day—she wants to talk about how the day went, while he wants to watch the news. Such couples may evolve a daily ritual of returning consisting of an argument over how to greet each other. When a couple can begin to examine such an argument as showing a need to develop a mutually satisfying ritual of reconnection rather than as an inevitable power struggle, new possibilities can emerge. For instance, a couple may decide to alternate his way of reconnecting and her way of reconnecting. Or, as one wife told us, "I found that if I left him alone for just fifteen minutes when he got home, he was then ready to *really* be with me. I also used those fifteen minutes for my own 'end of the day' thought-gathering. It's much more fun than our previous fights!"

Important changes in family relationships and individual development may first appear in difficulties regarding rituals of good-bye and hello. When the Carelli family experienced a divorce, Ms. Carelli began to work outside the home for the first time. She was able to continue a morning parting ritual of breakfast with her children, but she was no longer able to be home when they arrived from school. She told her two children that she needed them to do some chores after school and that she would be home at suppertime. Every day when she returned home, the chores were not done. She and the children would fight, and everyone remained angry for the rest of the evening. At first, the issue simply appeared to be one of children not wanting to do their jobs. However, the children quite willingly did several jobs before school and on the weekends. In a discussion focusing on the family's daily rituals, the children began to talk about missing their mother after school, having a hard time getting used to seeing less of her, and very poignantly spoke about being worried about her since they knew she was sad. Not knowing how to cheer her up, they preferred to get her angry every day, since this was better than seeing her sad. As the family reflected on the need for a new daily ritual of reentry that would express their changing circumstances, they settled on the children making a telephone call to Mother when they came home from school, in order for all to touch base, and they agreed to spend fifteen minutes together when Mother came home from work, sharing one humorous incident that happened during the day to each. As this new ritual of saying hello at the end of the day provided a way of reconnecting that was mutually satisfying, the children began to do their after-school chores and the fighting stopped.

Some families do not have any established rituals for leaving and returning. In such families, members are less aware of comings and goings. Family members may not even know who is home and who is not. In such families, individual choices count more than connecting with family members.

While this may be satisfying in your family, you need to be aware of transitions in individual and family life, when it may be important to implement such rituals. When families veer to an extremely independent style, it is often hard to know when a member is feeling lonely or vulnerable. Touching base with each other in a daily ritual of "hello" or "good-bye" can provide an opening, and a place to notice changes in one another that might otherwise be missed.

Single adults also need rituals for leaving and returning. These rituals often function to create a bridge between home life and work life. For instance, Karen Clinton takes a special coffee mug out of the house every day. The mug was given to her by a dear friend and symbolizes the warmth in that relationship. When she returns home, she washes the mug and gets it ready for the next day. She explained, "I like taking a piece of my home life with me on the way to work. It's comforting. When I get home at night and wash that mug, it's like I'm washing off the cares of the day. It's a small way I have of taking care of myself."

The rituals of leaving and returning in your life as a single adult may reflect unsettled relationship issues. Every day when Paula Allen arrived home, she was expected to call her mother. If she didn't call by six-thirty, her mother phoned her. Paula was living in her first apartment, and in the beginning, she found the daily telephone call ritual to be supportive and comforting. Gradually, however, as she felt more confidence in being on her own, the call became a burdensome and obligatory ritual, rather than voluntary. She began to feel she was being "checked up on" by her mother, and she resented it. Finally, she got her courage together to tell her mother that she no longer wanted to call every day. To her surprise, her mother was actually pleased, since she had secretly felt the calls were a burden, too, and was waiting for a sign from Paula that she no longer needed this particular daily ritual.

Some families develop rituals of leaving and returning that are extremely rigid, obligatory, and devoid of meaning. As one man complained, "When I was growing up, we all had to kiss my parents good-bye in the morning and kiss them hello in the evening. We had to do this even if we were mad at each other, if they had just punished us, or if we simply didn't feel like it. I came to hate those kisses, even when I wanted to kiss them!" Here a daily ritual of "hello" and "good-bye" had lost its intended meaning as an expression of affection, and had become empty, hypocritical, and routine.

It is important to ask yourself what really matters, so that your ritual can be constructed to express what you desire. If you are unsure about what would satisfy you or your family members in a daily ritual of reconnection, try an experiment that dramatizes each member's preferred way, and then evaluate the outcome. One of the wonderful aspects of daily rituals is that they occur with such frequency, and can allow for immediate reflection, feedback, and change.

As you examine your rituals of leaving and returning, ask yourself what you are hoping to express through this ritual, whether the ritual is alive, and whether you can change it to meet changing life circumstances and demands.

RITUALS FOR FREQUENT SEPARATIONS:
MAKING A SPECIAL BRIDGE

Divorced and remarried families have special issues regarding rituals of leaving and returning, since parents and children may say good-bye and not see each other for several days, weeks, or even months. The Cole family is divorced. Mr. Cole picks up five-year-old Billy at Ms. Cole's house every day to take him to school. This arrangement allows Dad and Billy to have daily contact. The ride to school is brief, and when it is time to say good-bye, father and son have a special "good-bye" ritual called "thumbs up." Billy gives his father the "thumbs up" signal as he leaves the car. Dad returns this signal when Billy is about to enter the school building. This comforting and familiar sign tells father and son to have a good day until they meet again, and connects them while they are apart. Such familiar rituals provide a sense of continuity in a relationship that is crucial to parent and child.

The movement of children from one household to another requires special attention to the rituals of leaving and returning, as these express more complicated issues of family membership, loyalty, or unresolved conflicts between parents. Children may receive the hidden message that they are not to express sadness in leaving one household to go to another, and that their good-bye ritual should be swift or secretive. Parents may complain that children take a long while to "settle down" after visiting the other household. This is often an important signal that a reentry ritual is needed that creates a bridge from one household to the other, enabling children to talk about the transition experience, rather than showing it in upset behavior. A simple ritual that acknowledges a child's life in two families—such as fifteen minutes with milk and cookies to talk about what it is like to go from Dad's house to Mom's house *this time*, what will be missed, or what's being looked forward to, as well as what went on while the child was away—provides permission to move between the two worlds. Sara Delanty bought cinnamon graham crackers that she and her son, Don, ten, eat only during this reentry ritual, enabling them to mark this time as special.

Your family may have longer time periods between "hello" and "good-bye" if family members are traveling. Parents who must travel for work and be away from children can design special rituals that keep them connected during these absences. When Janine travels away from her daughter, Natalya, she leaves a "notebook" with a message for each day, including what she's doing that day, where she'll be, and what she'll miss about Natalya that day. When Evan travels, she often leaves little notes in unusual places, such as the freezer or dishwasher, for family members to find. In return, her family members sometimes surprise her with notes in her suitcase! Other families make nightly phone calls during travel, or put photographs out. Following a trip away, a returning ritual may involve small gifts from the traveler and an established time to regroup and catch up on what's been happening.

EXAMINING YOUR RITUALS OF HELLO AND GOOD-BYE

If you would like to reflect on your leaving and returning rituals, here are some questions:

• In the families that you and your spouse come from, how did members go apart from each other? How did they greet each other at the end of the day? What did these rituals express about the families?

• How similar or how different were the rituals of leaving and returning in your families-of-origin?

• How do the members of your current family say good-bye to each other? Are there special phrases used, physical expressions, etc.? Is this satisfying? If not, what ways might be more satisfying?

• How do members of your current family say hello to each other after being apart? Is this satisfying? If not, what might be more satisfying?

• Has conflict become your daily ritual of returning? If so, try to consider this as an expression of dissatisfaction with the returning process. What might you develop instead?

• If you are single, what rituals of leaving and returning to your home have you created? Are these satisfying? How might you change these to be more satisfying?

• How have your rituals of leaving and returning changed? What has caused the changes? Divorce? Children growing? Remarriage? Are there aspects of your previous rituals of hello and good-bye that you would like to recapture? Do you need to create new rituals of hello and good-bye for special family circumstances, such as when children go from one household to another, or when family members travel?

Say "Good Night"—Bedtime Rituals

BABIES AND YOUNG CHILDREN

In every culture, parents create bedtime rituals for babies and young children to ease separation from the parent and the passage from the waking state to the sleeping state. Such rituals may include a playful bathing, a bedtime snack, telling or reading a story, saying prayers, singing songs, holding and cuddling. The familiar repetition of such bedtime rituals marks and defines the parent-child relationship as one where comfort, reliability, and safety are available.

While parents initiate such bedtime rituals, children very soon become their co-creators. They may insist that a particular story be told over and over. They may determine a certain number of times that the lights be turned on and off, or that three trips be made to the bathroom, or that stuffed animals be placed in a particular way in order to complete the bedtime ritual. As children grow and learn certain skills, they may want to read the story out loud to the parents, or they may initiate a mutual storytelling process.

Bedtime rituals may serve as a lens for child development and mastery, as over time a child will insist on completing certain bedtime tasks alone that previously were part of a parent-child ritual, such as bathing or changing clothes. Earlier aspects of a joint ritual, such as reading, will be taken over by the child, and often will continue when the child grows into adulthood. Gradually, a child will signal less and less need for many aspects of the bedtime ritual, until finally she puts herself to bed, with a ritual consisting of "Good night, Mom, good night, Dad." Often parents may miss the bedtime ritual that the child has made clear he no longer needs.

In addition to the bedtime rituals cocreated by parents and children, siblings often create bedtime rituals to work out aspects of their relationships, including conflicts and jealousies, while also expressing affection and caring. Siblings who share a bedroom may create playful bedtime rituals that are kept secret from parents and express a special sibling bond. When Evan was growing up, she and her older brother established a bedtime ritual of playing tricks on each other, such as putting cooked spaghetti, paper clips, or live turtles in each other's beds. These tricks were kept secret from the parents and enabled sibling rivalry to be expressed with much harmless creativity!

ADOLESCENTS

While adolescents may fiercely guard the territory of their own room and not welcome parents for anything resembling the bedtime ritual of a younger child, many families of adolescents are able to create a nighttime ritual *before* bed, often in a particular place, such as the parents' room or the living room, that allows for a comfortable discussion of concerns.

FAMILY CHANGES AND BEDTIME RITUALS

When families are undergoing intense change, such as the birth of a new baby, the departure of a sibling to camp or college, and especially separation and divorce, children's bedtime rituals may need special attention. A toddler can be helped with a transition of a new baby by creating a special bedtime ritual marking the unique place of the toddler in the family. Sometimes the three-year-old can be given a special part in the new baby's bedtime ritual before having her own bedtime ritual. Children with new siblings may insist that part of their bedtime ritual be exactly like the baby's. You should both honor this request and add some new aspect of the ritual that marks the special status of your older child.

Families undergoing separation or divorce may find that children's bedtimes become extremely problematic. If the parent who has most participated in the bedtime ritual has left the home, the children may feel especially lonely and upset. Families may approach this issue in a number of ways. When the parents are able to cooperate, the parent who is not living with the children may want to institute a nightly telephone call as part of the bedtime ritual. It is extremely important, however, that parents agree on this and that the telephone ritual occur with consistency. More often, the parent with whom the children live will need to cocreate a new bedtime ritual that can acknowledge the changes going on in the family. When children travel from one household to another, usually two different bedtime rituals will be elaborated that, in fact, express the differences in the households. It is very common for children to be the voice for wanting some common aspects to the two bedtime rituals, and they may do this by, for instance, choosing a special stuffed animal to carry from house to house to utilize in both bedtime rituals.

Step-families may want to create new bedtime rituals that help to build new family relationships. The Carsons are a remarried family. Ellen Carson has two children, Scott, six, and Stevie, eight. Bill Carson has one daughter, Naomi, who is eight. When Ellen and Bill married, each child wanted to retain their old bedtime rituals, and the bedtime hour was very tense and difficult. One night, Ellen and Bill called all three children into the living room and asked them to get their sleeping bags, which were normally reserved for camping. The children were excited by this unusual action, which broke the nightly tension and marked the occasion as something new and different. Each parent then read a story. Following the stories, Ellen talked quietly with Naomi, while Bill, Scott, and Stevie wrestled a bit. Finally, both parents took their own children and put them to bed. At eight the following night, all three children appeared in the living room with their sleeping bags. A new bedtime ritual was born, one that enacted new family relationships and preserved special parent-child bonds.

The normal fears of childhood that often emerge at bedtime can be effectively addressed through rituals. For instance, the Cowan family created their own version of Guatemalan worry dolls. In this bedtime ritual, a child tells his worries to each of five tiny dolls who work all night to solve the problems, freeing the child to go to sleep without worry. Paula Cowan encouraged her children to use their stuffed animals in a similar way, and in so doing, allowed for an open expression of concerns through an easy conversation with stuffed animals.

A family's special heritage may also be expressed in bedtime rituals, as when parents create a ritual that involves the telling of family stories from their own families-of-origin, their childhood, and the creation of the present family.

BEDTIME RITUALS FOR ADULTS

While parents generally pay a lot of attention to creating bedtime rituals for their children, adult bedtime rituals may go unnoticed. In an era of two-career couples who often have little time together during the week, it becomes all too easy to forget about creating a ritual to close the day and go to sleep. The television may intrude late at night, such that your adult bedtime ritual becomes the eleven o'clock news and no conversation.

Janice and Frank Engleman noticed that they had slipped into a very dissatisfying rut. He watched sports every evening and fell asleep in front of the TV, while she took care of the children and then went to bed alone. They grew more and more distant and alienated from each other, although this was not what either one wanted. One day after a particularly angry argument in which each accused the other of distancing, they sat down to look at how much time they spent together during the week. Since each had careers, they were often not home for dinner together. They left the house at different times in the morning, each taking children to day care or school. This left only the late evening for some connecting time with each other, which they realized they no longer had. They agreed to create an adult bedtime ritual. "I suddenly remembered the wonderful bedtime ritual I had as a child," Janice said. "It was a time when my mother would sit on my bed and we would just talk about everything that happened that day." From this memory, they constructed their ritual. First, Frank agreed to help Janice put the children to bed. This gave them more time together. Then they decided to have a cup of tea together and talk about their day. Following their nightly tea, they began going to bed together as they had earlier in their marriage.

While adult bedtime rituals can disappear due to sheer busyness and lack of attention to this potentially important time together, some couples never create bedtime rituals because they didn't learn about these in the families in which they grew up. Certainly not all children come from families where there are warm and loving bedtime ritual experiences. If you grew up in a family where bedtime was fraught with tension or arguments, or where people were distant and children simply put themselves to bed at an early age, you will need to think carefully about what a satisfying adult bedtime ritual might be.

Other couples have extremely different rhythms, with one being a "night owl" and the other being an early riser, and so may never go to bed at the same time. Such couples may need to work out a ritual to close the day with one another in order to prevent becoming too distant and disconnected.

An uninvited change in a previously satisfying adult bedtime ritual may be a signal of problems brewing in your relationship or in your spouse's life. Kyle and Elinor Lincoln always cuddled and talked in bed before going to sleep. Gradually, over a period of about three months, Kyle began coming to bed later and later. At first, Elinor tried waiting for him, but as the time grew longer, she began falling asleep before he came to bed. She missed their previous closeness, but when she tried talking to him about what was going on, he dismissed her concerns, saying, "Things change—it's okay—just go to sleep." A month later, Elinor found out that Kyle was having problems with his boss and was, in fact, about to lose his job. He had been too ashamed to tell her, and so began distancing during the one part of the day when they were always close.

How Do Bedtime Rituals Work for You and Your Children?

Here are some questions to help you reflect on bedtime rituals:

• What bedtime rituals do you remember from your own childhood? What did these bedtime rituals do for you? How did these rituals shape and express parent-child relationships? Sibling relationships? Adult relationships?

• What bedtime rituals do you do with your children now? Are these satisfying to you? What parts of the bedtime ritual have you created? What parts have your children created? Ask your children how they feel and think about the bedtime rituals—do they want to change any parts of it?

• If your family is undergoing stressful changes, you may want to examine bedtime rituals as a place where these changes can be expressed, talked about, and eased. Think through with your children how the bedtime ritual might change as the family is coping with separation, remarriage, etc.

• What adult bedtime rituals have you and your partner created? Do you need to pay some new attention to shaping a mutually satisfying bedtime ritual?

Family Meal Rituals

Sally Moore was twelve years old when she began to insist on eating a baked potato every night for dinner, and refusing to eat what the family was having for dinner. The oldest of three children, Sally sat between her mother and father at dinner. When she began her baked potato campaign, her father insisted that she eat what the family was eating, while her mother urged that Sally be allowed to make her own choices. Soon, mother and father were arguing every night at dinner. This argument, seemingly about baked potatoes, actually signaled much more about family relationships. Sally had always been very close to her father, and never differed with him. As the first child to begin growing up, Sally's new food preference symbolized her beginning to make choices that were not her father's choices. At the same time, Sally's mom was just beginning to work outside the home, and her siding with Sally and disagreeing with her husband was also an expression of her own new autonomy, along with reaching for more closeness with Sally. Sally's father felt tense about all the changes happening in his family, and expressed his nervousness through the nightly struggles with Sally and his wife. Insisting to Sally that she eat what the family was eating was his way to tell her that he was afraid he was losing her as she became a young woman.

The family meal is a ritual through which you can learn about many aspects of family relationships, including gender roles; boundaries around individuals, pairs, threesomes, and the whole family; allowable topics for conversation; the range of permitted emotions; and changes in family members. Although it is estimated that as many as sixty-five percent of American families no longer sit down together every night for a meal, nonetheless, most families do manage to eat together a few times a week. Simply gathering at the dinner table creates an invisible boundary around the family. A sense of family membership and identity is evoked.

Many families develop specific seating patterns at the dinner table, either by design or default. Such seating patterns silently tell family members many "rules" about family relationships. For instance, in some families, the father is designated as sitting at the "head of the table," symbolizing his position as "head of the family." Conversely, many families have deliberately done away with such a designation as they are defining relationships between men and women as equal in the family. The Hawkins family wanted to get away from "Dad at the head of the table," but even shifting seats didn't quite work, since this seemed to put another family member in the "head" spot. Ten-year-old Cathy solved the dilemma one day when she suggested the family get a round table like her friend Melissa's family had.

In many families, the mother sits in a seat nearest the kitchen or stove, symbolically announcing that the kitchen is her domain, while other families have consciously done away with this sexist seating pattern. We have been told stories of family dinner seating patterns in which the mother *never* sat down during the meal, and the family accepted the narrow definition of her role as the "one who served others." The seating pattern will tell you about who is close to whom in the family and who is more distant, who is encouraged to talk to whom. Family threesomes or triangles, in which two members are close and a third is on the outside, or two members join to fight a third or protect a third, are often visible in the seating arrangements at the dinner table. For instance, is a particular child always seated between the parents and the subject of their intense concern or anger in a repeated fashion? In some families all the males sit together and all the females sit together, while other families express age and power hierarchies through the process of who sits where.

Who is present and who is not present at the meal may tell a family about relationship changes and development. As children grow, and especially as they become adolescents with friends outside the home and after-school jobs, they may be less present for nightly meals. Some families are able to adapt to this shift easily, while others continue to insist that all members be present for dinner even when this is no longer possible. In the popular film *Saturday Night Fever*, the older adolescent, played by John Travolta, has a job and cannot make the nightly dinner, which has always been set for six o'clock. Rather than change the dinner hour, the rest of the family remains angry at him every day for his inability to make dinner on time. This small vignette expresses the family's larger struggle with children growing up and leaving home.

In many families, parents may need to work late, necessitating change in who is present. Some families require children to wait until a parent arrives from work, making the dinner hour later than young children can tolerate. Other families deliberately design their dinner hour with more flexibility such that certain nights may have children and parents eating separately, while other nights are reserved for whole family dinners. What is important is creating a situation that works for your family and for all the individual members, rather than imposing a format that may have worked at an earlier time.

Like many rituals, meals require a preparation phase and a follow-up. Preparation includes shopping, setting the table, serving the food.

Follow-up includes cleaning up, after-dinner discussions, etc. You can learn a lot about family relationships, particularly beliefs about gender roles and parent-child relationships, by looking at what happens before and after a meal.

MEN, WOMEN, AND CHILDREN

Despite many changes in women's roles outside the family, the lion's share of food shopping and preparation still falls on women in most families. Through the daily repetition by women of either shopping or making sure the shopping gets done, cooking, serving, and cleaning up, gender "rules" are invoked in families. Yet heterosexual couples who are trying to make changes in the gender patterns in their families often hold powerful memories of mealtime arrangements in which mother cooked and served, and father was served. Karen Dole came from a family where both men and women were expected to participate in meal preparation. She married Kevin, in whose family the men snapped their fingers to signal the women that a cup of coffee was required. When she refused to participate in this demeaning gender arrangement, terrible arguments ensued, but she stood her ground and began to change the gender expectations in her current family.

In addition to gender, beliefs regarding the responsibilities of children in the family are communicated in the preparation and follow-up phases of the meal. In many families, young children begin to learn to participate in family responsibilities through setting the table, simple cooking, and helping to clean up. In other families, the message is sent that children are not expected to have such responsibilities, and a more rigid boundary is drawn between adults and children. As you look at your family meal ritual, think about what you want your children to learn, and whether your current nightly meal imparts what you are hoping to teach.

CREATING YOUR FAMILY'S "CULTURE" THROUGH MEAL RITUALS

The family meal communicates "rules" regarding allowable topics for conversation and allowable emotions to express. In the Jonash family, the meal is spent discussing each one's day in turn, while in the Sparks family spirited discussions and arguments about politics are allowed.

When Mary England was growing up only adults were allowed to speak, while children were required to listen. In Sam Stone's family, children totally dominated the meal to the exclusion of adult concerns.

In the wonderful film *Annie Hall*, a marvelous dinner scene is shown illustrating the cultural differences in two very different families. First we see a somewhat exaggerated version of a white Anglo-Saxon Protestant upper-middle-class family at the dinner table. Their topics are limited to external events, such as "swap meets and boat basins"; each person speaks only after another person has finished, symbolizing very clear and somewhat rigid individual boundaries, and the range of allowable emotion is constricted and largely unspoken. Then we see a similarly exaggerated version of a Jewish working-class family at dinner. Here, members speak while others are speaking, and comfortably reach into each other's plates. These symbolic actions portray a family where individual boundaries are loose, and where moving into each other's territory is easily tolerated. Topics include a focus on people, including their illnesses and employment, and emotion is easily expressed, including anger. Each family is comfortable with its own dinner ritual arrangements and appears strange and different in comparison to the other family.

In some families, anger can be expressed at the dinner table, while other families have a rule against the open expression of anger, even if people are seething. Conflicts and differences may be suppressed, or they may emerge night after night, often symbolizing an array of unspoken issues. In short, examining your dinner ritual in order to examine allowable topics and allowable emotions will tell you a lot about the relationships and beliefs of your family. Ask yourself what topics *never* come up, what emotions *never* get expressed at mealtime in order to learn what your family taboos might be. This reflection, in turn, may enable an expansion of what topics and emotions can be expressed.

Since hidden or not-so-hidden loyalties to the families that we come from can lead to an imbalanced ritual style, couples who are struggling over the "right" way to organize their dinnertime may profit from a discussion focusing on what dinner was like in the families they come from and comparing this to their current dinner ritual. You may want to experiment. Have a dinner exactly like the one in your family-of-origin, alternated with one exactly like your partner's family-of-origin. This can lead to developing a ritual that is preferred by each.

Many families replicate patterns from their families-of-origin during the daily dinner ritual without realizing they are doing so. Sometimes a deliberate effort to "do it differently from my family" ends up repeating the very form one wishes to change. One young mother, Karen Delaney, told us that it was very, very important to her to establish a nightly dinner for her daughter, Jennie, her husband, Michael, and herself because when she grew up, anger and conflict permeated her household and her family *never* ate together. She consequently placed a very high value on what she called a "peaceful dinner hour" in which all members were present. This meant that even when Michael was late from work, Jennie had to wait in order for them all to eat together. Karen insisted to Michael and Jennie that there be absolutely no conflict at dinner. The family dinnertime was tense, however, as family members tried to honor her request. This tension, in turn, often led to Jennie frequently being naughty at dinner and being sent away from the table, after which Michael and Karen would argue about her and Michael would leave the table. Without realizing it, the family was repeating a familiar pattern. Their nightly dinner had become a way for the mother to try to settle old hurts from her family-of-origin, instead of being an opportunity to build current relationships. Upon some reflection, the couple were able to settle on a very different dinner ritual, including certain nights just for the adults to eat together, and a relaxing of the "no conflict at dinner" rule. As tension eased, Jennie's behavior at the table improved, and the family began to enjoy meals together in a ritual that more adequately reflected their current needs.

SYMBOLS AND SYMBOLIC ACTIONS

As a ritual, the family dinner contains many symbols and symbolic actions. Food is one such symbol, taking on multiple meanings in families. Thus in one family, food may symbolize nurturance, while in another food may symbolize rewards and punishments. Food may symbolize the family's connection to a specific ethnic tradition, such as challah bread in Jewish families, or pasta in Italian families. Arguments and a lack of confirmation of individual differences can also be symbolized through food, as when a food is pushed on a family member despite repeated statements that this food is disliked, as when parents insist their children eat cauliflower.

Food preferences may come to symbolize the expression of individual differences that are easily tolerated in one family, while in another family, food preferences may symbolize rejection of being "like the rest of the family," and may lead to terrible arguments and power struggles. Often children and adolescents who begin to eat at friends' homes will attempt to expand the food repertoire of the family, symbolizing the natural process of children bringing information from the outside world into the family. Many families are able to adapt to this, while other families resist and fight. As one woman remarked to us, "Dinners were the place of the greatest family contact and conflicts as my brother and I tried to grow into individuals. We were beginning to emerge with our own opinions, different from 'the family opinion' and our own habits, as I stopped eating meat. Both parents tried to dismiss our differentness. 'I've been around a lot longer than you, so listen to me,' said my father. 'If you eat something different from us, it's like you're not part of the family,' said my mother."[1] It is important to ask yourself about the meanings of food in your current family and in your family-of-origin. Some foods come to have a special meaning of comfort, often relating to particular traditions—for instance, Grandma's macaroni and cheese. Other foods come to symbolize fights and arguments. In step-families, children may express loyalty to a biological parent by wanting food cooked "the way Mom does it." A stepmother can show her permission for such loyalty by honoring this request, cooking certain foods "the way Mom does it," and introducing her own ways through other foods, thereby avoiding needless battles. In some families, new food preferences are experienced as a frightening change, the announcement of an intolerable difference, while in other families, they are seen and experienced as opportunities for growth and development.

In addition to food, a family may have other mealtime symbols, including china or silver or candlesticks handed down from earlier generations and symbolizing elements of tradition or connectedness. The appearance of new items on the table may also symbolize important family changes. When Linda MacIntosh bought a new set of dishes and put them out for the first time, her husband, Todd, was furious. "What's wrong with the dishes my mother gave us?" "That's precisely what's wrong with them," Linda replied. "Your mother picked our dishes, our silverware, our glasses, even our furniture—it's time for something new, something that reflects my tastes!" Linda's bold move initiated a discussion of long-held but never-before-spoken resentments of how much their family life had become imbalanced, expressing beliefs, values, and ways of being that came exclusively from Todd's family. Changing their dishes simply began a much longer process of family change.

Your family's dinner ritual may need to undergo changes when your family is experiencing profound developmental change. Children leaving home, divorce, mother starting work outside the home, or creating a step-family all require new daily rituals. When families are unable to adapt to these changes, the dinner ritual may be one of the first places that difficulty will emerge. Susan Ames, a divorced mother, spoke about a meal ritual in which she cooked dinner after work every day and took her portion of food to her room, while each child also ate separately whenever he felt like eating. Asked when the last time was that the whole family sat down together for a meal, she said, "Not since my husband left a year and a half ago," and went on poignantly to explain that she did not know how they could still be a family and that only families ate together. Here the divorce created a terrible disjuncture in the family's sense of itself, symbolized in their now eating separately and alone. Her three children, Sam, Bill, and Jerry, expressed a wish to eat together again, beginning with an upcoming meal on Mother's Day, and Susan agreed, signaling that the family was ready to begin the difficult process of becoming a single-parent family with its own right to family meals together.

Remarried families have the developmental task of working out mealtime rituals that affirm ways of relating in the prior family, while creating a new sense of cohesion. Since children may be moving back and forth between two or more households, the dinner ritual needs to be flexible in order to accommodate different groupings for meals. In the initial phases of forming a remarried family, a daily dinner ritual in which all members of the household are present can begin to build a sense of family connectedness. In her research on newly remarried families, Mary Whiteside describes a family in which the mother and stepfather very deliberately chose to focus on the nightly dinner as a place to form relationships. For many months, the mother's children refused to talk to the stepfather during dinner, symbolizing the often-tense state of relationships in new remarried families. Mother and stepfather continued the dinner ritual, however, and gradually tensions eased and conversations became more relaxed among all members, including the adoption by the children of the stepfather's ritual of saying grace.[2]

If you are in a remarried family, it is important to review the differing dinner rituals from the prior families and the still-existing families to which children may belong. Then family members may decide together what elements are important to preserve, enabling children to express their loyalties to multiple family systems, and what new elements to design in order to express the new family's identity.

Family meals are a time and place to discover a lot about your family. You may find stuck and repetitive patterns which are unpleasant and which you can work together to change. Or you may see how mealtimes illustrate particular issues for your family, such as family members growing up, new members entering the family, or people leaving. Your dinner ritual can provide a sense of connection, of family cohesion, of members' interest in and concern for each other. Daily meals are changeable rituals, so that with a bit of work and attention, you can use your family dinnertime to shape relationships, cope with changes, and celebrate your family.

EXAMINING YOUR FAMILY MEAL RITUALS

You can learn about your family-of-origin meal ritual and your current family meal ritual with these questions:

• In the family that you come from, did members have specific seats? In the family that your spouse comes from, did members have specific seats? What do you imagine would have happened if you had sat somewhere else? Take a moment and draw the dinner table from the families you and your spouse come from. Compare the two drawings. Are they quite similar or very different?

• Do people in your current family have specific seats? If so, compare this arrangement to the families you come from. Is your current seating pattern more like that of your family-of-origin or more like your spouse's? Have you replicated your family-of-origin without even realizing it, or have you created something quite different? Try an experiment with different seating arrangements for several nights and reflect on what begins to happen.

• In the family that you come from, what were the allowable topics of conversation at dinner? How did you know this—explicitly or implicitly? In your spouse's family, what were the allowable topics? Compare these to the allowable topics at your family dinner now.

• In the family that you come from, what emotions were able to be expressed at dinner? Were there "rules" against anger, etc.? In your spouse's family, what emotions were able to be expressed? Compare these to the allowable emotions at your family dinner now.

• What were the "rules" regarding gender that were expressed in your family-of-origin through the nightly dinner ritual? Who shopped for food? Who prepared the food? Who served? Who was served? Who spoke and who was listened to? Who cleaned up after the meal? Compare these gender rules to the ones in your current family. Does your nightly meal ritual implicitly express equality or inequality between males and females? What are your children learning as they watch what men do and what women do every night at dinner?

• Did the dinner ritual in the family that you come from express aspects of your family's ethnic and religious identity? In what ways? Compare this to your spouse's family. Does your dinner ritual now express aspects of your family's ethnic and religious identity? If your present family is a combination of ethnic or religious identities, can this be expressed in your dinner ritual?

• What were the symbolic meanings of food in your family-of-origin? In your spouse's family? What are the symbolic meanings of food in your family now?

• Were members in your family-of-origin allowed to have differing food preferences or was difference seen as somehow threatening? What kinds of discussions ensued when a family member either disliked a food that others ate, or brought home a new way of eating, such as vegetarianism? Compare this with your spouse's family. How are differing food preferences handled in your current family?

• How was the dinner ritual different in your family-of-origin when company came to dinner? Were you easily able to bring friends home for dinner? How was the dinner ritual different in your spouse's family when company came for dinner? Compare this to your family now—

what changes occur when there is company? Do the changes differ depending on who the company is?

• How did the dinner ritual in the family you come from change as the years went by? How did the family adapt the ritual as children grew and left? Were there profound developmental changes like divorce, remarriage, or death of a member that affected the dinner ritual? In what ways? How has the dinner ritual changed in your current family? How have you approached key developmental changes and how have these been reflected in your dinner ritual?

Creating "Daily" Rituals Once a Week

While all families have some daily rituals, many families also choose to create rituals that occur once a week, such as Friday night dinner, Sunday pancake brunch, or an evening without television when the family can simply be together and talk. These weekly rituals have many similarities to daily rituals, while also preserving special time every week for family members to come together, which can be especially important if individual members are extremely busy with work or school activities. Weekly rituals may also be an important time for you and your family to express values and beliefs, such as going to church together or spending time volunteering.

The Donegal family's weekly ritual is described by Susan Lieberman in her book *Let's Celebrate*. This family chose Friday night to make a weekly dinner ritual, both to honor Rebecca Donegal's Jewish heritage and to mark the end of the school week when both were in graduate school. They symbolized the specialness of this weekly dinner with cloth napkins, candles, and flowers. In order to keep current with one another's busy lives as graduate students and young parents, and to bolster hopefulness on a regular basis, they devoted time during this dinner to share with one another the "best thing that happened this week."[3]

Weekly rituals can provide a time when individual family members are given a special voice in how things go in the family. In the Colling family, Saturday night supper is alternately prepared by individual family members, giving each member an opportunity to make favorite foods for the rest of the family. In the McAllister-Albioni family, Sunday dinner is ethnic heritage time—Mike McAllister makes Irish food one week and his wife, Maria Albioni, makes Italian food the following week. The dinner conversation is devoted to talking with their children about each one's heritage.

Some families create weekly rituals that include extended family members. In our workshops we have been struck by how often people remember such weekly rituals as "Sunday dinner at Grandma's" with great warmth and fondness. At the same time, we have also heard stories regarding obligatory and imbalanced weekly rituals, when all were required to show up for a weekly gathering with Dad's family that left Mother feeling alone and excluded. You may want to take a moment to reflect on the weekly rituals that occurred in the family you come from and decide what aspects of these you might want in your own weekly rituals and what parts you would like to leave behind.

In addition to weekly rituals that include all family members, some families create weekly rituals in order to keep special time for certain relationships. Mark and Susan Donner have a weekly "adults-only dinner" when their three school-age children eat earlier, and Mark and Susan have a lovely dinner after the children have gone to bed. "We found ourselves with less and less adult time," said Susan. "We needed to preserve Tuesday night as sacred—no interferences, no telephone calls. I find that even if we've been angry with each other, our special Tuesday time enables us to come back together." In Jodi and Cal Spencer's family, Jodi and their two daughters spend Saturday morning "women's time" while Cal and their son have "men's time" three weekends out of four. On the fourth weekend Jodi goes off with their son and Cal goes out with their daughters. When Evan's children were small, she and their father divorced. When the children reached school age, Evan initiated a weekly "out for breakfast" ritual, taking Jason one week and Jennifer the following week out to a favorite restaurant for breakfast before school. Since children in divorced families often get taken everywhere together due to custody and visitation arrangements, this weekly breakfast alone with Mom allowed for unique relationship time.

Weekly rituals have a lot of flexibility. You can choose a day and time that works best for your family. They also give us a sense of reliability—no matter what happens in a given week, we can count on some special time together to reconnect.

The Power of Daily Rituals

Daily rituals offer an opportunity to shape family relationships every day. Their repetitious quality means that daily rituals powerfully tell us who we are to each other, sometimes without our even realizing it. Satisfying daily rituals often do not even get noticed by the family, while they are in fact shaping and expressing family relationships, beliefs, and values. Discomfort, tension, and conflict in daily rituals are an important signal that your family is struggling to shift relationships or to undergo a difficult developmental change. Since daily rituals occur with such frequency, they can be a vital resource to your family, a place where the family can easily learn about itself and can experiment with new relationship opportunities.

7

Birthdays

REMEMBERING LIFE'S BEGINNINGS
AND AFFIRMING RELATIONSHIPS ACROSS THE YEARS

IMAGINE THAT YOU are a member of the Rivera family and you are awakened on your birthday with family members gathered around your bed, each with a lighted candle and serenading you with "Happy Birthday." For the rest of the day you have no chores to do and they make you whatever you want for any of your meals. Whenever anyone has a birthday in this family, no matter their age, the day starts off in this way. Stories are told about the time Yolanda's hair caught on fire while she was singing, and the year Luis wanted nothing but spaghetti to eat all day. Family members feel uniquely connected to each other with this ceremony because they do not do it with anyone else. They have found a simple way both to demonstrate the importance of the birth of each person and to affirm family relationships.

With events such as birthdays, each family creates its own special *inside* calendar. Family birthdays happen each year on the same day. You will not find these days marked, like Thanksgiving or Fourth of July, on calendars that you buy, but families know when these days come around on their internal calendar. Other events that might go on this family calendar include anniversaries of marriages or deaths, or the day we stopped drinking or smoking. Vacations, family reunions, and seasonal traditions, such as apple picking and pie baking each fall, can be found on this inside calendar as well. (See Chapters 8 and 9.) These traditions offer a lot of flexibility in choices of symbols, symbolic action, and use of time, and provide a strong sense of identity to families.

What Do Birthdays Mean to You?

Birthdays can be an important time for individuals and families not just to honor the actual birth date of the person, but to mark new family relationships, honor the aging process, remember the birth parents, reconnect when there has been loss or cutoffs, and just have fun. But different people will have varying concerns about what is happening in the family as well as different values about how to celebrate birthdays. Here are some ways to think more about what is important about birthdays in your life.

Take five minutes by yourself or with your partner and/or your children and see where your values about birthdays are the same and different.

• Scan the list below and cross off lightly with pencil any values that are not important to you.

• Add any values that we have overlooked.

• Beside each of the remaining statements, assign a number from 1 to 10 that shows how important it is to you. A 10 is high, a 1 is low.

• Repeat these three steps with other family members.

• Where are your values similar and different?

_____Birthdays are a time to remember the sacredness of life.

_____Birthdays are a time of activity and festivity.

_____When it is someone's birthday, he or she should be able to gather together friends and family and do special activities.

_____Birthdays should be family celebrations focused on the home.

_____The people who gave birth should also be remembered on that day.

_____Presents should be small, handmade items.

_____Presents should be practical.

_____Presents should be exchanged just within the family.

_____Presents should be special things that the person wants.

_____Birthdays are mainly for small children.

_____Adults' birthdays should at least be acknowledged with a card.

_____Birthdays of older members of the family should be especially marked.

As you read this chapter, think about which of your values are currently expressed in how you celebrate birthdays. Are there any changes you would like to make so that birthday rituals reflect more of your beliefs?

Birthdays: Affirming Life

Birthdays indicate that we have spent one more year on this earth and that we are progressing through the years that we each have. They are a time to be reminded of the gift of life. They honor the particular day, time, and place when each person entered the world. Some of the symbols of birthday parties such as blowing out candles on a cake demonstrate these themes. Candles contain light and so can symbolize birth and at the same time, they burn down and go out, symbolizing death. By adding one each year, candles symbolize our progress through the life cycle toward death, and when we make a secret wish over them and blow them out, it is a small way to assert control over the inevitable.[1] Most people sing "Happy Birthday" with the candles lit, and the birthday person is supposed to blow them out with one breath. Often the number of candles represents the number of years the person has been on this earth. This kind of repeated symbolic action across birthday years and across families is familiar and known and helps us to move into the unknown of the future year. It also marks the change in age status of the birthday person.

The modern birthday cake was supposedly invented by German bakers in the Middle Ages. To call upon good spirits for the birthday person, the cake would be surrounded in the morning by burning candles in a kind of protective circle. The candles would burn all day until dessert time at dinner.[2] A variation of this practice was the use of a long twelve-year candle, one-twelfth to be burned at each birthday until the children entered the adult world at age thirteen. In present-day times the candles got smaller, and the symbol of the birthday cake has become so common that it comes in many variations, such as pie, ice cream, and bread. As Humphrey and Lin state in *We Gather Together*, "The tradition is so solid, in other words, so widespread and so observed that as long as the context carries other signs that signify 'birthday,' the actual form the cake may take is very free."[3] Also, birthday cakes can appear almost anywhere—at celebrations in homes, offices, schools, and restaurants. They can even be taken to hidden adolescent camps in the woods. Elliot Hardy planned his thirteenth-birthday celebration as a survival weekend camping out with a couple of friends in the woods near the house and eating food found from the land. However, he gladly accepted the offer of a birthday cake brought by his parents to the camp. Of course, candles needed to be a part of it and presents brought, too, but useful ones like rope and fish hooks.

Mock spankings are often another part of the celebration—a spank for each year and then one to grow on for the next year. Tad Tuleja, in his fascinating book *Curious Customs: The Stories Behind 296 Popular American Rituals*, links this activity to the three parts of traditional rites of passages where first a person is separated from the community; then new information and identity is passed on to him; and finally, the person is reincorporated into the community with a new status. Tuleja sees the spanking ritual as a mini-version of this pattern where the birthday person is separated from the rest of the group with a public spanking. This marks his or her special status. Then the birthday person is invited back into the group by offering luck, another mock spank to grow on, and congratulations.

Because of their movement through time, birthdays are good markers of developmental changes in families as children pass through childhood, the teenage years, and into adulthood. Birthdays are celebrated very differently for a one-year-old than for someone turning twenty-one or seventy-seven. The first birthdays of children are often more focused on adults coming together than on children playing with each other. For instance, when Zoe, a little Greek-American girl, was one, the family that took care of her one day a week was invited, as well as her grandparents, her mother's best friend, and one set of neighbors who had just had a new baby in the last year. Emphasized in the get-together was the safe passage of Zoe through the year. People admired her various accomplishments, such as saying "Ma-ma" and "Da-da," and Zoe played more with the wrapping paper than with her presents.

As children grow older and interact more with peers, birthday parties often shift to be more child-oriented with games, noisy party favors, and present opening as key parts. Adults take on a more supportive role. Children also begin to have a say about who they want to invite and what they want to do. When Janine's daughter, Natalya, was younger, she already had a sense of what was and was not appropriate for birthdays. Her six-year-old molars came in with no calcium on them so she was very limited on the sweets that she could eat. For Natalya, having a piñata full of candy at a birthday party was a very big deal. At seven, Natalya said to her mom, "I would really like to have a piñata at one of my birthdays. Can I, for special?" Janine agreed. Then Natalya said, "I'd better have it at my eight-year-old or nine-year-old birthday because after that I'll be too old for it." Soon after, she had a piñata at the party for her eighth birthday. Natalya asked if she could have a dancing party for her twelfth birthday. By then she had been at two dancing birthday parties of her mother's. Natalya's imagining of future birthdays in this way helped her to mark her own development. As children grow older, they shape how their birthdays change, too. Listen over the years to what your children want for their birthdays and negotiate it with them. They will remember this as a special time that they were felt, seen, and heard as unique individuals and communication lines will more likely remain open. When Evan's son, Jason, turned twelve, he decided he wanted to make a dinner party for five of his seventh-grade friends. He had been learning cooking in school, and had recently started to make and sell chocolates in the neighborhood. He called three girls and two boys for what he termed his "gourmet" birthday. He told his friends to dress up for the occasion. Evan helped him shop, and then, on his own, he prepared cornish hens, potatoes, and vegetables, with his delicious chocolates for dessert. Other mothers called Evan, wanting to know how she had convinced Jason to do this, but all of it was his idea that simply required some support for a birthday that allowed him to experiment a bit with being more grown up. Planning a birthday celebration can provide a time to find out what the interests of your child and his or her friends are, how their friendship network is organized, and what your child thinks about growing up.

Rick O'Leary, an Irish-American father, found out about what their son thought about growing up the hard way. When he and his wife showed up at their son Dan's college dorm for his nineteenth birthday with the same baseball figurine on his cake that Dan had had since he was five, Rick was taken aback when his son grabbed the figurine off the cake and threw it in the trash. That figure was a symbol to Dan of his childhood family birthdays at home and Dan was now a young adult at college. Later, Dan's father quietly rescued the baseball player from the trash and took it home to put in the family keepsake chest to pass on to Dan when he has a child of his own.

As family changes over time are highlighted by how birthday celebrations shift, there may also be key milestones that families want to mark in an individual's life such as the eighteenth or twenty-first birthday (entering adulthood), decade birthdays (turning thirty, forty, fifty), older birthdays, such as seventy-five or eighty, or making it all the way to one hundred. There are few good rituals in our society to mark the transition from adolescence to adulthood. Some of the age markers that we do have, such as turning sixteen and being able to drive or gaining voting privileges at age eighteen, are minimally ritualized. Since the line between adolescence and adulthood is quite unclear as children live at home longer, or are in school well into their twenties, you might want to celebrate some of the young-adult birthdays with family, teachers, and friends more intentionally, emphasizing how your child is entering the adult world. Birthdays provide us with age labels that help to explain both to ourselves and others our various responsibilities and possibilities in life.

As we reach the upper limits of the life span, birthdays are more likely to be honored by the community as well as by family. Newspaper interviews are often done with people who reach ninety or ninety-five or one hundred. In the town of Leverett, Massachusetts, a golden cane is presented on the birthday of the oldest member of the community.

How Killarney Cake Got Its Name and Other Customs

As you think about how birthdays are different for people of different ages in your family, it may also be useful to think about what central family symbols or festivities change or are the same. For instance, in Janine's family, the Killarney Cake (a lemon sponge cake) has been made now for four generations of birthdays. It was originally made by Great-grandmother Elma Heaton after an aluminum pot salesman came to her door in the 1920s and sold her a "chube" (tube) pan for making sponge cake. Aluminum was all the rage for cooking then as a new lightweight metal, and Janine's mother begged her mother to buy it. So she did and Great-grandmother Heaton began to make lemon sponge cakes. When Janine's mother married and had four children, the family lived on Lake Killarney in western Washington. The lemon cake was traditionally made on each child's birthday but it had no name; over time, it became Killarney Cake. Interestingly, Janine never knew the cake's story until 1987, when she asked her mother how it evolved into the cake for birthdays. Her sister Tanya didn't know the story until 1989 when Natalya wrote up the Killarney Cake story for a school recipe book. When you ask, who knows what stories you will find!

Butter on the nose of the birthday celebrant has been a custom in other families. When it was someone's birthday in Cathy Condon's family in St. Louis, Missouri, in the morning before the birthday person woke up, someone would sneak into his room and put butter on his nose. This led to a lot of kidding and good-natured fights among the siblings. None of them would take responsibility for putting on the butter. As Cathy said, "There was nothing you could do about it because it was traditional. It's true, it's true, there was nothing you could do. It was the tyranny of tradition!" This same custom was found in Judy Kopff's family on the East Coast. In her family, people said that the reason they did it was so that the birthday person would have a shiny day and would also be asked during the day, "Why do you have butter on your nose?" The birthday person could then reply, "Glad you asked, you know, it's my birthday."[4] This is a unique way to advertise that it is the birthing day of someone.

A certain amount of advertisement usually needs to be done to help others remember and plan for birthdays, especially for adults. If you are living alone, you cannot necessarily expect that someone else will remember. When Amy Medine Stein turned forty, she invited forty of her friends to celebrate with her. During the party, she presented affirmations to each of them that she had created, "telling each how much he or she meant to me."[5] By organizing an event yourself and inviting friends and family, you can make sure that the day does not pass unmarked.

Other families have traditions of wrapping presents in three or four layers of paper or boxes before the opener finally gets to the present, or they set up treasure hunts for the presents complete with clues. The Santanas let the birthday person pick the menu for the birthday meal. In the Brown family, the day after the birthday, the birthday person is allowed to have a piece of cake for breakfast. Single adults can share these traditions by asking friends who come to a birthday gathering to bring or do something that was particular in their own family. This not only creates a festive atmosphere but provides a way for persons to get to know one another better as they tell the story of why they brought candles that cannot be blown out or homemade birthday cards or a birthday cake sculpted out of fruit.

These traditions underscore the uniqueness of each family's history and experience. Participation in the birthday rituals can help families to voice their own identity, mark membership, and honor individual members. Because birthdays come on a regular basis for each person in the family, they offer a lot of possibilities to help with family changes. We usually think of them as a time to celebrate the birthday of just one person, but they can also be a time to honor the birthing parents (the next generation up), in-laws, and aging and step-family members. They are an underused resource for linking people in intricate family groupings.

Separation, Divorce, Remarriage: The Birthdays Still Continue

When there is divorce or some other family disruption, passing on traditions, staying connected across generations, and using birthdays to help us be aware of our movement through the life cycle can become more complicated. Still, there are many options. When separated or divorced parents have worked out a cooperative relationship, the party can be done together. Or there can be two parties in two locations. One might be a family party and the other a party with the child's friends.

Some families might plan just one party with one parent. All of this depends on what stage of the divorce process the family is in, the ages of the children, distance between the parental homes, and the kind of parenting relationship the mother and father have.

When there is a divorce, children often live in two locations, while the adults live in only one. The birthday plans will have to take this into account. Ideally, the children need connections to both households and support from the adults involved. You may need to hold separate celebrations, but it is critical that a child's birthday not get totally lost in adult tensions. Birthday celebrations offer children reminders of their specialness in your life and how you will always be their parent. Even if you do not live with them all the time, such celebrations will go a long way toward helping heal their hurts over the divorce.

CHANGING BIRTHDAY RITUALS

Siyu Cheng separated from her husband when her son, Doug, was five. His sixth birthday was at his mother's house with his school friends, but his father came and participated in it as did his nineteen-year-old half-brother. Doug very much wanted them there and they did one of their usual customs at the party, telling the story of Doug's birth from the father's and the mother's perspective. Over the next year as the couple divorced and settled into the custody arrangement of Siyu as the primary caretaker, Doug did not bring up his father's or half-brother's coming to his next birthday party. Nor did they ask to come. Doug had a swimming party with many of his friends. The following year, Doug's mother was dating someone with a daughter, eleven. They decided to have a family birthday dinner for Doug, along with the usual party with his friends. Meanwhile, Doug went out to eat for a separate birthday meal with his father. The shifts in who is at what party or meal reflects the changing membership and relationships in the family.

The Belsons, an English-American couple, separated when their daughter Alicia was two. As she lived primarily with her mother some five hours away by car from her father, birthdays were quickly established as something that were only celebrated at her mother's house. For the Peterson family, where the parents had joint custody and their two children went back and forth two miles between two homes, the parent who had the child for a birthday would typically arrange the party and the other parent attended. This went on for several years until each spouse became involved with another partner. Then the children began to have two separate celebrations in each of the households.

In situations where one parent has custody or parents live long distances apart, the other parent may forget or ignore a child's birthday. If this happens, the custodial parent often has to deal with the disappointment, hurt, or anger of the child. If you know from previous experience that this is likely to happen, you can gently remind your child not to get her expectations up, while focusing on the things that you know will happen. You can also help your child write or call the other parent to express her distress so that it is not all focused on you.

Birthdays can hold within them memories of happier times, wishes for lifelong connections, and an awareness of loss for both adults and children. Using birthdays intentionally to make realistic connections that honor what you currently have, without glossing over the very real changes, can be helpful for everyone. No matter what else shifts in a family, birthdays remain on the same day. They can be used as a steadying point. For Tess, a young woman in her twenties who lived through two divorces and in three different family configurations growing up, the fact that her birthday was celebrated no matter what else was going on helped her to feel connected through all the changes. When the family grew to six children with the addition of half and step-siblings, birthdays became even more important to her as a time that she was singled out among all bustle of the household to be especially feted and remembered.

STEP-FAMILIES: MAKING NEW CONNECTIONS

Almost a year after Janine and David met, David's daughter, Heather, was about to be seven. Janine's daughter, Natalya, figured out that her birthday was exactly six months to the day behind Heather's. When Heather was turning seven, Natalya was turning six and a half. The kids decided to have a half birthday party for Natalya at the same time that Heather's birthday was celebrated. The newly forming family had a whole birthday cake and a half birthday cake and sang "Happy Birthday" as well as " 'Halfy' Birthday." During the dinner, for which the girls picked the food, Heather's father, David, told how they came home from the hospital with her the same day she was born because she was such a strong, healthy baby. Janine told how she was unable to hold Natalya when she was first born, because her arms were full of tubing from the emergency caesarean. But when Natalya was laid next to her, she looked straight at her and reached out and touched her on the cheek. And how she looked like a little elf in her father's arms. They also talked about celebrating Heather's half birthday when Natalya was seven, and then discovered that Janine's sister's birthday was exactly six months to the day after David's birthday.

A simple celebration, but a lot of step-family work was happening. First, the past relationships of the children were honored through marking their birthing days and stories. History was also being shared. Second, the family expanded the common ritual of birthday parties to create a celebration that is unique to step or adoptive families. (It is next to impossible biologically for two children to be born six months apart in a nuclear family!) Third, a cycle of birthday parties was started that anticipated future gatherings. Later, David's half birthday was celebrated at Janine's sister's forty-sixth-birthday party. This was a way to begin to link in-laws.[6]

Honoring Birth Parents

When we think of birthdays, we most often think of the person who was born on that day. However, it is also a possible time to honor the birthing parents. Selina, who came to this country from Brazil, was returning home on a family visit at the time of her twenty-fifth birthday. Her parents had divorced several years earlier, and she was still feeling her way with establishing separate relationships with her mother and father after the divorce. As she thought about her birthday, she saw it not only as a celebration for herself, but also for her parents as they were finishing their first quarter of a century of parenting. She decided that on her birthday, she wanted to honor both her mother and father by giving them gifts that acknowledged their different ways of being her parent and also as a thank you to them for their love and care. Selina made and gave a book of photos to her father with captions from a trip she had taken with him earlier, the first time the two of them had ever traveled together without anyone else. She gave her mother a copybook with short stories, songs her mother used to sing to her, and phrases and drawings about different times of their life as Selina remembered them.

After Selina gave these gifts to them, she noted that it also seemed to mark a shift in her own view of herself in the family. The ritual worked to change her identity and to mark new relationships. As children grow older, there needs to be a shift in who are the ritual givers and creators. Selina saw herself as moving beyond being just on the receiving end in the family. She felt that she was saying, "Now that I have grown up, I want to give you back some of the support and help you gave me."

Marcella sometimes sends her mother a birthday card on her own birthday, thanking her mother for her birth, or she calls her mother-in-law and thanks her for the gift of her husband on his birthday. At times, Marcella has also made a cake for her mother on the birthdays of one of her siblings when they were far away and were unable to get together to celebrate.

These small gestures all honor the connections between generations. With the overemphasis in our society on youth, a way to hear from and acknowledge the role of elders in our world can be very important. Oscar Goldfarb described another way to link generations as well as keep a historical record:

I do tape a lot, every birthday. We tape "Happy Birthday," and then we interview. Everyone in the family gets a chance to say how they feel and what the year was like. And we also tape when we have a religious holiday or something like that. And just every once in a while when the family seems to be in the right mood, we'll bring the tape recorder out, and we'll have interviews, and we'll sing. Then we'll listen to tapes from previous years. And you can hear the kids' voices change. The kids love it.[7]

Older Parents

As parents get on in years, their adult children often make more of their birthdays as a larger family occasion. As Delores, an African-American woman, said, "When the kids are little, we make a big deal out of each of their birthdays, that they have safely made it into the world. Then as we get grown up, we're too busy living it to do much with our birthdays. But when we're older, we become more aware again of the fact people won't be with us that long, and so we make a big fuss to acknowledge that we've made it through all those years."

For their mother's seventieth birthday, Janine and her sister planned a large surprise party. It was complicated because their mother lives in Seattle and both daughters live on the East Coast. The daughters found that they had to have a lot of contact with their stepfather, his daughter, and family friends there in order to pull it off. The party had the effect of making many more direct links between family members that did not ordinarily have much contact. The secrets that were shared and the lies that were concocted together made for lots of good humor. Originally the party was to honor their mother, but when the family looks back on it now, it is recognized as an event that helped to cement the step-family ties as well as put the sisters more in touch with people of the older generation.

At the actual party, Janine's sister, Tanya, showed slides of their mother's life from when she was a little girl until now. (The slides were made from old photos.) Janine even managed to get some photos that only her mother had by having her daughter, Natalya, call her up and ask her for some pictures for a school history project.

The family also told some stories that were remembered from when the now-grown children were little. This honored what a wonderful storyteller their mother was. Janine and Natalya played a Handel duet on their violins. She originally thought of the playing as a way to share with others the gift of music that her mother had passed on to her children, but as they played for everyone gathered there, Janine was aware that her own mothering relationship with her daughter was being honored as well.

The party was videotaped so that it can be shared later with other generations. You might want to think of elders in your family that you would like to acknowledge more fully and do something different for their birthday. When these elders subsequently die, your grief will probably be softened by the memory and record of small celebratory things that you did while they were alive to remember them.

This can be a very positive time, too, to rework past hurts or differences by sharing, without bitterness, that things have not always gone smoothly between you, or letting family members know that you are open to seeing their point of view in a different way. Anthony Andersen wrote a letter to his father, Ron, on his sixty-fifth birthday. For a number of years, they had had an estranged relationship because of religious differences. In his twenties, Anthony had left the Baptist

Church and converted to the Nation of Islam. After his father found out, they had almost no contact for a number of years. Now in his late thirties, Anthony wrote to his father that he understood, given that his father's father was a Baptist minister, how difficult it must have been for Ron to accept Anthony's conversion. He also talked about how he hoped that as adults, each could respect and agree to accept each other's religious differences. Using quotes from both the Koran and the Bible, Anthony spoke to how people at times needed to heal and come together. He also wrote about what he thought his faith had given to him in his life.

Parents may or may not respond directly to this kind of letter, but at least you know that you have stated your own position and hopes. The focus should not be on trying to evoke a certain desired response from someone, but rather on being clear about where you stand, how you see the other people involved, what you would like and what you can do. If birthdays have been occasions in your family with good memories attached to them, then such birthday letters carry the advantage of being connected to warmer times.

Birthdays and Adult Siblings

Maurice Kaplan, a construction worker in his forties, had never marked the birthdays of his two adult siblings since they were children. Growing up in a family where there was alcohol and prescription drug abuse, the three children, born over a span of four years, had not received much support for strong relationships among themselves. Rather, they had disengaged from one another as a reaction both to lack of reliable parenting and because each parent had played favorites among the children. It was only as adults in their forties and fifties that they began to talk with each other about the confusing patterns of their childhood home with its secret and shameful addiction. With little regular contact among the three of them, and wide geographical distances, Maurice decided one year that he would make an effort to visit his siblings around the time of their birthdays and give them each a present. He managed to have a party with his sister on her actual birthday and to make it to his brother's house two thousand miles away shortly after his birthday. For Maurice, this was a way to begin to acknowledge their special relationship of brother and sister.

Birthdays are a natural time for siblings to remember each other. However, as birthdays are often primarily facilitated by adults for children, you may not have had much experience in being celebration providers for your brothers and sisters. You may need some practice at it. Maurice waited as his own birthday approached to see if his siblings would initiate contact. They didn't remember his birthday, but they made renewed contact in some other important ways. He figures that maybe if he remembers their birthdays for three years running, they will start to remember his.

As siblings age, honoring each other's birthdays is a good way to keep connected. Appreciations can be given and old memories revived. Siblings can be an important supportive network over a lifetime. Because they have usually shared intimate experiences that are unique to your family, they can help you remember forgotten details or understand family stories with a fresh slant. Paying attention to the possibilities of sibling involvement, especially available through birthdays, opens new adult resources for you.

Birthdays and Losses

It can also be important to continue to mark birthdays when people have died or left the family, particularly when it is an unexpected death of a younger person, or what has happened to someone is a mystery. (This is also discussed in Chapter 10; see the section "Celebrating and Loss.") Rituals' capacity to provide healing can be tapped by especially marking the birth of a loved one who has died. A writer described how the family still gathered on his brother's birthday after he was killed as a young adult in a car accident. "Mom thought we should do something on Jim's birthday, rather than try to just pretend it wasn't happening, so the three of us got together. She also thought of the gifts, as a memorial to him. Dad gave me an arrowhead he found when they dug a cellar hole down by the marshes. Mom gave Dad a fountain pen with a mother-of-pearl handle. I gave Mom a swatch of Chinese silk that Jim had pulled out of an attic. And, since it needed to be renewed and wouldn't pass anymore, I gave her Jim's license. It had a good photo of him on it, a good rendering of his cockeyed smile, the smile that told me here was somebody who looked closely for the differences between things. Mom leaned back and closed her fingers over it." This first gift sharing started a family tradition. "We (still) get together on Jim's birthday, exchange gifts that remind us of him, gifts he would have picked out or made himself: a mushroom carved from pine, an antique button, a book on bird identification. Things like that, anything that speaks of Jim's curiosity."[8]

When there has been a loss, many families have a natural inclination to ignore and pass over what is missing around birthdays and other family times. They often think that by pushing the loss aside, that memories will be easier for people. What we find, though, is that people are each left very alone with their memories and hurts. This family found a way to come together and support one another by remembering some of the very positive parts of what Jim was like as a person and by acknowledging what he brought to their lives for the time that they had him. Birthdays are after all a time to be aware of the sacredness of life. In a couple where the husband's brother had committed suicide some fifteen years earlier, it was very difficult for anyone in the family to talk about this. They began to remember the brother again by first marking his birthday. This felt safer than beginning by remembering the anniversary of his death.

When older couples have shared their birthdays for many decades and one member of the pair dies, it's often very hard for the remaining partner to enjoy his or her own birthday. Merrill Chatham's beloved wife, Suzannah, died just weeks before his seventy-fifth birthday. Having a birthday party or even marking the occasion without her seemed impossible to him. Still his children wanted to honor his special day. His daughter, Anna, asked him what he would like for his birthday, and he replied that he just wanted to ignore it. Then she asked him what he thought Suzannah would have wanted him to do. He began to cry and said, "She'd want me to be with all of you and eat that cake she always made." Anna asked, "Can I try making that cake? It won't be as good as Mom's, I know, but what do you think?" Merrill agreed, and he gathered with his children to mark his seventy-fifth birthday. They told stories about Suzannah, who had been a most creative ritual maker, and in that way honored Merrill's birthday and furthered the whole family's healing. If your own aging parent finds it too painful to celebrate her or his birthday in ways that are reminiscent of previous birthdays, you will need to respect this, and search for new and unfamiliar ways to celebrate. Something as simple as shifting this ritual to a new location, or marking it with a different kind of food, can often make a birthday possible for a widow or widower.

REDOING A BIRTHDAY

Redoing birthday parties can also be important when there have been particular hurts and losses. You may have grown up in a family that, because it was not functioning well, made little of birthdays. Or, celebratory aspects of birthdays may have been lost with tension around other members of the family drinking at the party, refusing to come, or staying on the periphery. Economic pressures may have made it difficult to honor the growing child.

Mercedes, a Cuban in her mid-thirties living alone, had not been allowed by her family to celebrate her eleventh birthday. Two weeks before she was eleven, a neighbor man had molested her. Her parents were so upset about it that they canceled Mercedes's birthday party. This had remained with her as a very traumatic memory: she felt blamed by her family for what had happened, and her friends, who were then disinvited to the party, were all whispering and wondering what Mercedes had done. When she was thirty-five, Mercedes decided to finally have her eleventh birthday. Friends were asked to bring presents or symbolic items appropriate for a child. At the party they played musical chairs and pin-the-tail-on-the-donkey, wore party hats, and laughed and laughed! Some of Mercedes's friends knew the details of why she was having the party twenty-four years later; others did not, but entered easily into the playful atmosphere. This party allowed Mercedes to move beyond painful memories and become more focused in her current life.

If you recall a particularly unhappy birthday, especially one that feels like it marked a turning point for you, such as a childhood birthday that became fused with a parental divorce or was ruined by parental alcoholism, you may want to consider ways to redo that birthday in your adult life. Use this ritual to close off old hurts and orient yourself to new possibilities.

Celebrating the Family Ritual Maker's Birthday

Many families have a person or one or two central people who do much of the ritual preparing for other's birthdays. Oftentimes this is the mother. So what happens when it is the ritual maker's birthday? There may not be mechanisms in place to structure the planning and organizing of her birthday. Sometimes little is done for her birthday. Many mothers have described their disappointment to us in words similar to Ellen Barnes's: "Everyone's birthday gets celebrated but mine!" Or the ritual maker gets pulled into working on her own event. Gina, a thirty-nine-year-old Italian-American and mother of two, was excited when her children announced they were going to cook her a meal for her fortieth birthday. However, on that day she found herself in the middle of showing them where things were, helping them to open things, figuring out directions, and running out to the store for what they had forgotten. It ended up not feeling very celebratory at all.

Bruce's father had a stroke and was unable to do much anymore around the house. Several months later, it was Bruce's mother's sixty-third birthday. Bruce realized that if he didn't pitch in to help that his mother would have to do most of the work for her own day. Since it took a lot of effort to get his father out of the house, he decided to transport the birthday celebration to his mother and father's house. Each year now he bakes a cake and gets ice cream, and everyone brings presents, birthday banners, and flowers.

If your family has one primary ritual maker for birthdays, you may need to think of ways to put a different structure in place for celebrating her or his day. It may seem a little unfamiliar at first, but they will appreciate it very much.

Unbirthdays

Birthdays are also unique because they have the tradition of unbirthdays. No other holiday has an "unholiday." Unbirthdays have unlimited possibilities. At twenty-one, Wendy Roges fondly remembered unbirthdays in her family.

> When I was little—I was one of six—my mother would come up with some day out of the year that was really far away from Christmas and

your birthday, you know, that endless stretch. You'd come home from school and she'd tell you it was your unbirthday. She'd cook your favorite dinner, whatever it was—even hot dogs. And you could watch all your favorite television programs. Nobody could argue with you about it. People sang "Happy Unbirthday" to you. There was a cake sometimes and presents, but it wasn't like a birthday when you got real presents. It wasn't every year that everybody had one. It was just kind of spontaneous. It came from Alice in Wonderland. Remember the Mad Hatter's tea party? "Have a happy unbirthday!"[9]

In families where a child has a birthday on or near a major holiday (like Fourth of July or Christmas), unbirthdays can be a good way to celebrate their birthdays at a quieter time of year when their celebration does not get lost in the other holiday or taken over by it. For instance, Maria, a young Italian-American woman born on July 4, finally revolted against the red, white, and blue flag motif of her birthdays that had been going on for twenty years. Last year she asked for, and got, a purple birthday, including cake, candles, and flowers, and in February! Unbirthdays can also be used to give people some special support or surprise when other difficult things are happening in their lives.

Another variation on unbirthdays is celebrating, for example, three-quarter or seven-twelfth birthdays. That means you can have a birthday almost any time of year. For single adults this can provide an excuse to invite people over to dinner, renew old friendships with a party, or gather your network together for a picnic.

Thinking More About Your Own Birthday Celebrations

Because birthdays are on the inside calendar of each family and there are not many cultural pressures on how they should be celebrated, they have a lot of flexibility to respond to differing family needs over the life cycle. They also can mark our shifting roles and responsibilities with ease. Ronice Branding of Florissant, Missouri, and her sister wanted to do something for their mother's seventy-fifth birthday that didn't add unnecessary things to her life but that would give her much joy. Unbeknownst to her, they "stole" her address book and wrote a letter telling of her activities to some two hundred friends, inviting them to take part in the celebration of their mother's birthday by sending a card.

At a family birthday dinner a few days before her birthday, we announced the surprise by reading the letter that had gone out. Then the mail began to arrive—170 birthday cards from all over the country and from people she had not seen in years! Her postman said she was the talk of the post office.[10]

Like Ronice and her sister, you can use the openness of birthdays as a time to make new connections or mark generational shifts. Or you might want to revive lost family traditions or connect differently with others in your community. Birthdays can be a resource for us to celebrate our various changes as people grow. Here are some questions to help you think and discuss more about birthdays in both your past and current life.

• What birthday traditions have been passed down or would you like to pass down? How do they represent either your mother or father's side of the family or different ethnic traditions?

• What do you know about how/why they have been passed down? Who can you ask?

• How has the celebration of birthdays for you or someone else in your family shifted over time in terms of *who gathers together, where you gather, foods, planning, symbols*? Who creates the celebration? Has that changed?

• How do birthday celebrations work for your family? (Do they help to bring generations together, mark the passing of years, or help you to remember the sacredness of birth? Or do they link step-family members, connect children with their friends, or . . . ?)

• What is the significance of gift giving in your family? Are there any hidden rules about the giving of gifts that you have fallen into that you would like to make more open? Or that you would like to discuss in order to change? (The older the child, the more expensive the gift? Gifts need to be given for all the cousins' birthdays? Mothers buy the gifts that fathers give?)

• What role does humor play in your birthday celebrations?

• How would you like to be celebrating your or someone else's birthday in the future? (Perhaps pick a time that has special significance, such as a decade birthday, or a particular year.)

Family traditions on the inside calendar are flexible enough and happen often enough in our lives that they can work with whatever issues are up for families. They are generally free from many of the constraints of events celebrated on the outside calendar—such as a period of time that is predetermined, and an emphasis on types of gifts to exchange, decorations, and foods that *should* be used. Birthdays offer prospects to highlight new identities, connect family members in unique ways, and honor the sacredness of life as people progress through the life cycle. While most families note birthdays in some fashion, there are many other events on the inside calendar of family life that may or may not be acknowledged. For instance, families have all kinds of anniversaries. In the next chapter, we'll look at ways that significant anniversary dates can become meaningful rituals.

ᄒ

Anniversaries

HONORING RELATIONSHIPS AND
MARKING PERSONAL CHANGES

THE WORD "ANNIVERSARY" literally means the turning of the year. Anniversary dates are sometimes like flags that stand out marking the passage of time. They often evoke strong memories of previous moments in one's life. While birthdays are usually remembered from year to year (the addition of another number to our age seems to keep us focused on the upcoming day and change), anniversaries of other important events are sometimes not marked. Yet anniversaries are particularly appropriate for reassessing the significance and meaning of key decisions or events in the past and in your current life, as well as their implications for your future.

The Importance of Milestones

Remembering milestones can provide reflective time and space to honor the positive aspects of one's life as well as look at possible changes. The significance of the original event may have expanded, altered, or been challenged by subsequent life changes. Or current relationships may be stuck around what happened at key turning points. An anniversary ritual can help you to express beliefs, redefine relationships, and heal from past hurts. The Chhoun family used the date of their move from Cambodia to the United States as a time each year to sit down and check in with one another about how all the changes had gone. They shared their original hopes and fears, as well as what had worked and not worked over the past twelve months. They talked about the adjustments they had had to make and discussed other ways they could continue to help each other. Time was also included to share memories in-depth of their previous life in Cambodia, as well as to write long letters and take pictures to send to those members of their extended family who were still living there.

We usually think primarily of wedding anniversaries in relation to families, but there may be other important anniversary dates such as the loss of a family member, divorce, or significant entrances into the family such as an adopted or foster child. If anniversaries of individual changes such as stopping drinking or smoking are noted, friends and family can honor what it took to make the change and offer continued support. Too often, when someone shifts his behavior, it can begin to be taken for granted and people do not have a place to share ongoing issues that accompany the change. A more public celebration of such an anniversary also highlights that it was a shift that affected others close to the person.

It may be important, too, to highlight a divorce anniversary in some way to enable people to heal and move on with their lives. Wedding anniversaries in remarried families can look quite different than anniversaries of first-time married couples. If either of the wedding partners brings children to the second marriage, the children may be important to include in the anniversary marking, as it is the time of the new family creation as well as the couple's marriage.

Anniversaries of pregnancy loss, deaths, and other traumas are often unmarked. The anniversary of someone's death can be a time to publicly affirm the loss that has been experienced by loved ones. A funeral helps to bring together community support at the time of a death. Anniversaries can be a time to reactivate this network. There may be unfinished business from the funeral as well. These issues can sometimes be addressed with an anniversary observance.

A FATHER WITH TWO LIVES

For Sara, the funeral for her father, Richard, two years earlier in her hometown was very difficult. No one acknowledged that he had died of AIDS. For her mother, who was going to continue to live in that small community, making that information public knowledge would have meant opening her marriage and life to a scrutiny that she did not need, given her own pain. Yet for Sara, who knew of her father's bisexuality and dual life, the funeral occurred without full acknowledgment of who her father was and what he had gone through. Two years later, upon the anniversary of his death, in her own community where she felt she could now be open about how he had died, she put together a memorial service for her father.

As guests entered the chapel, they received a program that included color photos of her father with her, her mother, with his grandchildren, and with a male lover. At the beginning of the service, both Sara and her children shared memories and blessings for Richard. Sara talked about what it took over the last two years to come to the point where she could openly mark a fuller version of her father's life and death. One of her children, with tears in his eyes, told the story of how, with his grandfather dying of AIDS, he had gone to the principal in his elementary school to try to get him to stop the other children from taunting each other with words like "Don't touch him, he's got AIDS," or putting each other down by using the words "queer" and "gay." He made a public plea for an end to this kind of behavior. This memorial service released the family from the secrecy of the original funeral, when the whole story of the grandfather's life could not be told. It also let Sara's immediate family share their own story more openly in relation to their grandfather, and lifted any vestiges of shame.

Anniversary traditions are unique in that the individuals and/or families who are involved in the event are often the only ones who are aware of them or remember them. Some advertising or sharing needs to happen for others to know about them. In talking with people around the country, we have been struck by the number of people who do not know when their parents' wedding anniversary is or do not celebrate it in any way. Traditionally, people have not looked to other generations of the family or to friends to support the hard work required in marriage. When a couple makes it to their fiftieth anniversary or other high numbers, then it is often more widely acknowledged. But most couples (as evidenced by the divorce rate) could use the community and familial support much more usefully *along* the way, rather than once it is clear a couple has "made it." An anniversary can be an ideal time to validate their work as parents, their commitment to each other, and what they have done for family members and community.

Wedding Anniversaries: Continuing to Be Married

Wedding anniversaries may be mentioned only in passing, celebrated with the same perfunctory flowers and dinner out, or a new and different event may be planned each year to highlight the continuity of a marriage and the changes of that particular year. Perhaps only the couple marks it, or maybe the children and other family members do something as well. Maria Rodriquez remembered her parents' wedding anniversary as virtually uncelebrated. Her parents would exchange cards and her father would sometimes buy her mother roses. A friend described how his parents' twenty-fifth anniversary was celebrated with a big family party and kept asking Maria what she and her siblings were doing for her parents on their twenty-fifth anniversary. She and her siblings, never having celebrated it, didn't know what to do. It ended up being celebrated in the same way, only her father bought a few more roses.

Danielle, a forty-four-year-old Jewish-American woman, described how her parents' wedding anniversary was never marked by their request because as children they had felt so pressed by their own parents to do something special for them on their anniversaries and birthdays that they became rigid and obligatory rituals. Each year Danielle's parents made a point of telling them that they did not want the children to do anything. They moved, in one generation, to a minimized ritual style, leaving Danielle to feel that there were few ways for her and her brothers to reciprocate in some small manner for all their parents had given to them. Children need chances to give and do for others, too.

JANINE'S MANY ANNIVERSARIES

When Janine and her future husband, David, told Janine's mother that they were going to announce their engagement around the time of David's birthday, September 15, Janine's mother said, "Whatever you do, don't make it September 16."

"Why not?" Janine asked.

"Because that *was* the wedding anniversary of your father and me." (Her parents were divorced over twenty years ago.)

"Gee, I never knew that," Janine responded. There are a lot of different rituals celebrated in Janine's family and she even has old home movies of her parents' wedding. And yet she didn't know her parents' anniversary and didn't have a sense that celebrating their marriage was a happy event for them.

In contrast, Janine realized she has marked every anniversary of her mother and stepfather for the last ten years with a variety of things, from cards to a gift of a two-night stay for them at an inn on Vancouver Island. They advertise their anniversary, not through saying that the children must do something, but through their affection for each other, their care, their playfulness. And with their words. As her eighty-five-year-old stepfather once said, "We can't count on fifty years together, so we celebrate each anniversary like it was seven years of being together." They typically take time to go on a trip for their anniversary, which seems to be the only way they can have some space from their extensive political involvements. Other couples go back to where they were married, or first met, or have a special dinner to remember when they first lived together. Others read letters they wrote to each other in earlier years. Some write new marriage vows. Since it is easy to take marriage as a given, an anniversary can be used as a time to remember changes across the years as well as renew the relationship.

Partners in a couple may have very different meanings attached to the significance of a wedding anniversary. There may be important gender differences. If the woman is the primary ritual maker for all of the other holidays and family events, the anniversary may be a place where she expects adult appreciation from her husband for all she does for others. Her partner may not understand the shift of roles that is called for in planning the anniversary ritual. She would like him to really put time and effort into thinking about their anniversary.

One partner may be more sentimental than the other and want a romantic anniversary. For their tenth wedding anniversary, Stuart Ulrich wanted to go away to a honeymoon hotel for the weekend. He kept telling about how this was their first decade together and they would never have a first decade to celebrate again. His wife, Karin, thought he was making a big deal out of what she saw as just another regular wedding anniversary.

If one partner is happier in the marital relationship than the other, he or she may look forward to the anniversary with quite different meaning and intentions. Jane Lerner did not feel that her husband, Tom, was taking some of her strongly stated concerns about their seven-year-old marriage very seriously. He felt that they had a solid marriage and that Jane was blowing things out of proportion. As is true in many rituals, his anniversary gift to her carried very different meanings for each. When he gave her an expensive necklace, Tom was hurt when she accepted it very coolly. Jane felt that a warm acceptance of the necklace on her part would be a statement to Tom that she was celebrating the marriage with him. At the time, she was not feeling very celebratory.

There may be significant gender differences in what partners want to do for a wedding anniversary as well. Richard wanted to go out with several other couples that they were good friends with, while his wife, Laura, preferred an intimate dinner with just the two of them. Patrick's secretary always ordered a dozen roses sent to his wife, Portia, on their anniversary. Portia spent hours refurbishing furniture (including a roll-top desk for his use at home) and making other very personal gifts. Sylvia, twenty-two, found herself one summer in a jewelry store on Cape Cod buying the wedding anniversary gift for her father to give to her mother. Their twenty-fourth anniversary was in November and Sylvia was already planning ahead. She had taken on the role of buying and wrapping the gift for her father in her teen years after he repeatedly told Sylvia he had no idea of what to get for her mother. Watching her mother's disappointment with the plants and cookbooks that came her way, Sylvia took it upon herself to "help" her parents out. A mythology had grown up over the years that her father did not know how to shop for her mother. This put Sylvia in the middle of her parents' marriage, trying to interpret for her father and mother what gift would symbolically mark their current relationship. Her father lost the opportunity to let his wife know that he really "saw" her and had something to communicate through the gift giving, both about her and their marriage.

CAREERS, CHILDREN, AND THE COUPLE, TOO?

Doug and Jan had been married for eleven years. It was a time that had been very focused on their careers as they married just out of junior college. They were also very involved with caring for their two children, Jeffrey, age six, and Pam, age four. Parenting and work responsibilities seemed to take precedent over their couple relationship. They had never spent the night together away from their children, nor had they done more for their anniversary than the usual going out to dinner. For their eleventh anniversary, they decided to go camping overnight and leave their children with friends. This helped them to focus on the fact that they were moving out of the time in their lives where their children needed them the most and that they had an important relationship as spouses that needed to be taken care of, too. A different frame marked the beginning of their second decade together. They started the second ten years enjoying something they had done a lot together before the children were born. Their relationship was honored as being as important as their parenting and work roles.

In Phil's West Coast family, the wedding anniversary of his parents was focused on the couple in a different way. It was typically a time when extended family members would get together and write poems and songs about Phil's parents' relationship. As a family with a number of members involved in show business, quite a few occasions were celebrated in this way. Events or issues were presented in a public fashion where people could laugh together about them and release some of the tension that always ensues when there is a long-term intimate relationship. Phil experienced these spoofs as a place where parents and children could look back and laugh about the sore spots together. This helped to place these in the frame of the normal ups and downs of life.

There are a variety of ways to celebrate a wedding anniversary. It can be with the couple alone, with friends, or with extended family. It can be a quiet marking of an important event, or it can be a time to refocus a marriage, work some things through, and get some closure or new direction. Think about your previous anniversaries. How have they worked for you? If you find yourself and your partner expressing a lot of differences about the meaning of anniversaries, it may have to do with what you have learned in your family-of-origin about the significance of them or ways to celebrate them or not. It may be useful to go back in time and understand what you were taught about anniversaries, in words or by example. People know their preferences intuitively for doing things in particular ways, but often these are not verbalized or understood in the context of what people experienced growing up. Here are some questions to help you think about what you were taught about anniversaries:

• Which anniversaries were celebrated in your family-of-origin? How was your parents' anniversary marked (just with the couple, with others, special location, cards or other symbols, foods)?

• Which anniversaries were celebrated in your partner's family-of-origin? How was their parents' anniversary marked (just with the couple, with others, special location, cards or other symbols, food)?

• What anniversaries were forgotten, ignored, or unable to be marked?

• How alike or dissimilar are the patterns that you and your partner learned growing up about anniversaries?

Anniversaries can also be an opportunity to mark relationship changes in a marriage. With thoughtful planning, these changes can be honored and shared with others.

OLD ISSUES AND FRESH VOWS

Sam and Susannah had been married for almost twenty-five years. They had two teenage children. Their marriage, like most marriages, was not without its ups and downs. For their twenty-fifth anniversary, they wanted to do something that would respectfully observe their many years of marriage as well as facilitate some shifts in their marital relationship. A theme that had emerged for them at various times was whether or not they should continue to be married. Intertwined in this issue was a concern about whether either of their families-of-origin had really accepted the marital partner each had chosen. As an interracial couple, they had experienced both hostility and mixed messages from both sets of parents about marrying outside of their own "group."

In order to think about what they might do for their twenty-fifth, they first sat down and went back over their wedding pictures and talked about what had happened then. Sam's parents had come only reluctantly. At the reception, Susannah's mother had made a long toast supposedly to the couple. But she had gone on and on about her own life and her life raising Susannah. With some irony, both Sam and Susannah remembered wondering at the time how the other could marry them, given how each of the families had behaved. They also talked about what the ceremony and the words and rings they exchanged had meant to just the two of them. They were reminded of their youthful hopefulness and chuckled about their naïveté about marriage.

As they talked, they realized that vows made now to each other would be even more meaningful than their original vows. After twenty-five years, they truly knew what committing themselves to each other meant. They decided to write reaffirmation vows that focused on how they were connected to each other, knowing both their strengths and each other's foibles and weaknesses. This helped them move beyond the issue of each of their own families accepting their choice of marital partner to a focus on their own commitment to stay married.

After sharing these reaffirmation vows with each other, they decided they wanted to read them publicly as a way to have witnesses to their recommitment. They also decided to have their wedding rings cleaned and polished so as to give them to each other "anew." At the same time, they had two small sapphires added to Susannah's ring to represent their two children. They invited a small group of friends to dine with the family. After the group ate together, Susannah and Sam read their recommitment vows and exchanged their old "new" rings. Their twenty-fifth anniversary was much more than a perfunctory dinner or flowers. It was a time to look at the meaning of being married, both originally and now. It was also a time to move past what others thought about their marriage. To themselves and to others they named and shared the significance of their relationship.

Divorce and Remarriage

Divorce, single parenthood, and/or remarriage all bring with them more complex family configurations that sometimes need thoughtful care to help people hold membership in two or more family units. Anniversaries can be key times to reach out and make contact with different parts of the family or to acknowledge shifts and changes that have been made. Because anniversaries are not too tied to set symbols or ways to celebrate, they offer a lot of flexibility to create new traditions.

FROM A FAMILY OF FIVE TO TWO FAMILIES OF FOUR

It was important for Ramona to mark the time that her family separated. She wanted to create an anniversary ritual to specifically address complicated relationship changes in the family since, as she described it, "the five of us split into two families of four." She wanted to celebrate what they had created and gained, as well as note what they missed. "I want to let them know that although I think we're better off now, I still feel the loss and can tolerate their ongoing feeling of frustration and sadness." Using their shared interest in reading and writing as a starting point, Ramona began assembling a book that they could add to at the end of each year. Pages were included for each of them with subheadings such as "Memories," "Changes," "Good Times," "Hard Times," "What I've learned or done this year," "What I wish for in the coming year," and so forth. Contributions to each of these sections have included writings, drawings, and photographs with captions. As part of this family tradition, they have a special dinner together and go over what they have done and play games. These kinds of activities helped a changed family unit to rebuild a sense of connection and new identification.

With a very painful separation or divorce it may be impossible to do something like this in the first few years, or ever. What may be most important is ensuring that the parent in the family gets special adult support and contact around the separation or divorce anniversary. The adults involved are likely to remember the exact day of when someone moved out, or the divorce was final. The children will probably not remember the exact date, but more than likely they will have some emotional response near the anniversary of the profound changes in the family. Everyone in the family may need more support and reassurance at this time. Such extra attention can help normalize the intense and often ambivalent feelings that arise.

It can be important for remarried families to celebrate the day that all members met for the first time. Step-families have a unique history in that there are often children who are old enough to have experienced the creation of the new family. By making a family celebration of this anniversary, the children's memories are honored as well as the special-ness of their role in the new family.

Meryl Butler describes making anniversaries a family affair in remar-ried families by having family-oriented activities or gifts. In their family, they save candles from each family member's birthday cake and melt them into one big candle to burn on the wedding anniversary day.[1] Using birthday candles to symbolize each individual and the symbolic action of melting these together creates an anniversary ritual that speaks to the issues of individual differences and connectedness in a remarried family.

Celebrating Life as a Single Adult

Anniversaries most often conjure up images of marriage or committed relationships. Janice Barker, forty-seven, often felt that her decision to live her life as a single woman was not honored, especially by her family. Her parents readily assumed she was available to come to their home at any time, since "she didn't have a husband who needed her." Janice decided that a way to address this and to affirm her own decision to be single was to make a ritual. She sent invitations to her family and friends that read "Please come to my fifth anniversary party, celebrat-ing five years of my decision to live my life as a single woman!" Some people were startled to receive these invitations, but Janice's single friends were delighted. When her father complained, "But what if you get married someday?" Janice calmly replied, "Lots of people have wedding anniversaries and someday get divorced. This is where I am in my life now—let's celebrate it!" When her family came to the party, this was the first time that they actually witnessed the loving and active social network of Janice and her many single friends. Their tendency to assume that Janice "had nothing to do" abated after this ritual. During the party, Janice spoke about what it meant to her to stop living her life waiting to get married and to embrace what being single offered her, a decision she had, indeed, made five years earlier, but had never spoken about openly. Other people in Janice's circle of friends began making their own "anniversaries of singlehood."

Loss and Anniversaries

For many losses and traumas, we do not have structured rituals to help us remember and grieve what we have been through. Sometimes this is because secrecy silences the loss, which is not uncommon with sexual abuse or familial violence. Or perhaps there is a sense of guilt and shame about the event, as occurs with the suicide of a family member. Other times, what has happened is ambiguous and no one knows how to name it. This might be the case when a family member is missing in action in a war, or someone in the family disappears.

Possibilities to heal and move on can be found within anniversary rituals. The date of when the silence was first broken about the traumatic event may be marked. Or the anniversary date to be remembered might be when a person entered therapy or joined a therapeutic group. If someone has disappeared, the date they were declared missing might hold possibilities to gather people together, both to remember the person in a public way and to provide support for ongoing life and relationships.

BROTHER OR FIANCÉ?

Marissa, in her late thirties, had lost her brother some twenty years earlier when he had committed suicide. Her fiancé, Howard, had the same first name as her brother, and she wondered sometimes if she was confusing her past relationship with her brother with her current relationship with her fiancé. Marissa and Howard both had questions about whether they should get married. The birthday of her brother was not marked in any way, nor was the anniversary of his death. She almost never went to the cemetery where he was buried. Her brother was not usually mentioned on family holidays such as Thanksgiving and Christmas, though his presence was strongly felt by all.

Each fall, the time of her brother's death, Marissa would get depressed. This fall, she and her fiancé, Howard, decided to do something different. The week of her brother's death they lit a candle for him each night in Marissa's apartment. Marissa shared memories of her brother, getting clearer about the very real differences between the two Howards in her life. She put up pictures of her brother, which up to this time had been kept hidden. She was also able to call her parents and talk about what she and Howard were doing, and she shared some of her sadness and heard some of her mother's pain for the first time in years. A year later Howard and Marissa married. The pictures of her brother remained out in the open.

CREATING HEALING ANNIVERSARIES

In every human life, there are times when personal and relationship healing is needed. Some cultural rituals, especially ones created for a person's death, make use of anniversary dates for healing rituals. In Catholicism, survivors may request that a Mass be said to commemorate the anniversary of a loved one's death. On All Souls' Day (November 2), the whole community in Mexico goes out to the cemeteries and makes flower bowers, decorates the graves, and together honors the souls of the dead. In Judaism, a special ceremony is held to place the headstone on a grave a year following the death, and family members recite the Kaddish prayer both on anniversaries of the death and on certain holidays. These anniversary markings give protected time and space and support from family and community members and religious leaders to continue both to grieve and connect with others as life continues. Culturally common symbols such as the grave headstone may be available as a marker to gather people around, and to signify the importance of the event.

Families who do not have this kind of support available to them from the outside may need to structure their own ceremonies and give meaning to their own symbols. Peg Mayo created an anniversary remembrance day of her son's death. Patrick died at age twenty-three some years ago. Peg celebrates his birthday (her birthing day) each December 22. She usually calls a close friend in the morning who was born on the same day, and then she goes out into the woods for a walk, remembering the happy times of his life. She has planted a candle-red rhododendron in his memory because Patrick had given her a big fat red candle for a present his last Christmas. Buried around the rhododendron are some of Patrick's treasured books "feeding the roots."[2]

Symbols such as the rhododendron with the books feeding it can be key parts of an anniversary event because they transform meaning. The red candle given by Patrick to his mother can burn down, but the candle-red plant continues to grow and blossom each year. The photographs of Marissa's brother symbolically brought his death out in the open, and clarified the differences between her fiancé and her brother.

A lesbian woman was in a long-term relationship that was not legally acknowledged. When her lover was killed in a car crash, she received a black shawl from her brothers and friends "that represented her mourning and acknowledged her widowhood." A year later they gathered "to mark the end of the formal period of mourning and presented her with a many-colored shawl that represented healing."[3] Symbols can hold these multiple meanings, and an agreed-upon gathering provides a sense of safety and protection for the strong emotions that can arise.

ANNIVERSARIES TO MARK KEY CHANGES

Anniversaries also have a lot of flexibility to create traditions in other parts of our lives that are often minimally ritualized, such as sobriety or stopping smoking. They can be marked by just the people involved, or a wider network of support. Alcoholics Anonymous (AA), using the structure of birthday celebrations, encourages people to mark the anniversary each year of the day they stopped drinking. When an alcoholic connects with a sponsor, a key support person, he or she gives the sponsor his or her date of sobriety. The sponsor is often the person who brings a "birthday cake" to the AA meeting on the anniversary of when the person stopped drinking. The symbolism of the cake and candles and singing to the person is all used as a way to mark the rebirth of the person as one who no longer drinks. This highlights a central event in people's lives, and reminds them of the need to continue to monitor it.

People in AA have developed their own personal rituals around this date as well. Bob, who stopped drinking some fifteen years ago, often gets in his car with his young adult son and drives out of town. When he gets to a city where he has never attended an AA meeting, he calls AA and finds out where people are gathering that night. He then goes to that meeting with unknown people, as a way to remind himself of this larger community to which he is connected by virtue of his stopping drinking. Allison, who has found it hard to nurture herself, took a childhood doll and named it Sobriety. Sobriety then went with her on the anniversary date when she stopped drinking and Sobriety was feted, along with Allison. The doll has become her concrete symbol of taking care of herself.

There may be other kinds of changes that are not celebrated that can benefit from an anniversary marking. For instance, Jim and Alex, who had lived together for five years, had never had a wedding or commitment ceremony. Feeling that they were starting to take each other for granted, they began to celebrate the spring day they had met some six years before. One of the things they took time to share was what had attracted them to each other at the beginning, and ways they still appreciated those parts of each other now.

Jennifer's Adoption Day—a Special Kind of Anniversary

Many families we have talked to who have adopted children create special family tradition rituals to mark the adoption. In Evan's family, Jennifer was adopted as an infant. Although Jennifer was born in October, she entered the family in November 1970, just after Thanksgiving. Her family created a ritual called Adoption Day to celebrate Jennifer's adoption. This day is different from her birthday and occurs every year during Thanksgiving weekend, when the whole family has some time off together.

Adoption Day has been an evolving ritual with many facets. By family agreement, Adoption Day developed as a ritual just for immediate family, in order to affirm their mutual relationships, mark Jennifer's place within their family, and because Jennifer's adoption was a personal decision made within the boundaries of the family. This special day always includes whatever Jennifer's favorite food happens to be that year, ranging from peanut butter and jelly to pizza to Chinese food, and a small gift to symbolize her special place within the family. When Jennifer was a little girl, her Adoption Day was both a fun time and a time to introduce the concept of adoption to her. By having one day in which time was especially given over to the subject of adoption, the family found that it became an easy topic to raise at other times as well.

As she grew a little older, Adoption Day became a time to talk over Jennifer's questions about where she came from, why she was given up for adoption, and why Evan decided to adopt her. A little later the family began to talk about her birth parents, whom none have ever met, and to honor them in absentia. When she became a teenager, Jennifer began to take charge of how she wanted to shape her Adoption Day ritual. One year, Evan started to think that she might feel she was too old for this ritual, but that was the year she came to Evan and told her that she was, indeed, anticipating a very exciting Adoption Day, and could her mom please get tickets to a Broadway show for it!

Last year, when Jennifer was twenty, she changed Adoption Day very profoundly by making a decision that she wanted to "adopt" the family. As the family sat around the table, Jennifer read a document that spoke of her love for her mother; Lascelles, her stepfather; and her older brother, Jason. She said, "Since you adopted me, now I want to adopt you," and with that one sentence expressed the mutuality in their relationship, and her own sense of choice. She gave each family member a little gift, changing the previous pattern in which only she received a gift on Adoption Day. With that symbolic action, altering who gave and who received, Jennifer was able to express the more adult-to-adult relationships toward which the family was moving.

If your own family has been formed by adoption, you may want to create a family tradition ritual of your own to mark the anniversary of adoption. Since there is no culturally agreed-upon ritual for this unique anniversary, you actually have a tremendous amount of freedom to shape a ritual that can express your own circumstances. In our view, families formed by adoption are *both* exactly like other families with children and different from other families due to the fact of adoption. Since rituals can so nicely capture and express contradictions, you can create a ritual that speaks to both sides of this duality. Jennifer's Adoption Day, for instance, both celebrates a parent-child relationship *and* the special relationship of adoption.

Reflecting on Anniversaries

What happens with anniversaries in your life currently? Here are some questions for thought and discussion.

• Which anniversaries do you celebrate in your own and your current family life? What aspects of the celebrations work for you? What aspects seem obligatory, minimally ritualized, or imbalanced?

• How are they influenced by what you learned about the significance of anniversaries when you were growing up?

• What gender roles are enacted in your anniversaries? What kind of initiating do men do? Do women do? What kind of planning do men and women do? Are you satisfied with the gender patterns?

• Are there any anniversaries currently not acknowledged that you would like to mark in some way? How might they be important to your partner, you, your children, other family members? What symbols, symbolic actions, foods, special locations might you use to mark them?

Celebrating anniversaries allows the public affirmation of key milestones in one's life. While anniversaries probably take more effort and advertisement on the part of family members than other traditions such as birthdays, public acknowledgment of these milestones can expand an individual's view of them. It is possible to revisit and rework the meaning of a significant event, and to focus on how it is affecting current relationships. As the year turns, so people can turn and look forward and backward—understanding things from different perspectives.

In the next chapter, we'll look at other family traditions on the inside calendar: vacations, reunions, and seasonal events. Most families celebrate the birthdays of their members in some way, and anniversaries are at least remembered, even though it is sometimes after the fact. But because of their less obligatory nature, the open-endedness of these last family traditions provides a wide arena to create family meaning in the realm of play and relaxation.

9

Vacations, Reunions, and Seasonal Events

MAKING SPECIAL TIME FOR YOURSELF
AND YOUR RELATIONSHIPS

Vacations

In Evan's family, yearly vacations to Florida *always* meant waking up in the middle of the night to be on the road by 4:00 A.M. "before the traffic." Family members couldn't drink their usual daily orange juice because they might get carsick. Repetitive games like counting cows or license plates linked the three children who were otherwise too far apart in age to play together. The day proceeded with brief arguments over driving too fast and usually ended with a grand fight over how far to go before stopping. But the most fun was starting out from Chicago bundled in winter clothes, and gradually disrobing as they reached Georgia. These vacations are forever in Evan's memory, too, as the times when her parents became her best teachers, when the three children learned directly that "colored" and "white" drinking fountains were wrong, that the legacy of slavery still needed to be overcome, and that responsibility for change belonged to them.

Vacations often offer the most dramatic shifts for people out of regular time and locations into special protected time and space. Possibilities open up for all kinds of daily rituals to change including the roles people take in those rituals. New rituals quickly emerge, frequently around the themes of relaxation, doing things on a different time schedule and without the intrusion of work responsibilities. Morning rituals shift so that people can sleep in later if they like, or do things like have breakfast in bed. Bedtime rituals become more flexible. Meals often become less formal. Daily rituals can be a low-keyed, restful, and playful contrast to day-to-day rituals during the rest of the year.

There may be the creation of new yearly vacation rituals as well, where people return to the same resort area, revisit restaurants, or return to museums or parks. Or a family may do the same types of activities year after year. How family members choose (or do not choose) to spend time together on vacation expresses a lot about family identity.

Vacations are among the most flexible of family traditions. There is little intrusion from the larger culture on what one *has* to do on one's vacation. Societal messages are more about having a good time, playing, breaking with usual routines. And what each family sees as relaxing can be quite different. One family may picture themselves lounging by a pool a short drive out of town, not stirring far from their hotel, and getting lots of sun. In contrast, another family may envision themselves driving seven hundred miles to have their dream vacation—a strenuous ten-day hiking trip on the Appalachian Trail.

Given the open-endedness of vacations, why is it they are not always relaxing? Why is it they work for some families and not for others?

When Is a Vacation a Vacation?

Harold grew up with his younger sister in a working-class family on the East Coast. They could not afford vacations. His father was a musician and once in a while their family car would be packed up and he and his sister and mother would accompany their father to one of the hotels where he was playing. These were their only vacations. His wife, Cathy, grew up on the West Coast, and her somewhat larger family often took short trips and vacations in the woods camping and hiking. Many times they visited cousins and aunts and uncles on these trips, or went with friends. Vacations were seen as possibilities for lots of people to get together. When Cathy moved to the East Coast and went on visits back home, people would gather for similar kinds of vacations. Harold and Cathy married and had a son and began to go back West for two-week summer vacations. And every year, after the first week, Harold would buy an expensive one-way ticket and fly home alone. Cathy would stay and come home at the end of the vacation with their child, very angry at Harold. It would take them some time to reconnect again as a couple. What was happening in this family?

Vacations had become an imbalanced ritual to fit more with the patterns Cathy was familiar with in her family growing up. Harold's family was much more private, stayed close to home, and did not gather often with extended family and certainly not on their times away from home. After a few days on the West Coast, Harold started to feel closed in and obligated to interact with lots of different people—for him that didn't feel like a vacation. Cathy and Harold had to work out different vacations that combined more of both of their styles of finding a break from day-to-day obligations. First, they shortened the time they spent on the West Coast. Then Harold, who had grown up near the ocean, asked for a week with just the three of them somewhere near salt water. This was to be a quieter, more slowed-down vacation.

When two people join in an intimate relationship, they each bring a vacation history from childhood. What is a vacation for one person might not be relaxing for another person at all. For instance, some people don't think of going to visit relatives as a vacation. Steve, talking in a workshop about his vacations, realized that he had forgotten to mention that his family went for a week every winter to Florida to visit his in-laws. His wife considers this a vacation, but he doesn't.

Last summer in the middle of her vacation, Janine was talking with an old friend, Bill. He and his wife had just come back from a week on the beach in California. "That was a real vacation," he said.

"What do you mean?" Janine asked, "I thought you took a lot of time off to go up to your family's house on Whidbey Island."

"You know," said Bill, "I have decided that that is *not* really vacation. I mean I'm always trying to help my mom and do things for her that she'd like Dad to do. And I cook and clean a lot because I don't want anything to be too difficult for them with the extra work of our being there. So I don't really get a vacation."

When Janine came home from her vacation, which included visiting four sets of parents (both of her remarried parents and remarried parents-in-law), she thought a lot about what Bill said. On the vacation, she had worked hard at trying to be a good daughter as well as show her parents that she was a good parent. All those helpful things Bill described himself as doing seemed very familiar. Bill had a point. Was family time with parents and other relatives really a vacation?

Vacationing with family-of-origin, especially when it is done in the parental home, sometimes makes it more difficult to really have relaxing vacation rituals. Rather, you can find yourself trying to fit into the rhythm of their daily rituals—with little chance to experience a real change from your own. Family vacations can reactivate memories as well, of family rituals that may or may not have worked for you growing up. You may find comfort in hearing the same grace at the table again, sitting in your old seat, and having the traditional Sunday spaghetti and meatballs. Or it may be painful for you to see your mother waiting hand and foot on everyone during the meal, hardly sitting down to eat herself. Or you may be upset to see how much longer the predinner cocktail hour has become. Family-of-origin vacations may not have the benefits of a real break from daily known routines and responsibilities.

People who vacation together may have quite different opinions about what is and is not a vacation. If parts of your vacation time are not working well, it may be because you have different ideas about what a vacation should look like. This exercise can help you clarify your beliefs and the beliefs of others. Take five minutes with your partner, friends, and/or your children that you vacation with, and see where your values vary and where they are the same.

• Scan the list below and cross off lightly in pencil any values that are not important to you.

• Add any values that we have overlooked.

• Beside each of the remaining statements, assign a number from 1 to 10 that shows how important it is to you. One is low and 10 is high.

• Repeat these three steps with other family members.

• Where are your values similar and different?

_____Vacations are a time to get together with extended family members and friends and renew our connections with them.

_____Vacations are a time to have protected space and activities with just our own family.

_____It is important on vacations to have a break from phones, newspapers, TV, computers, mail, etc.

_____On vacation, I don't want to have to do the ordinary tasks like cooking, cleaning, yard work.

_____Bedtimes, meals, morning routines should all be more flexible.

_____Physical activity is a very important part of vacations (outdoor sports, hiking, jogging, etc.).

_____I like to be in a large city on vacation with access to cultural activities, restaurants, etc.

_____Being surrounded by nature makes for a better vacation.

_____I like to go back to the same places each year for vacation.

_____Vacations should be at a place where there are structured activities for the kids.

_____It is good for adults in the family to have separate vacations sometimes.

_____People should have some alone time on vacation.

On the Road

Every year for vacation, Sheila's parents would plan a camping trip to see some other part of the United States, so for three weeks, she and her two brothers would live with her parents out of the car. The morning vacation ritual included eating cinnamon buns and hard-boiled eggs in the car (the only time they were allowed to eat in the new Ford). The children would then go back to sleep. At each night's campsite, her father, who had been in the military, organized everyone to help set it up. And in the morning, they would "break down the tent, clean the mess kits, and scout the perimeters" before they hit the road again. Every year, they would go too far and try to see too much. Her father, who was the exhausted driver, would end up sleeping on the beach or in the campsite of their final destination for most of their time there. As a child, Sheila felt like the vacations were more work than fun for her parents, and in her own family now, she is trying to avoid this.

Families may find it takes more preplanning and time during the vacation to organize when they don't go to other family members' homes to visit. It may also be more expensive and the family may find themselves more on the go. One family found a creative solution to these dilemmas.

VACATIONS AT HOME

The Robinson family plans a vacation at home each year. They started doing this after they came back from vacations out of town both exhausted and feeling the financial strain of supporting a family of six away from the house. For a home vacation, they cook large batches of food together ahead of time like chicken, potato salad, and macaroni and cheese. They also eat out more than usual, make an agreement to *not* do house chores, suspend their regular bedtime and cleanup rules, turn off the phone to incoming calls, and limit TV time for the week. Each day they do different activities either at home or nearby, especially finding things that groups of them enjoy. The family has created a meaningful annual ritual that enhances relationships and expresses their unique values and beliefs.

It takes discipline on this kind of vacation to not fall into everyday responsibilities, like painting trim that has needed attention for the past year. Setting aside a certain amount of money to spend on eating out and another pot of money for doing fun things can remind you that you are outside of your regular life. Then you just have to make sure you spend it. When people are "caught" doing work, they can be made responsible in a playful manner for planning another of the family outings for the week.

REMARRIAGE: BLENDING THREE OR MORE TRADITIONS OF FAMILY VACATIONS

When there is divorce and remarriage the logistics of working out a vacation can get even more complicated. Not only is there a vacation history brought along from each family-of-origin for the parents, but the children may carry a picture of how a vacation should go from their first family as well. And there are more relatives to consider as well as former spouses and their schedules.

"The first camping trip we went on as a family was a disaster! We made the mistake of going to a spot which had been a favorite in my first marriage. Memories kept interfering, nothing seemed to work right. Sam and I got into

*our first big fight. Our kids refused to sleep together in a pup tent, so we ended up
with his daughter in the tent with us. . . . It was weeks before we recovered from
that experience."*

—Andrea, describing her first summer in a remarried family[1]

Vacations usually happen over a longer period of time than other
family traditions like a birthday or anniversary. Special issues of
remarried families may be exacerbated because of the lengthened
time. Scheduling over several households, honoring traditions from
previous families as well as current families, and planning together are
all more complex. Vacations may need to be scheduled a year or more
in advance to accommodate the different schedules of other parents
that the children are living with part-time. And if each partner brings
children to the relationship, it may take a lot of effort to schedule time
when all the children can be there together. If families vacation with
members of their extended families, then there may also be lots of
relatives to visit.

What has been a fun vacation for one family may be downright
boring to a family with whom they become joined. Stephanie and her
two children liked to camp, hike, swim, and do active things on their
vacation. She married Paul and found out that he and his son had a long
tradition of going to New York for a few days each year, spending time
at museums and parks and taking in the sights. And children may have
lived in single-parent homes for a number of years where they did not
have to negotiate with other children, may not have been able to afford
vacations with the financial strains of divorce, or where they would go
to their grandparents' house for time away. Going on vacation together
as a family, while usually thought of as a fun thing to do, may really
mean a loss of special connections such as a particularly close relationship between a parent and child. Some remarried families deal with
this important issue by taking special weekends for the biological
parent and children to be together, or by reserving time within a larger
family vacation in order to reaffirm that these relationships remain
special.

Meeting new people in a different place often also raises questions
about the family by strangers. The first time Jody went away with her
husband, Steve, his two children, and her two children, everyone at the
lodge where they were camping asked if the four kids were all theirs. As

Jody's daughter and Steve's daughter are less than a year apart and near the same height, people naturally wondered about them. They were trying to define the family. With the questions, Steve and Jody found that they were also being asked to define their relationship. For instance, when Jody said that Steve's children, Amira and Ken, were half hers, Jody's daughter, Tatiana, questioned it. Tatiana said that she was one-half her mother's and one-half her father's so how could Amira and Ken be one-half Jody's? Jody said, "Well, they feel like half mine."

Isabel and Bob are a recently remarried couple with three children. When they went together on their first long vacation to the Midwest, they visited three sets of grandparents, three siblings and their families, and saw some twenty cousins. That's a lot of people. They were worried about the children staying in so many different places and seeing so many different faces—but they did fine. What was trickier was handling all of the emotional responses of the adults, including their own. It was the first time many people were meeting them as a couple and as a family, which brought up a lot of feelings about former spouses and their first families. Extended family members experience loss, too, when there is a divorce. They may have close relationships with the divorced spouse, their own interpretation about what caused the divorce, and their own feelings about the new marriage. Isabel and Bob discovered that they had to support each other when parents told stories about former spouses and prior wedding gifts, or they found themselves sleeping in the same rooms that they had slept in with their previous wife or husband. They and the people around them were literally reworking their links and connections to each other as the new son and daughter-in-law were being met, the new step-grandchildren introduced, and former spouses were concretely envisioned as more out of the picture. Not surprisingly, they found themselves reacting more intensely than usual to issues such as whether they were equally holding up their share of the travel arrangements and planning. A vacation can be much more than a vacation!

BREAKING NEW GROUND:
PUTTING TO REST BAD VACATION MEMORIES

Raul and Josie and their two children came back home to Nevada from a ten-day vacation in northern California. They had not had a good time. First, their five-year-old son, Ben, came down with a stomach virus. Then it rained for three days while they were camping out. The last part of the vacation they went to the home of Raul's sister. Josie felt really unwelcomed by her. The kids, picking up the tension from the parents, were very crabby and picky with each other. They returned exhausted. Josie and Raul described it as the worst vacation they had ever had.

As the next summer approached, Raul's parents called and asked when they were going to come to visit. Josie heard about a wonderful new campground near Mt. Shasta. But when the two of them tried to talk about what they might do for their next vacation, they found themselves unable to agree on what to do and really procrastinating on planning it. They realized that they were stuck, remembering how awful their last vacation was. You may find yourself in a similar situation, which can color where you will consider going on vacation, affect whether you even want to think about one, or leave you with a set of expectations that the next vacation is not going to be a good one. Some boundary needs to be put around the old memories. One of the things Josie and Raul did was to gather everyone together and talk about the best and the worst parts of their previous vacation. Some of the good parts had gotten lost with the emphasis on what had gone wrong. Some of the more difficult parts, such as the small stream that appeared through the middle of their tent one dark night when Ben was sick, had some humorous possibilities as they exaggerated and retold their vacation stories.

You can also talk about your worst fears for your next vacation and play them up based on vacations that did not go well. Or you might take photos, postcards, or other vacation mementos from a really bad vacation and "put them to rest" in a "Memories I'd Just as Soon Forget" folder. Most importantly, you can plan vacations that will minimize what led to the previous one not working out. An important part of that planning can be finding out what is really a vacation to different members of the family.

WHAT DO VACATIONS MEAN TO YOU AND YOUR FAMILY?

We can feel in our bones when a vacation is right, but rarely do we talk beforehand about what our ideal vacations are with other family members. Yet vacations tell a lot about family identity. Here are some questions to think about the picture you have of your family.

• What is it I/we like to do together as a family?

• What kinds of activities are relaxing?

• What is a break from everyday responsibilities?

• What fantasies do I/we have about what we are like or would like to do on vacation? What image do I have of myself or others on vacation?

• How are we intimate with each other when I/we don't have the pulls of work and other daily requirements?

• What does it mean to be more fully with our children when they are not going off to school, to baseball practice, to spend time with friends, and so on?

How might *someone else in your family* answer these questions? How are their responses the same or different from yours? Use the information you learn to help you plan your next vacation. And remember, vacations can be a break of routine not just from work responsibilities but also from usual family patterns. All patterns, no matter how interesting, can become worn out and too known over time. Take advantage of vacation time to introduce some variety into typical family exchanges. Doug and Lynn let their two adolescent children plan two days of their vacation one year. They went to hear a rock band and to a water park that they would have never have gone to if the parents had remained in charge of all the planning. And their teenagers enjoyed having a reversal time when they could tell their parents what to do.

Family Reunions and Seasonal Celebrations

Reunions are a family tradition that usually happen less often than birthdays, anniversaries, or vacations, but they can be very important, especially for maintaining extended family relationships. In some families reunions happen on a regular scheduled basis, such as every five years. In others they occur sporadically when someone has the energy to organize it. And in some families a central event, such as a wedding, or a grandparent turning ninety, provides the push to gather together.

The Wilson clan of five siblings—three living in the North and two in the South—have a reunion every three or four years alternating between one of the siblings' houses in the North and then in the South. Their first reunion was when their grandfather, getting older and not in very good health, had a birthday. They planned a reunion under the cover of his birthday and then surprised him by having most of the clan appear. The reunions have continued since then for the last seventeen years. They have found it important to have at least three or four days for the reunion. Food has been a key focal point. Old family recipes are resurrected and shared and at least one meal is typically Southern, with collard greens, black-eyed peas, rice and ham hocks, and sweet potato pie. And they usually have different activities for the different generations to do. If you look at photos over the years of their reunions, you get a wonderful sense of the passage of time. Clothing, cars, hairdos all change. You see, too, the development of the generations with parents now holding grandchildren. And you'll see year to year the big watermelon fruit salad with the watermelon rind scooped out to be the bowl and the Wilson name carved in the handle. Computer innovations have been added to reunions in the 1980s. Banners welcoming kinfolk have been put up in different languages, and one member has put what he knows about the family tree on a computer program and set it up in the living room for other people to see. In the future, the computer may be on and ready to take people's reminiscences or stories right during the reunion.

Here's how one family described their annual reunion:

Roberta: It's like every member of the family . . .

Jerry: . . . has a special thing.

Roberta: Each one of my mother's brothers and sisters and my mother also has got their own traits and peculiarities. And all put together it makes for a unique affair. My uncle Jimmy is always screaming about the dirty rotten stinking cards, whenever he's playing cards.

Jerry: And there's always a pitch game going. The women play poker, and the men play pitch. Then there's the election every year, that's one of those things . . .

Theresa: Oh, it's all in fun, we elect a president of the family every year.

Roberta: Well, there's kind of a tradition here. The elder is the head of the family anyway, he's the don. He always has been and he always will be. But every year, he's got to get elected! And every year a couple of the brothers will put up a fight, and they'll mount a campaign to get themselves elected president. They will go through all kinds of contortions and slogans and campaign songs and everything to get themselves elected. Then comes the day of an election and everybody will listen to their slogans and appeal and promptly vote Uncle John president again.

Theresa: And every year they raise our salaries.

Jerry: Every year they double the salaries.

Theresa: 'Cause we get nothing. And so they double it every year.

Jerry: You got to picture this family. Most of them are elderly, in their eighties.

Theresa: Not most of them, Jerry, there's only a few.

Jerry: All right, many of them. And they're—no, not very square— they're the most energetic people you've ever seen for their ages. That's basically it.

Roberta: They are people who enjoy themselves and they have a spirit of fun about them and a spirit of nonsense. And the thing is that it never seems to surface until they get together—if you talk to one of them by himself he is a pillar of the church, as Ma says, just as square as the day is long!

(Roberta and Jerry Wilson, ages thirty-eight and thirty-six; Theresa Roach, age sixty-four).[2]

Summers or holiday weekends when people can travel are often good times to have reunions. In 1986, President Reagan proclaimed the first weekend in August as "National Family Reunion Weekend," but you certainly don't need to be bound by this. Other dates to consider might be an anniversary of the arrival of some branch of the family to the United States or the date of a crucial event in the family's history. People will need to be in touch with each other to figure out the focus of the reunion as well as to carefully delegate and share responsibilities. Some families like doing lots of shared history with old home movies and photo albums; others like to go where they can research the family roots, and yet others want a more social, active event. Following the death of one of their aunts, the Gonzales family decided to make writing down the oral history of their family the central part of their next reunion, before more people from that generation passed away and their stories were gone.[3]

Other families have had family "fact finding" contests to help people reconnect, and treasure hunts where teams are made up of multigenerational groups including grandchildren, nieces, uncles, and grandparents. Cookbooks can be made that include things such as the recipe for foods brought to the reunion or family recipes that have been passed down, stories surrounding the recipes, old photographs, copies of the family tree, or excerpts from family letters. Including the children in writing down the recipes can be great fun. Eight-year-old Jacob Singh wrote the following:

RAJ'S KILLER COOKIES

(Raj is the name of Jacob's dad)

Cream about 1 lb. soft butter so that there are no lumps. Add 1½ c. brown sugar or ¾ c. honey or maple syrup or a combination of those and molasses or other sweeteners. White sugar or brown sugar make the next step more fun and the cookies less crumbly! (But that stuff is not supposed to be good for you.) Beat this greasy stuff until it gets lighter in color and, if you use sugar, until the stuff gets a shiny sheen like satin. Take a couple two or three eggs and mix them in. You can beat the eggs first if you want or just plop them in. Either way, it looks gross until the eggs are completely mixed in. Now you can throw in a couple teaspoons vanilla, and three point 5 heaping tablespoons of peanut butter or tahini. That's the wet stuff.

Now, pull out another bowl for the dry stuff. Start with about 3 c. oatmeal, and add another 1½ c. flour and/or bran or wheat germ or dry cereal (Grape-Nuts are great!). Throw in a tbsp. of cinnamon, one of ginger and one of nutmeg. If you want salt, throw in one of that too. Also, throw in a tbsp. of baking powder. Now you can mix the dry stuff, a cup or so at a time, into the wet stuff. The combined stuff should be goopy and sticky kind of like peanut butter. If it's too sloppy, add some oats or other dry stuff; if it's too dry and hard, add a little water. Now comes the best part. Now you can throw in a package of good chocolate chips and/or chopped nuts and/or raisins and/or other dry fruit and/or sunnies, etc., etc.

Oh, yeah, at the top of this recipe, pre-heat oven to 325°. O.K. Now using two teaspoons, drop your favorite cookie-sized drops of goop onto ungreased sheets. Bake for 15–20 minutes, or until you can touch the tops lightly without denting them. Recipe will yield about 50 2-inch cookies or 33 3-inchers or 20 5-inchers or 24 4-inchers or 2 50-inchers or 1 100-incher or 100 1-inchers . . . YUMMY!!!

This recipe me and my dad made up one day when I was seven years old. We were really, really, really bored. So, my dad made up Super Duper Killer Cookies. We have them all the time now.[4]

REUNIONS AND UNEXPECTED HAPPENINGS:
WHEN REUNIONS PROMOTE HEALING

Janine's extended family's last gathering was thirty-two years ago at her grandparents' fiftieth wedding anniversary. In planning a reunion in the summer of 1990, her sister mailed out a sheet to all possible participants with questions about when and where they might like to gather and what they would like to do. Using this information, she then found a location for the reunion and different people took charge of organizing potluck lunches on the beach, a hot dog and marsh-mallow roast, a games night, and putting old home movies on video to watch. Many families made a photo board time line with captioned pictures from the early days until now. These were laid out at a reunion dinner which also included a skit by the youngest generation of Great-great-great-grandpa and Great-great-great-grandma Roberts's wagon train journey from Kansas to Washington territory back in 1882. One or two people seem to be needed to start to get things organized, but then responsibilities can be delegated to other people.

This reunion ended up being a very healing event for the family when Janine's younger brother, Mark, reappeared shortly before it was scheduled. An alcoholic, he had disappeared some eight and one-half years earlier and no one was sure whether he was dead or alive. Sober for almost nine months, Mark was able to come to the reunion for two days. He had not seen people there for from eight and a half to twenty years. He had a lot to say to his family, yet this was not the time to share all that had happened to him in the last nine years. How could he communicate that he was open to sharing where he had been but still be there primarily for the reunion activities? He started the formal dinner out by saying, "Hi, I'm Mark and I'm an alcoholic. Whoops—wrong meeting!" He got a big laugh. Mark then went on to read a poem he had written called "Balance—Acceptance." It ended with the lines:

> *Emotions stirring, I feel alive—*
> *love, wholeness, humanness—so long denied.*
> *A growing sense that I'm all right,*
> *I find some roots in family ties.*
>
> *I still don't know the answers "why?"*
> *Yet on this journey, we can fly*
> *on a broad highway deep inside—*
> *breathless wonder, seeking to the day we die.*

By reading this poem, he created a bridge between the last nine years of his life and the extended family that had gathered. He told a small piece of his story, let people know it was okay to ask him about it, and also communicated how he wanted to be relinked with family. Now there were many tears in the room.

ORGANIZING A FAMILY REUNION

Expectations and scheduling need to be flexible for reunions, and people need to remember in planning that there may be different economic levels among people coming. Reunions more typically involve people who are not in as close contact as those that might celebrate anniversaries or vacations together. People need to be clear about what they want as well as tolerant of various styles. Reunions may need to be scaled back when some family members do not want to come. A smaller event can be planned with those who really want to be there. Or people can keep laying the seeds for a larger reunion when family members are together for other occasions. The capacity of rituals to define relationships, enable change, and express beliefs all come into play in family reunions. When reunions work, they can capture a sense of identity and connection, with a feeling that you are in a very known place that is different from being at any other type of gathering.

Especially careful planning is needed when there have been family cutoffs or different factions within the family. There may be ways with the planning to make some small changes in alliances within the family as well as how people view each other. Thoughtful consideration should be given to choosing a location that is neutral. It should not be seen as a place that is more convenient or more important to certain sides of the family, nor should it be a family home that is not seen as open and available to all. Provide a mix of activities with some more intimate than others, and additional ones with a large group focus. Let people choose what parts of the reunion they want to attend. This can give them a sense of control over how much contact they want to have with the clan.

When people are invited, think carefully about the best way to make contact. Should a letter go out with the names of people from different generations in the family? Should phone calls be made by certain central family figures? Is it best to invite people with some acknowledgment of the particular skill or historical information they would bring to the reunion—thus letting them know how much *their* presence would mean? It is also important to build in ways to get participants' views and ideas on what to do at the reunion. If some people are unable to come or choose not to come, remember them at the actual event with a toast, or ask them to send pictures that can be out for others to see. Or they may want to send a greeting to be shared.

For a stirring description of planning one of the largest family reunions in the country, read Dorothy Spruill Redford's *Somerset Homecoming: Recovering a Lost Heritage* (Doubleday, 1988). Inspired by Alex Haley's *Roots* and wanting to be able to tell her daughter about her family history, Ms. Redford, an African-American woman from North Carolina, traced her family tree back to the plantation called Somerset Place. She gathered information on twenty-one different family lines that had come off that plantation, with many of the descendants still living in the immediate area. As she pieced it together, she was struck by how few people knew anything about their ancestors who had been slaves or about their lives. Certainly local history gave them no credit for the growth of North Carolina. And yet without them the state and the nation would never have been able to do the things they did. She wanted to convert a sense of shame about the past into a sense of pride for what the slaves had given to their country. She began to envision a multiple family reunion at the plantation itself. For months, she talked at churches about her plans, she went to the homes of descendants, she talked to the people that ran Somerset Place as a national park. But few were interested. Finally, newspapers like the *Washington Post* and *USA Today* started to pick up on the story. Now people began to be curious. In the end, two thousand descendants of slaves of Somerset Place came to the reunion. Descendants of some of the slave owners came as well. Ms. Redford described her feelings at the end of the day:

> The need to belong. That's what this was all about. Not just my need, but the need of our entire people, whose destiny was out of our hands for so long, and who are still struggling to shape our identity, our sense of place in a society that was not of our making. In the beginning, when we were first brought to these shores against our wills, our strength was in ourselves, in our bonds with one another. Somewhere along the line, in complex and subtle ways, those selves were severed, the bond broken. My journey, climaxed on this day, was a reunion in every sense of the word.[5]

Questions to help begin planning a reunion:

• What family events are coming up that might provide a point around which to organize a reunion (e.g., wedding, christening, vacation time when some members will already be getting together)?

• How can you best contact people in the family to encourage the sharing of responsibility?

• What time of year is easiest for people to get together?

• What might you include on a simple list of questions to people to get their input on what kind of reunion they might like?

• How can you then share this group information with everyone?

Rites of the Seasons

"During the first snow of the year, we would always run barefoot around the outside of the house. This was a lot of fun until my younger sister was in college and her home was a dormitory. It's a very long way to run around the whole dormitory with your shoes off."

—Doug and Laura McDowell
ages forty and thirty-nine, Annandale, Va.[6]

One of the most open-ended traditions can be seasonal family observances. Many of the holidays on the outside calendar, such as Thanksgiving, Christmas, Hanukkah, Three Kings' Day, and Passover, have roots in celebrations long ago of seasonal changes. For some families, incorporating an awareness of the cycle of nature enhances the holidays. The meaning of Christmas may be deepened by tying it to the solstice, or Thanksgiving may take on another level of significance by linking it to previous harvest festivals. Other families have seasonal traditions that have been passed down, or outdoor activities they have found they enjoy doing year after year. They find that they develop their own spiritual expressions as they stay in close contact with nature. Some other families have developed seasonal rituals because of a conscious intent to move away from the religious overtones of holidays that occur when the seasons shift. Michelle, who grew up in an Irish-Catholic working-class family of nine children, liked much of the symbolism and pageantry of the Roman Catholic church but not some of what she personally saw as its rigidity and lack of awareness of current social issues. When her daughter, Elaine, was born several years ago, she missed the church rituals even more. As Elaine grew older they began to develop spring and fall family outings. In these outings, Michelle especially wanted to incorporate time to reflect, examine, and appreciate the interdependence of life. In the spring, they would take a day to plant bulbs, go to the animal barns to see new baby animals, and walk in the woods to discover what plants were coming up. In the fall, they went apple picking (complete with a pizza picnic) and came home and made apple pie and apple butter. They created their own honoring of the earth's cycle. The pictures that they take each year of these activities have been put into a special book.

Looking at it, you see the changes of this family over time with the backdrop of each spring and fall.

An inspiring book for children that can help you think about what seasonal rites you might want is Byrd Baylor's *I'm in Charge of Celebrations.*[7] The main character creates her own New Year's celebration when the white-winged doves are back from Mexico and dirt is warm to bare feet. She tells why she has Rainbow Celebration Day to remember the first day she saw a double rainbow filling the sky. She whirls and dances on Dust Devil Day, celebrating the dryness, dust, and wind of summer in the Southwest. The book gives good ideas on how to choose to ritualize something that is happening in nature around you.

RITUALS AND BITTERSWEET CHANGES

Each year Jolleen collects things from the woods and uses them for various decorative purposes. For instance, in December she gathers greens, red berries, and pine cones, and in the spring she looks for the first pussy willows. In October as the leaves fall and the woods become more stark, she always looks for bittersweet, a bright yellow and orange berry, to put in a vase in her home. This excursion went through a series of changes when she divorced several years ago. The first fall, several months after the separation, she did not do it at all. In all the welter of other things to do with moving, making a separation agreement, working out the visitation schedule with her son, it went by the wayside.

In the second year, Jolleen found herself going back to the woods behind her old house where her ex-husband still lived. She gathered bittersweet there from the same large plant where she had cut it for the nine years she had lived in the house. There was some comfort in doing this as those woods had been an important place for her in those nine years, and besides, she knew exactly where to find it. Later in the winter of the second year after the divorce, she found herself scouting the woods near her new home for bittersweet. She found two big plump patches and now knows where to go the third year to get them. With time, the ritual gradually transformed, marking the changes occurring in Jolleen's life. Temporarily the ritual was dropped as energy was needed for a major transition. Then the ritual was resurrected, but in a form in which it bridged two locations—Jolleen's former home and her new one. Finally, with the locating of bittersweet in the woods near her new home, the ritual had moved fully into Jolleen's new life.

Families or individuals may or may not have reunions or celebrate seasonal rituals on any regular kind of basis. Reunions can be a powerful way to learn about extended family relationships and history and also to see the wider context for why you or your family do some things the way they do. Seasonal rituals can be an important alternative for people wanting simple ceremonies that provide some of the mystery and excitement of more established holidays, but without consumer or church pressures about how one should celebrate. Reunions and seasonal rituals have movable dates and can be incorporated into individual or family ritual life at any time during the year. They are also the most open-ended and flexible and can thus be shaped by your family into something that is uniquely their own.

This contrasts with holidays on the outside calendar that arrive each year with fixed dates and times, and often with expected types of gift giving, decorating to do, foods to eat, and other holiday observances. In Chapter 10, we'll look at how we can experience both support and pressure from our families, neighborhoods, the media, and religious institutions during holiday celebration rituals.

10

Holiday Rituals

Celebrating with Merriment, Memory, and Meaning

Christmas Then and Now

For Tania Cisneros, Christmas was the most magical of the holiday celebrations. On Christmas Eve, she and her two brothers and sister hung up the red velveteen stockings their mother, Aristi, had sewn for them with each of their initials embroidered in white angora yarn. Then they heard once again how Santa would come down the chimney that night, fill the stockings, and put up and decorate the tree he had brought with him on his sleigh. Just before they went upstairs to bed, they always wrote him a note, asking him to say hello to the reindeer for them, or telling him to *please* wake them up so they could go with him just once and see the North Pole. They left the note on a plate along with his milk and cookies.

Six o'clock in the morning always found the children huddled on the stairs, all holding their pillows. Strict instructions were given by their parents not to go downstairs before 7:00 A.M. Sometime, usually shortly before seven, they crept downstairs to the living room, which had been transformed overnight. In the corner where the rocker used to be was a large tree covered with brightly colored ornaments and circled with mysterious packages. The stockings were now lying all humpy and bulgy on the floor. After a few shakes and pokes to the presents and stockings, Tania and her siblings loaded up with more pillows from the sofas, then crept to their parents' bedroom. They threw open the door and flung the pillows all at once onto their parents' bed while shouting, "Merry Christmas! Merry Christmas! Santa has already been here— time to get up!" After their parents threw the pillows back at them, everyone rushed to the living room where the children opened their stockings. Then they went off to the kitchen to help their father, Don, make waffles. He was on the road a lot in his work as a book salesman, and this was one of the few times he was in the kitchen cooking first thing in the morning.

After breakfast, their dad donned a Santa hat and distributed the presents one by one. First, each person had to read the cards or notes that had been put on many of the packages. Some of them were clues about what was in the box; others were rhymes and special messages to the person receiving the present. And then there were the love notes that Don always put each year on the presents to their mom. Things were not always tranquil between Don and Aristi, partly because he was not around a lot to help with the family, but this was a time of year when he found a way to communicate his care to his wife. The children would watch their mother read them silently to herself, a smile softly spreading over her face. Aristi and Don would exchange glances, or she would go over and kiss their father tenderly. Tania's family spent hours slowly opening and sharing all of the presents. Each of their relation- ships was marked by the giving and receiving of things picked out or made for each other. This day symbolically showed the connections between one another that existed all through the year.

Tania is an adult now, married and with three children of her own. Five years ago in early December, her father had a stroke. He was immediately hospitalized. While alert, he was unable to speak or move on his own. As had been his custom, he had already bought and wrapped Christmas presents for Tania's mother. Tania knew they were home under the guest bed in the study. At Thanksgiving, her father had shown her each carefully wrapped present with the usual love notes fastened on top. These had been painstakingly written, as he had developed Parkinson's disease in recent years. As the family gathered in the hospital room, it was clear that he was not going to live until Christmas. So his children, now all adults, asked him if he would like their mother to open her presents from him. He seemed to indicate that he would like her to and the next day the family brought the gifts to the hospital. She opened each one with love, care, and pleasure, just as she had done so many Christmases before. This time, she read each "love" note from him out loud and back to him. Tania wrote, "The process broke our hearts and yet somehow was healing—it was a fitting and proper way to spend our last day with our father."

The family was not only there, in a hospital room with their father in bed. They were surrounded by memories and echoes of years of previous family holidays together. The simple reading of the love notes and opening of gifts evoked connections with many family Christmases. And Tania's parents publicly shared a part of their years of intimacy, giving all of them the opportunity to witness and honor the vibrancy of that relationship.

Now, at Tania's home, her husband wears the Santa Claus hat each Christmas and hands round the presents. They tell the story of Santa's journey to their house. Their three children write to Santa Claus and leave out milk and cookies. Tania and her husband write back "thank you notes" from Santa in disguised handwriting. And they find themselves, parents and children, writing notes to each other on the presents they exchange. Each year Tania tells the story of how her father wrote notes to their grandmother. The heritage goes on.

Often, our most vivid memories are of holidays. And they may carry some of the deepest emotional meaning of families. When parts of our ritual life that have worked well are passed on to the next generation, people feel comforted. When holidays are filled with tension or unspoken conflict, the very relationships holidays are supposed to celebrate can become frozen. Why is this? What happens with family meaning making at holiday times?

Cultures and Community

Holidays that are marked on the outside calendar, such as Martin Luther King Day, Valentine's Day, the Fourth of July, Labor Day, Christmas, and New Year's Day, are occasions that everyone knows will come just once each year. Typically, people are given time off from work, and daily routines are usually changed as many schools, offices, and stores shut down. These days may also bring prescribed traditions from the larger culture on how they should be celebrated. This may mean lots of festivity as people see other people decorating, or preparing special food or clothing, or planning for the holidays. Connections across households are built as people know that others are celebrating in similar ways or at the same time. There are likely to be group events at libraries, religious centers, town meeting places, theaters, and parks where families can celebrate with others. Workplaces and schools may organize special events and themes around the holidays as well, such as school programs and office parties.

At the same time, families may also experience a lot of pressure about how to celebrate. There may be strong media messages about what to do or buy. High levels of anticipation may also accompany some holidays with images pushed by television, magazines, and newspapers on what family togetherness looks like and how happy people should be at these times. Families may feel pushed to spend more money than they have available.

Set holiday dates can mean less flexibility for when and how families celebrate. For instance, if a child lives in two or more households, there can be competition between the two families for which household has the child on the actual day of Thanksgiving or New Year's. Because holidays provide a kind of snapshot memory of the family, they may also be focal points that remind people of family changes. Strong feelings or memories may be evoked of people who were once in the family, or people who are unwilling or unable to be there.

In addition, as it is common for generations of families to gather for many of these kinds of celebrations, possibilities emerge for both generational connections and differences to be highlighted. There may be expectations of particular ritual observances such as religious services that may be meaningful to some family members and not to others. Familiar family patterns may become more intense with the

increased proximity that often happens at holiday times. Old unresolved issues and losses may come to the surface. Holidays involve
many sensory elements with their emphasis on foods, activity, special
clothing, words, and music. Because of these visual and aural elements,
intense emotional memory can be evoked by holiday activities.

"We're just pleased he can still get into the Christmas spirit."

There is tension sometimes, too, when holiday celebrations are not
equally recognized in a society. Some holidays are by governmental
decree and are found printed on most calendars, while others are
dependent upon family members to explain and try to get time off from
day-to-day obligations in order to celebrate. For instance, not all groups
celebrate Christmas. Other holidays may be much more important in
different cultural and religious traditions. These holidays are not noted
on the "outside" calendar of the dominant culture. If your family has
such holidays, you will need to put in extra effort to create possibilities
to commemorate these days.

CAMELS AND HAY OR MILK AND COOKIES
Luis was five when he migrated with his family from Puerto Rico to
Connecticut. He remembers his family trying to celebrate Three
Kings' Day on January 6. In many Hispanic countries, Three Kings'

Day is much more important than Christmas. Presents are exchanged on this day, and in December and early January people are wished Happy Three Kings' Day, not Merry Christmas. It celebrates the arrival of the three kings in Bethlehem with their presents for the Baby Jesus. January 6 fell on a day in the middle of the week, so there was no time off from school or work for Luis's family to celebrate. Special foods that they needed to buy to make traditional dishes from Puerto Rico were not available in the stores. When Luis tried to explain in school that he had put hay and water under his bed for the camels to eat and drink, his classmates were confused and teased him, asking him if he had put milk and cookies out for Santa Claus. The larger culture, so focused on Christmas, did not offer support for customs from other cultural and religious traditions.

There may be problems of competition between holidays as well. This has happened with Hanukkah, which is a relatively minor Jewish holiday. Because of its proximity to December 25, many families have felt compelled to have similar activities to Christmas so that their children do not feel left out. Cherie Killer-Fox and her husband, Everette Fox, were "appalled by the Americanization of the holiday, which had come to center on the lavish exchange of presents."[1] They decided to intentionally organize each of the eight nights of Hanukkah around a theme that would move it away from a copy of Christmas strung out over eight nights. So, with their three young children, they now have Homemade Presents Night, Food and Fire Night, Music Night, Book and Story Night, and Tzedakah (charity) Night. They focus on Jewish songs, games, foods, and stories each night, so Hanukkah can take on its own definition.

In this chapter, we will look at both the possibilities and the difficulties that arise when there is a larger community sharing something together. When holidays are marked in many households at the same time, families can feel supported because there is some common purpose, vision, shared activities, and images. Indeed, a holiday that may be celebrated at the same time in different parts of the world can help us feel connected to millions of people we will never meet. Difficulties can arise if the celebratory events become rigidly prescribed, or there is not room for a variety of holidays based on the cultural, religious, and historical background of people. There can be tension, too, between the religious nature of a holiday and secular life. This tension is embedded in even the roots of the word "holiday." It comes from the Anglo-Saxon words *halig daet*, or "holy day." Originally, holidays were always either a religious event or marked the special day of a holy person.

In the United States, usually the only religious holidays that people are given time off for are Christian holidays. Also, some of the secular holidays such as New Year's are actually part of the Christian calendar. For instance, we celebrate New Year's on January 1 rather than in September, which is when the Jewish New Year, Rosh Hashanah, usually falls. Yet at least fifteen percent of the population identify themselves as non-Christian, and a number of those who do identify themselves as Christian do not have a formal religious association. The fastest growing religious group in the country is Muslim. Yet dates of central Muslim celebrations such as the three-day Festival of the Breaking of the Fast (celebrated at the end of Ramadan, the holy month of fasting) are not marked on calendars, and few people are aware of Muslim holidays. Many of the symbols of Christmas have come to dominate the culture such as the Christmas tree, Santa Claus, and Baby Jesus and the Holy Family. This was not always the case in the United States. We used to have a predominantly secular calendar.

THE COMMON CALENDAR IN EARLY AMERICA

Historically, Americans had a festival calendar that was very pared down compared to Western Europe's or England's. As Margaret Hall wrote in the 1800s, "[The people of the U.S.] have few holidays and the few they do have are going rapidly out of use."[2] In contrast, in many of the countries that people had emigrated from to the United States, the months were filled with saints' days and feasts and long-honored festivals of particular villages. But these days did not survive in the New World, especially under the early influence of the Puritans and the Quakers. For instance, the Puritan government in England under Cromwell banned trees and Christmas festivities as "rowdy" and "pagan" in 1642. "People were to work as usual. Stores were to be kept open. Anyone caught lighting a Christmas candle or eating a Christmas cake was punished. Town criers went around crying, 'No Christmas, no Christmas!' "[3] A law was passed in Massachusetts in 1659 that set up a series of fines if Christmas was celebrated.

Civil holidays such as the Fourth of July were more commonly celebrated. Bonfires, wrestling, parades, and pony and foot races might all have been found as part of Independence Day celebrations as well as at seasonal militia drills and court meeting times.

Many of the Native American groups in North America had their own elaborate festival cycles including hunting and planting ceremonies, rain dances, and harvest festivals. The four- to eight-day Green Corn Dance of the Eastern Woodlands Indians celebrated the first corn crop of the summer. Past wrongs were forgiven at this celebration. The Buffalo Dance of the Plains Indians was done to ensure good hunting as well as visions for the warriors. The Pueblos of the Southwest had religious societies such as the Kachina Masked Dancers that performed to ask for good crops. But almost none of these customs found their way into the national calendar of the United States. The native culture was denigrated and destroyed rather than respected and seen as something from which to learn.

It can be fun to share some of this early history of holiday rituals with family members because all too often we assume that how something is currently being marked is the way it has always been celebrated. Janine's three children were quite taken aback to hear that Christmas had been banned in Massachusetts. Take a moment now to imagine what it would be like not to have any decorations up, no Christmas tree lots, and to continue our normal day's activities through Christmas and New Year's. Sarah and Bill Langston's two teenage sons, who had both recently entered the world of work, were intrigued to learn about the early history of Labor Day. After hearing about how it really was a holiday marking important gains in workers' rights and solidarity with workers over the world, they decided to do more with the day than just taking a day off. First, they read some of the history out loud to each other on Labor Day morning.[4] Then their older son, Zachary, had the idea of interviewing their parents about their first work experiences when they were teenagers. They heard about how their dad had worked after school in a soda parlor making "short and thick" (vanilla ice cream with malt) and "black and white" sundaes (chocolate and vanilla ice cream with fudge sauce and marshmallow sauce on top). Their mom talked about her first job picking blueberries. She would sit on an upturned bucket and slough the berries off into another bucket on the ground. She described how it was solitary work but peaceful, as she was outdoors at the end of a small bog. Both parents talked about what it was like to shift into having to be more responsible, to try to save money, and to get along with others on the job. Zachary and his brother were able to imagine their parents somewhat in the same position as they now found themselves. They talked some about what the meaning of work was for them, and what it meant, as they grew up, to have to start making more choices about what they would do.

The Langstons ended up going out and buying blueberries, malt, chocolate and vanilla ice cream, and fudge and marshmallow sauce and making sundaes that night for dessert in celebration of first jobs. Labor Day became a chance for this family to connect the generations and understand some of the history of work in this country. The two young adult sons were helped to make meaning of changes in their own life as they heard how their parents had coped with making similar kinds of changes.

Planning for Holidays Today

The outside calendar today includes both secular and religious holidays. Also, many holidays, such as Christmas, have both religious and secular elements. Some secular holidays have little meaning for people because the original intent of the day is too removed from their day-to-day lives, or they do not stop to think about its meaning. They also carry more of a press from the larger culture on how things should be done than do daily rituals or family traditions. One way this is strongly communicated is through the media. All families need to decide what their relationship is to the outside calendar in regard to the the idealized images and commercial pressures put out by newspapers, magazines, movies, and television. Families have to create their own reality, one that differs from the glossy touched-up pictures of magazines and retakes of TV. Families live with all the preholiday preparations and postholiday cleanup and fallouts. We certainly never see people washing dishes for hours on end on Bill Cosby's show, nor do we hear the Huxtables arguing over their invitation list for a New Year's Eve party! Today's children who are growing up in a media-driven culture can easily assume something is wrong with their own family's holiday when it doesn't match what's on television.

There are also TV specials for each of the major holidays, and often parades or sports. Ads on television and in other media communicate that the holiday is really a shopping event. Look at any major newspaper around a holiday time and you can get a sense of how the holiday spirit and their symbols are used and manipulated for advertising. Here are some samples from the *L.A. Times* on Thanksgiving Day (November 22) 1990. THIS HOLIDAY SEASON ALL OF L.A. IS GIVING *THANKS*! GOBBLE UP TO *70% OFF* IN BRAND-NAME FASHIONS. Or look at Santa Claus, phone in hand at the top of the ad, saying, "Santa Loves the Extraordinary COOPER BUILDING. HE SAVES A BUNDLE AND SO WILL YOU! THE PLACE FOR YOUR HOLIDAY GIFT SHOPPING. HERE'S WHY!" On the next page, find a cornucopia with a bunch of furniture in it and a few Pilgrims standing around trying to sell Angles Furniture. And so on. The bulk of the newspaper consisted of After Thanksgiving sale ads. The essence of holiday symbols can become watered down when we see them being used this way all around us.

Each family needs to find its own relationship to the possibilities of the media and technology that we now have available. Certainly the development of lightweight VCR cameras and computer geneology programs has added rich resources to augment ritual making. On the other hand, media is so dynamic and so much a part of our lives that it can slip into center stage sometimes without our awareness.

Here are some suggestions your family might want to try for dealing with commercial and media pressures:

• Decide ahead of time on a limit of how much you will spend on presents. Stick to the limit by only taking that amount of money with you when you shop.

• Make things to give to each other. Have some afternoons or evenings set aside when you can work on things together.

• Ask people for lists of practical things they need.

• Try just one major shopping outing, but plan it as a family event when you go off in different groupings to shop, then regroup and have lunch together, and go off with different family members. Have fun hiding things from each other by doing things like putting them in different-sized boxes or putting presents in bags from stores where you have *not* shopped.

• Discuss with your children what is missing from those holiday TV shows.

• Share with other families the real joys and frustrations of holiday making. Let your children hear about the realities from another family's perspective.

• Talk ahead of time about how the TV, VCR, or computer will or will not be used on the holiday. What are ways their use enhances your time together, detracts from it?

STARTING OUT THE NEW YEAR IN A NEW WAY

The Munroe family had celebrated New Year's Day for years by having an open house. They invited friends and neighbors to share food, games, and socialize. Originally, they had viewed it as a time to touch base with people, look back over the past year, and look ahead to future plans. As their three children grew into their teens and were into sports, they began to turn on the TV during the open house to watch the Rose Bowl, Sugar Bowl, and Cotton Bowl games. Their friends also began dropping over to watch with them—cheering and yelling for their favorite team and making bets on them.

After a couple years of this, their parents, Bob and Dinah Munroe, realized that they were not looking forward to their open house, nor did they enjoy it. With the television constantly going and all the energy focused on the football games, they felt like there was little space to talk to one another and enjoy the spirit of a more reflective time.

When Bob and Dinah brought it up with their children, they were really surprised at what their parents had to say. Over the years, their house had come to be known as *the* house to come to on New Year's Day. At first, the teenagers didn't want to make any changes. Monica, their oldest daughter, said, "It works for us. Why don't you guys leave and go out and do something else if there's too much going on here?" "It's our house, too," her mother admonished her. Gradually, they worked out a compromise that included elements that would work for everyone. The children agreed to watch only one of the bowl games, and to make it one that began later in the afternoon. They decided to start the day off more intimately with a brunch with some of their closest friends. Each of their three teenagers asked to invite one friend, and the parents invited two other families. Their fifteen-year-old son, Russell, had an idea for the brunch—to ask everyone to write down on cards two or three things they had particularly appreciated over the last year. They did this without signing their names or putting in information that easily identified them. During the brunch they put the cards in a hat, mixed them up, and then each person pulled one out and read it while the rest tried to guess who had written it. This set a tone for the day of thinking about each individual person and what the year had been like. The day became more balanced with both a quieter small-group and more boisterous large-group time. The TV, rather than dominating the day, added to the rhythm of meaningful group activities.

With the addition of more technology, you may need to plan ahead on how it can enhance rather than detract from your activities. In the Tep family, they found that their children and their cousins were not getting together to do things on holiday gatherings but instead were fussing over who could play what computer game next. They decided to limit the computer, only turning it on the last two hours of the day when things were winding down and it was dark outside. They posted a sign-up schedule for twenty-minute slots for each person to choose a time, and kept a kitchen timer out next to the computer.

REDISCOVERING THE SECULAR CALENDAR

There are many secular holidays in this country that are minimally ritualized. For instance, few people do things on Flag Day, June 14, or Citizenship Day, September 19. Yet, they can be days that are very meaningful. Joanie Doughty, a teacher in a local elementary school in Philadelphia, used Flag Day as a time to tell the story of Betsy Ross's first design for the flag, how the flag evolved over time, and the meaning of the symbols on the flag today: fifty stars for the fifty states and thirteen stripes for the original thirteen colonies. She also showed them other flags from around the world and asked them to think about what the symbols and colors on them communicated. They talked about why nations might have created flags in the first place. Next, she asked her students to think about important symbols in their own lives. The children then designed their own flags to commemorate some things about themselves. Shoshana Coulter drew a soccer ball, the tree house she had made with her sister and brother, and the recorder she played.

These were all things that she felt good about learning to do over the past year. The children learned about the day and some of its history, but they also applied the idea of symbolic representation to their own lives.

There are a host of many other less well-known secular holidays. If you are looking for some new ways to do things with friends or families, you might find that one of these holidays has some particular attraction for you. What about celebrating Day of Remembrance for Japanese-Americans (February 19), Pan American Day (April 14), Arbor Day (April 24), International Jumping Frog Jubilee (end of May), Hiroshima Day (August 6), Native American Day (end of September), or World Food Day (October 16)?[5]

Or perhaps you would like to refocus known secular holiday celebrations so that they are more meaningful to you. For instance, some people in Georgia have tried to recreate Memorial Day so that it emphasizes peace, rather than glorifying war with military parades and music. They spend some part of the day asking questions about what war has really accomplished, as well as learning about the lives of children in this country who have lived through war. They have talked to children from Cambodia, Vietnam, El Salvador, Northern Ireland, and Lebanon, and asked them to share their stories.[6] They feel that this is closer to the original meaning of Memorial Day, when southern women during the Civil War went to the battlefield of Shiloh to strew flowers on the graves of both Union and Confederate soldiers, trying to reconcile the two warring sides.

Here are some questions to help you think for a few minutes about the secular holidays that are important in your life.

• What meaning do they have for you?

• How do they fit in with secular holidays that others in your community celebrate?

• What aspects of them do you want to be sure to pass on to your own children?

• What secular holidays might you like to make more personally meaningful? How might you begin to do this?

Religious Holidays

Some holidays that families celebrate may have religious significance. This can have different implications for families depending on whether different religions are represented within the family itself, or different levels of religious faith exist, and how the larger community responds to varying religious traditions. Where there is an interfaith relationship, partners will need to work through what holidays they will celebrate. Some families combine and celebrate the holidays from both traditions; others choose to mark the holidays from only one religion, while still others separately celebrate the two different traditions.

DOUBLE FAITHS, DOUBLE HOLIDAYS

When Rachel's mother (a Lutheran) married her father (who was Jewish), she agreed to keep the house kosher and he agreed to celebrate the Christian holidays in the house as well. As a child growing up, Rachel remembered holidays that had their own unique blend of these two traditions. For instance, at Christmas, her father always sat in the other room watching TV, while she and her mother and brothers decorated the tree. When it was all done, her father would come out and admire the tree and listen to her mother tell stories about each ornament, where they had come from, and what they represented. But he himself would never decorate it. They would always have turkey for dinner, but it would be a kosher turkey. Also, they would always wait several hours between dinner and dessert so that if there was any dairy in the dessert, they would not be mixing dairy and meat. Her family found a way to combine their various traditions in an agreed-upon pattern each year. While this left Rachel as an adult with the task of sorting out her own religious values, she never felt pulled by her mother or her father. "I saw a marriage where respect for differences came first," she remarked.

Changing religious beliefs in the O'Callaghan family led to different issues. The four O'Callaghan children had been raised Catholic. Over time, the oldest son, Kevin, and the oldest daughter, Bridget, chose not to go to church. When religious holidays were celebrated in the family, a great deal of tension emerged. One year when Bridget and Kevin decided to go to the Easter sunrise service, their parents kept asking them why they went when they did not go near the church the rest of the year. On years when Kevin and Bridget did not go to services, a pall hung over the family that somehow they were not really a family anymore. Everyone was miserable. The family needed to work out some minimal level of acceptance of the different beliefs in the family, rather than letting the holidays be the time when the issue emerged. They did several different things. First, they decided that holiday times were not the time to be trying to hash out how they felt about religion. Other times before and after the holidays were set aside for discussion about their beliefs. Second, Kevin and Bridget explained that they wanted to feel free to go to services with the family out of respect for the family. They did not want this necessarily interpreted as a change in their religious beliefs, nor did they want to be reminded that they had not gone other times that their parents wanted them to go. The family found ways to reduce some of the tension about different beliefs that arose at holiday times.

Sometimes a family that has a set of shared beliefs will find themselves in a community that has celebrations different from their own.

"Can I Wish You Happy Father's Day Today or Not?"

Anastasia and Mike Ventura were Greek Orthodox. They lived in a primarily Catholic neighborhood. Because of the calendar that the Greek Orthodox Church follows, the Greek Orthodox Easter is frequently celebrated on a different Sunday than the Catholic Easter. No one in their neighborhood seemed to understand this, and their two young children, three and five, seemed to be getting confused as to why they did not celebrate Easter along with most of the rest of the kids around them. So Mike and Anastasia decided to share some of the rituals from their Easter with the neighborhood to let them learn about the Greek Orthodox customs. They had a neighborhood open house and invited the children to dye red eggs, which are particular to the Greek Orthodox celebration. They taught the children to say some of the blessings in Greek that children exchange over the eggs. Using a calendar, they also showed them how various religious traditions divided up the months and days differently. The children, including six-year-old Dan, took their eggs home and shared some of what they had learned.

A couple of months later, Dan rang the doorbell at Anastasia and Mike's house. He wanted to play with their oldest son. It was Father's Day. Mike answered the door. "Hi, Dan," Mike said. Dan looked up at him. "Can I wish you Happy Father's Day? Do you have it on the same day or not?" Dan had gotten it. The six-year-old was learning a basic respect for differences.

If you have religious differences within your family, you may have fallen into some patterns that may or may not be working for you. Think about what holidays you celebrate that have religious significance.

• How do they reflect the beliefs of your family?

• Are there variations on how family members get involved in them, depending on the differing beliefs? Are different beliefs accepted? Can these be spoken about?

• What religious beliefs do you want to be expressing in your holidays?

Family Change, Family Variations

When there have been major family changes, issues of membership, loyalty binds, and reworking family dreams can arise during holidays. These may emerge in ritual making and at the same time can be worked out through the planning and ritual process.

ONE HOLIDAY CELEBRATED IN TWO HOUSES

When Sherry Stembridge and her husband separated, she found that holiday times were very disorienting. Holidays had typically been organized around doing things with their two children and other families out in the community. Symbolically, this was represented in things like sending out family photos each year for holiday cards. In the first fall of their separation, Sherry found herself with a photo that had been taken of the four of them on Mother's Day all dressed up to go out and eat. She had set aside this photo as a possible one to have made into holiday cards. However, she felt that she couldn't use that picture, and not knowing what to send, she ended up sending no cards at all. Also, that first Christmas, Ed had the children for the initial part of the Christmas vacation and Christmas day. He had been the person who usually got the tree and put it up. Then they would all decorate it together. This year, he asked for the ornaments. Sherry did not feel like putting up a tree herself, and besides, she had no ornaments to put on it. The house remained undecorated. Financially, things were also very tight because of setting up two households, and fees for mediators and a legal separation. Yet Sherry found herself spending more than she could afford on presents for the children, because she felt so responsible for the hurt the children were expressing about the separation. She found herself trying to make it up to them with fancy gifts.

Planning for holidays became more complex. Basic assumptions about who would be there and who would do what could no longer be made. As she and her former husband shared the custody of their two children, they alternated the holidays each year. One year Ed had them for Thanksgiving and Christmas and she had them for New Year's. This was reversed in the following year. This meant that one year in Sherry's house they could have a family holiday on the actual day of the holiday, and the next year they couldn't.

Sherry found that whether she had the children or not for the holiday really seemed to set the tone. If she knew the children were not going to be there for Thanksgiving, she found it harder to get into thinking about the holiday. She also found that she had to make sure that she had planned to be with other people on Thanksgiving Day; otherwise she sat home and was upset about the divorce and subsequent family changes. Generally, holiday times seemed to restimulate the childrens' memories of when the family was all together. They would even get out old picture albums to look at photos of previous holidays, which Sherry found upsetting.

The third year after Ed and Sherry's separation was the last straw. Ed was going to have the children for Christmas. Sherry would have them for New Year's. First, her eldest son asked to take his Christmas presents from her over to his father's where they were going to celebrate "real" Christmas. Then Sherry's mother sent presents for the two children to their father's house. Sherry felt her mother still blamed her for the divorce, and this was just another way she continued to communicate it to her. Then Sherry heard from the children that their plane back from their father's parents' hometown was not arriving until 10:00 P.M. on New Year's Eve. Sherry had assumed they would come to her house by five that afternoon, the usual time she and the children's father exchanged the children. She had already planned a special New Year's Eve dinner. Sherry knew they were on the wrong track about how to celebrate holidays.

Over time, Ed and Sherry, with the help of friends and other family members, figured out some strategies to be celebrating with two families in two houses. Holiday dates became more fluid for them. One year Sherry had a Thanksgiving eve dinner since she did not have the children on Thanksgiving day. Another year, Christmas was celebrated on New Year's Day. She and her former husband began working out the children's visitation schedule more directly with each other. The actual times children moved from one house to the other were written in on the schedule. They did some minimal coordination of holiday trips and vacations, so that the children did not find themselves coming back from one trip and immediately setting out on another.

Sherry talked to her parents and asked them to send cards or gifts for the children directly to her house. She also started buying less mobile presents that could not go as easily to the other household, never to be seen again. Previous aspects of the holiday were modified to reflect family changes. She began to send out photo cards at Christmas of just the children. She bought small live trees to decorate each December, and then set them out in her yard. She reclaimed her right to have family holidays with a changed family.

Families can find many different ways to work with the changes when there has been separation and divorce. It depends on how recent the change is, the age and number of children, the amount of conflict around the separation, and what other support networks are available to them. In the Saari family, even after the mother had moved out, they kept having holidays together in the family home for a number of years. She would come to the house where the children lived part-time with their father. In the Corliss family, the parents always coordinated their Christmas shopping so that the parents, even though living apart, did not duplicate what they gave to the children. In the Redford-Nichols family, there was so much tension between the parents that they did no planning together. Rather, they each looked to their own network of friends and families to help them organize the holidays.

Find the way to rework the holidays that fits for you. What is most important is that the celebration of holidays does not stay rigid, frozen, and static, unable to reflect family shifts. Holidays should honor the strengths and resources of your current family. They need to take on their own integrity and history, not stand juxtaposed against what has happened before in the family. It is also important that the children are kept out of the middle of differences that parents have. Try to put a boundary around tensions or ongoing conflicts, so that they do not directly intrude into the holiday time. Children and adults need to have protected time and space to enjoy these special events together.

HOLIDAYS AND A MISSING PARENT: OUT OF SIGHT BUT NOT OUT OF MIND

Other issues arise when there is separation or divorce and there is little or no contact between the child and one of the parents. The child may be hurt or angry when the parent does not contact him on a holiday. The parent who lives with the child may then be left to deal with the emotional reactions. The child may have fantasies that the holiday would be much better with the missing parent. Or he may blame the parent he is with for the fact that the other parent is not there.

Ignoring the emotional intensity around the absence of a missing parent at holidays and hoping it will go away only increases the child's sense of being left alone to try to figure out how to handle their reactions. With a separation or divorce, a key emotional element is the child's sense of loss of control. Children often feel that the adults are making major decisions about their life over which they have no say. When a parent is absent, use small ways to help children feel that they have some control.

You might sit down with your child and look at a few pictures of the missing parent and talk about what it would be like to have contact with him. To do this, you will need to set your own anger at your former spouse aside, and simply listen to your child's feelings. You can help a young child write a letter to him. This gives your child a structured format to express herself. Help facilitate contact with relatives of the missing parent if they want to see the child. This can help a child feel less cut off. If there is no possibility of your children reconnecting with an absent parent at holiday times, it is best to have an honest discussion about this. As the sole parent, holidays will pose a special challenge and can become a time to discover the unique strengths of your single-parent family. Virginia Estes began a Thanksgiving dinner with three other single-parent families in which the fathers had completely disappeared. This dinner continued every year until all of the children were grown. "At first it was quite difficult—we felt odd, almost handicapped. During our third year together, my son, Terry, who was fourteen, said, 'I'm just thankful for our mothers,' and then I knew we would all be just fine!"

The custodial parent can also initiate contact with the absent parent as well, so as to have some control over it. For several Christmases, Bill Wilson felt a real pall had fallen over Christmas Day because his son, Michael, kept waiting for his mother to call and she never did. So the next Christmas, first thing in the morning, Bill Wilson called his former wife himself with Michael and they wished her a Merry Christmas. Not easy, but better than sitting, waiting to see if she would call.

SECOND CHANCES:
REMARRIAGE AND THE JOINING OF SEVERAL FAMILIES

Remarried families often have to deal with many of the same issues as families where there is separation or divorce. But besides issues of scheduling across households, divided loyalties, and restimulation of previous holiday memories and meanings, there are particular issues for remarried families. There are new extended family members with whom to become connected. There is a prior history of how family holidays should be done. Not only are there ideas from each family-of-origin about what constitutes a "good" holiday, there are living memories that the children carry about how a holiday should be celebrated. Particular foods and activities may be seen by children as essential while being strange and uncomfortable for step-parents, and vice versa.

Fortunately, holidays have a lot of potential to facilitate healing and make new connections. The same action elements that give us powerful memories about special days and the way things used to be also make it possible to create vital new meaning.

JAMES, DIESNER, HOLDZKOM, BOGGS FAMILIES, INCORPORATED

Incorporation is the name of the game in remarried families. In one family's experience with remarriage, they consciously set out to build networks of contact and create new histories of family holidays. For instance, at their first Thanksgiving together, they made big THANKS cards for each other by making the letters of "thanks" out of potatoes and printing them on large pieces of folded paper. Just before dinner, they circulated each person's card and everyone wrote a message on each card about what he or she appreciated and was thankful for to one another. Before they ate, they sat down at the table and read them out loud. For instance, on Rand's card (age fifteen at the time), his new step-sister Kerja (age eight) wrote, "I like that you're active and like doing things." His father wrote, "Thank you for your creative shows and for including everyone so graciously in your play and ploys." Doing this acknowledged their small growing connections.

In another remarried family people were asked to name a favorite dish that they wanted included, as a way to honor foods from previous families in which they had lived.

At the same time that you might be doing this family building in remarried families, you need to respect other family configurations in which the children are members. For instance, when the children made placemats one Thanksgiving for each person, Janine's daughter, Natalya, made one for her father as well with a picture of her father and his bike in Rhode Island. Then she wrote on it, "To the best dad there could ever be!" She passed this on to her dad for him to use for his holiday. Later, when the family was making puzzles and tie-dying shirts for holiday presents, the children wanted to make presents for family members in their other households. They gathered the right size shirts and other materials to do this, as it seemed to be a way to help them think about and honor both families. It also appeared to help the children be less concerned that one of their parents might be left out. When children make something for the parent that is not there, this can help them feel the parent is included in some small way.

When remarriage occurs after divorced spouses have worked out a particular holiday pattern, initial reactions and changes may be startling. Karen Parsons and her two sons, Jim, twelve, and Jason, fifteen, had celebrated Thanksgiving with her parents ever since her divorce from John Parsons seven years ago. He never asked to have the children for holidays and saw them rarely. This year, John remarried in July. In October he began to insist that his sons come to his new home for Thanksgiving. "I feel it is for his new wife—he wants to act like he's a 'family man' now, but where was he for seven years?" Karen said. Jim and Jason refused to go for Thanksgiving, but each felt very guilty and confused. The argument started up again for Christmas. This time Karen knew she and John had better talk. Since anger was high, they agreed to see a counselor to work out a new holiday pattern. They went for three sessions, and then each parent went for a session with the boys. The counselor focused these sessions on past, present, and future holiday celebrations. This was the first opportunity any of them had to speak openly about holidays when they were all together, and to discuss their disappointment in a safe environment. Finally, the counselor met with the three adults in order to mediate a new schedule to which all could agree.

Holiday celebrations will often sharply focus relationship changes that are required when there is divorce and remarriage. Even well-established visiting and custody arrangements are often challenged and may need to be reworked, sometimes with brief professional help. Remember, too, that the relationship changes occurring with remarriage will likely take experiencing holidays over a number of years to become truly comfortable.

CELEBRATING WHEN YOU ARE SINGLE OR LIVING ALONE

For people who are not living with others, holiday times can bring up issues because of the expectations in the larger culture that these are times that families and groups of people celebrate together. There may also be familial pressures to return home and go along with whatever extended family members are planning because you do not have a family of your own. Certain holidays may also have meanings attached to them as well. Take Valentine's Day. The message is given that you should have a special sweetheart who will remember you on that day.

Yet precisely because they are not as intricately involved with a group of people that they live with, singles often have the possibility of more options and other choices to make around the holidays. They can join with members of their family-of-origin. Here the issue may be to make sure that some parts of the celebration with their family reflect their current identity. Reed Richter came from a traditionally observant Jewish family. While feeling spiritually and ethnically connected to Judaism, he needed his own rituals to reflect his social activism. Initially, his parents did not pay much attention to his requests for additions to their Passover Seder. Reed noticed that his married brother and sister-in-law and their young children were allowed to bring new symbolic actions to the Seder. When he spoke with his parents about this, they conceded that they had continued to treat Reed as if he were still in college, bringing home "radical student" notions. He was able to negotiate with them for some time during the recitation of the Ten Plagues in the Seder to voice his *adult* concerns regarding homelessness and hunger.

Single people can also celebrate with others who are single. Yvette Schutte found herself starting a tradition of a pre–Valentine's Day card-making party. She gathered a range of simple materials and invited about twenty of her friends over to make cards. They then sent these cards to each other for Valentine's Day as well as to other friends, and gathered for Valentine's Day at one of their houses for their traditional chocolate dinner party. One year they had chicken mole, fruit fondue dipped in chocolate sauce, and chocolate cake for dessert. As Yvette said, "This sure beats sitting home and feeling blue on Valentine's Day and waiting to see if anyone remembers me."

Other people make it a point to volunteer to help others on holidays and create a network of people with whom they are connected. In Bill Starr's mid-size city, the United Way organization always served meals on major holidays at the community center. Bill volunteered to help with the shopping and baking before the meals, as well as serving on the actual days. He felt that he had found the true meaning of many of the holidays: helping others.

A person living alone may make a conscious decision as well to celebrate a holiday alone. Cheryl Nash, who had had a drinking problem in previous years, did not like the emphasis in many of the New Year's Eve activities on drinking and partying. She preferred to stay home and think carefully about what the past year had been like for her, and what she hoped might happen in the forthcoming year. She let her friends know that this was a deliberate choice on her part to do what was meaningful for her.

Other singles find ways to connect with other families and join with their household for holidays. Lucille Aranyi felt welcomed by her friend, Dana, and her husband and two children. They knew that Lucille could be counted on to bring the chocolate-covered bunnies for Easter, and the Witches' Brew for Halloween.

PHOTOS ON THE MANTEL:
UNACKNOWLEDGED FAMILIES AND HOLIDAYS

When Kay and her partner of twelve years, Margaret, first lived together, they celebrated holidays separately at each of their parents' homes along with other extended family members. They did not yet feel comfortable sharing with their families that they were a couple, and they did not want to deal with issues like where they would sleep and how others would or would not value what they meant to each other. This pattern of holiday celebrating was very stressful for them. Kay found that it was hard for her to really enjoy the time with her family, when she was missing Margaret and resenting that she couldn't invite her along. Margaret worried that Kay was closer to her family than to her, and she also felt that the two of them were really missing out on some special times to celebrate their own unit because they did not spend holiday times together. They were always finding themselves in situations like opening Christmas presents to each other early, the night before they left to go to their parents. Then, when they were at their parents', they were not able to share the significance of the new sweater each had been given by her partner, or the new piece of jewelry. Or they found themselves cooking special holiday foods together after the occasion.

Over time, they each disclosed to their families that they were in a lesbian relationship. Kay's parents accepted them as a couple and showed this by now inviting the two of them to their house for family get-togethers. In contrast, Margaret's family backed away from the couple once they found out, and Margaret found herself spending very little time with them. Holiday celebrating shifted to becoming a part of Kay's extended family gatherings.

These gatherings were comfortable for the most part, but over the years they found that at Kay's parents, there were still lots of things that people there would not talk to them about such as having children, buying a house, life insurance, or putting away money for retirement. In subtle ways people communicated that they did not really expect them to be together for the rest of their lives, or they did not think Margaret and Kay wanted some of the same things that many families want. One day, Margaret brought to Kay's attention that this seemed to be symbolically represented by the family photos on the mantelpiece. Kay's parents had placed pictures there of all of their adult children with their spouses—except for Kay and her partner. Margaret also brought up how she was beginning to feel like their holidays were imbalanced because they centered much more on Kay's traditions and her family. Further, always being with Kay's extended family reminded her of her painful cutoff from her own family-of-origin.

Margaret wanted to back away from primarily celebrating at Kay's parents' and create more couple ritual times, including holidays with other friends at home. At first, Kay had a hard time understanding this because she felt secure with her family and she knew that both she and Margaret appreciated how they had been accepted by them. As she and Margaret continued to talk, Kay began to see how never celebrating in their own home marked them as different in a way that affected their own adult development. She also began to understand how they were subtly treated differently as a couple in her parents' home. They decided to do a number of things. First, they had a copy of a photo made of them at one of their anniversary celebrations in their apartment. They framed it and presented it to Kay's parents for the mantelpiece. They also decided to consciously bring up topics that people did not ask them about or raise. They had been thinking of adopting a child. At the next family gathering, they talked about some of the pros and cons of doing this. Finally, they decided to let Kay's parents know that they needed to celebrate some major holidays at their own home. As they did this, Margaret consciously tried to find ways to include connections to her own holiday history by recreating things she had enjoyed when she was younger such as going from house to house at night with a group of people singing holiday songs. She also began to send holiday cards to people in her family, even though she did not typically receive any from them. To her surprise, she received a Hanukkah card back from her mother, and later a phone call.

Kay's family slowly started to follow the couple's lead, asking them if they wanted to celebrate holidays at their apartment, or with them, or if they had other plans. This couple found ways to shift their ritual patterns around holidays to accommodate their changing relationship needs.

Here are a few questions to stop and reflect on both religious and secular holidays on the outside calendar. Think about your holidays over the last couple of years. What patterns do you see over several different holidays?

• How do you typically celebrate holidays?

• Who do you get together with?

• What works or does not work for you with this pattern?

• What do you see other people in similar circumstances doing?

• Are there any small changes that you would like to make in how you mark holidays?

Celebrating and Loss

"Christmas was my father's favorite holiday. Every December he went from being a serious businessman to becoming like a little child. His excitement captured all of us. How can I celebrate Christmas with him gone?" With these words, Mary Alice Lawrence expressed a dilemma that we all face at some point in our lives—how can we celebrate a holiday after someone we love has died? Our own sense of loss and grief can become especially poignant when it seems as if everyone around us in the wider community is happily celebrating a holiday.

During the holiday celebration rituals that follow the death of a family member or dear friend, two patterns commonly emerge that can impact subsequent celebration rituals for years and even generations to come.

"HOLIDAY BUSINESS AS USUAL"

In their struggle to figure out how to celebrate when everyone is mourning, many families establish an unspoken "rule" that there will be no conversation about their loss, especially during a holiday. They valiantly attempt to celebrate as if the loss had not occurred, and try to have what one family called "holiday business as usual."

In Andrea Simpson's family, such a pattern developed following the death of her eleven-year-old sister, when Andrea was thirteen. "My sister, Marcia, died in March, right before Easter in 1961. My mother was devastated, but everything in her background was 'stiff upper lip.' My father was in so much pain, but his primary concern was my mother. When Easter came, three weeks after my sister died, my parents made the same sort of Easter celebration we always had—they hid eggs and candy for me and my little brother to find, and none of us spoke about Marcia. I remember thinking about how she always found most of the candy and yet would share it with us, but it was like there was a rule that I couldn't say anything about that because it would upset my parents too much. My grandparents came for Easter dinner just like they always did. It was the one holiday when we all got together. I overheard my mother telling my grandmother, 'I want us still to be like other families at Easter. I want to make us be happy.' And so she did what she always did for Easter, which was to make three special side dishes, one favorite for my brother, one for me, and one for Marcia! No one said, 'But Marcia's gone.' No one said anything. We just ate in silence, pretending everything was still the same. The following year, Marcia's favorite food just disappeared from the ritual, but no one said a word about it. After that, all of our holidays went dead."

In subsequent years, tension would rise in the family before every major holiday and no one understood why. Like many families, the Simpsons' desire to protect one another from the pain of Marcia's death, in fact, left each family member isolated and lonely, especially during holiday rituals. Since there was a prohibition on talking about Marcia, including sharing stories about her and her place in the family's rituals during her life, the family was cut off from a key source of comfort and connection, and from the possibility of experiencing any new joy with one another.

If holiday celebration rituals in your family feel filled with tension, and your family has developed a rigid style in which everything must remain the same at holiday times for no apparent reasons, it may be that a death or other major trauma that cannot be spoken of has profoundly impacted your celebrations. It's possible that such a loss occurred many years or even decades ago. You may want to go back in time and talk with members of your family to find out when holidays were different.

Twenty-two years after her sister's death, Andrea Simpson decided that the time had come to change her family's celebration pattern. With sensitivity and care, she organized a family meeting well before Easter. She began the meeting by thanking her parents for their wish to protect the family from the pain of Marcia's death and then she spoke about her own memories of holidays when Marcia was alive. She brought out photographs of the children hunting Easter eggs and spoke about Marcia's generosity. Finally she gave her mother a beautifully framed copy of Marcia's favorite Easter dinner recipe. The family grieved openly together for the first time in twenty-two years. Several weeks later their Easter celebration was lively and meaningful. "Easter is supposed to be about rebirth and resurrection," Andrea's mother said. "I think we can really feel that now."

"LET'S CANCEL HOLIDAYS"

Other families respond to death or trauma by stopping their holiday celebration rituals entirely. Getting together with family members for Thanksgiving, Christmas, Passover, or other important holidays when a significant person has died may feel so overwhelming and painful that a family may simply decide, as one family told us, "to just cancel Christmas."

When Patrick Dinson's brother committed suicide in July, his family initially responded by coming together to comfort one another. Family members flew in for his funeral from many parts of the country, just as they always flew in for Thanksgiving at Patrick's mother's house. The Thanksgiving gathering had served as an annual family reunion, and had grown to include in-laws, spouses, and grandchildren. When October came, however, grown siblings began calling with various reasons why they would not be coming for Thanksgiving this year. One was going to his in-laws', another thought she would "just be with friends," a third said she couldn't afford it. Patrick's mother decided to "just sit Thanksgiving out this year."

This was the first time in the history of the family that they did not gather for the holiday. "Truly, it felt too painful—how could we celebrate? I was quite relieved that no one was coming," Patrick said. "Then the day of Thanksgiving came. The parade was on TV, the football games my brother had loved were everywhere, friends I called were busy cooking turkeys—the holiday was all around me. It actually ended up being worse without my family. It felt to me like we lost my brother *and* each other. I think we'd have done better to try being together."

The Dinsons had responded to the tragic death of a brother and a son by "canceling the holiday." Since our celebration rituals, however, are embedded in the culture at large and are going on all around us, the decision to opt out has a paradoxical effect, as Patrick Dinson realized. The Dinsons ended up doubly troubled, each alone with their grief, bereft of the support and love that was available in their annual gathering, while sharply aware that celebration was going on everywhere.

Following this attempt to "cancel Thanksgiving," Patrick initiated a conference telephone call with all of his siblings and their mother. He described his experience on Thanksgiving and asked if they would consider gathering for New Year's, which they agreed to do. When they got together, each one spoke about their seemingly separate decision to "cancel Thanksgiving." Coming together on New Year's and speaking openly about their dead brother lifted a rapidly developing taboo. They spoke about the next Thanksgiving and how they thought it would be different without him, but all agreed that it was vital that they be together.

When Patrick made his conference call, he interrupted what could have easily developed into a more ingrained family response of avoiding each other on major holidays because of the painful suicide. We have talked to other families who never get back together to celebrate holidays after the death of a family member. If your own family has elaborated a minimized ritual pattern around major holidays and you are not sure why, you may find that a death, even a generation or more ago, affected all subsequent celebration rituals. Just as you can intervene when the holiday pattern has become rigid and stereotypical after a death, so you can alter a minimized and avoidant celebration pattern.

WHEN THE RITUAL MAKER DIES

The loss of your family's "ritual maker," the person who has made sure that holiday celebrations happened, poses special problems. Often this person, usually a mother or a grandmother, has been a central voice for family cohesion. In the confusion following such a death, family celebrations may disintegrate, enlarging your sense of loss.

In the Connegan family, an intense but underground struggle ensued following the death of Grandmother Connegan, who had been the ritual maker. Her two grown daughters each declared that Christmas Eve dinner would be at her house. Aunts, uncles, and cousins called one another, expressing their bewilderment at the competition they felt between the sisters. The holiday gathering of the entire extended family fell apart, as some people took sides and others decided not to participate at all. In this family, previously unspoken relational issues of jealousy between the two sisters came to the fore following the death of the ritual maker. Struggles over where power would now be located in the extended family overwhelmed the previous meaning of holidays.

If your family has relied upon one person to create celebration rituals, and this person has died, it is extremely important to talk openly about the meanings of becoming the new ritual maker. Several questions are useful to consider in your negotiations:

• Does one person want to take on this position?

• What does that mean for family relationships?

• Are there struggles over this position? Are such struggles really metaphors for where power and influence are moving in the family?

• What might it look like if several people shared this responsibility?

• How can shifts be made in ways that both honor what has come before and acknowledge changing family relationships?

While it can sometimes be difficult to discuss questions regarding family ritual making, holding such a conversation about future holiday rituals can enable you to sort out many complex relationship issues.

RECOVERING FROM A LOSS: HEALING AND CELEBRATING

One of the most intricate and important aspects of rituals is their ability to hold and express contradictions for us. Since many of us are not aware of this potential in rituals, we commonly respond to celebrations as if they cannot also hold our grief and loss. In fact, any given holiday ritual *can* enable both healing and celebration. The starting place is an open acknowledgment that this year's holidays will be different because they are impacted by a death. Such a statement to your family and friends immediately prevents the pattern of "holiday business as usual." As you talk about how the celebration will be different, hard, painful, and/or sad, you may want to begin to build in a specific way to honor or memorialize the person you have lost, while still gathering for the holiday. Doing this begins to orient you toward ongoing life and prevents the pattern of "Let's cancel the holiday."

Recovering from any loss and reengaging with life is developmental, taking place over time. Your holiday celebrations can provide a measure of such change. Chin Woo reflected that when her husband died, she could see her own grieving through the lens of the Chinese New Year's celebration. "The first year I stayed home alone. I could not be with my family for our banquet. I felt guilty celebrating with him gone. The second year, I joined the banquet but I couldn't cook anything. I always used to prepare my husband's favorite foods—I just couldn't do it, so I went like a guest, but I felt very empty. The third year, I told my daughter I would cook one of my husband's favorite dishes. At the banquet, I told my grandchildren about this special dish, chicken in parchment. My husband had brought the recipe from China, from his mother. My granddaughter asked if she could learn to make it. Then I knew his memory would stay alive and I could truly celebrate the new year." The changes that Chin Woo described mirrored her healing process following the death of her husband. If you find that your holiday celebrations have become static and unchanging following a significant loss, it is likely that your own healing process and that of your family is not proceeding.

Try setting aside an agreed-upon amount of time, for instance an hour, on the evening before or the morning of the holiday. Ask that family members gather with the expressed purpose of telling stories about previous holiday celebrations when your loved one was alive. Share whatever stories come to mind, emphasizing this person's place in your celebration rituals. When you do this, you will find yourself honoring this person's memory, while simultaneously acknowledging that this year's holiday is going to be different, as will subsequent years'. Some families have gathered with meaningful symbols that speak about their loss in ways that words cannot. A simple ceremony in which such symbols are passed from one person to another can facilitate healing. A given symbol, such as candlesticks belonging to a grandmother who has died, may find its way to a holiday table as an enduring memory in the midst of ongoing life. Other families look through photographs or at videos taken on prior holidays. As you do this, likely you will find yourselves laughing one moment and crying the next. Moments of healing will find a place in your holiday celebrations.

We have found that when families take a prescribed period of time at the start of a holiday to mourn their loss together, authentic celebrating becomes possible once again. Your family can remain open to the changes that are required in the face of loss. Rather than attempting the impossible of celebrating as if there were no loss or trying to skip the holiday, rituals' capacity to heal and to celebrate can become available to you.

What Not to Say During Holiday Celebrations

Celebration rituals can provide a strong sense of family support and connectedness. They are also often a time when people experience a lot of family tension and anxiety, due to a combination of high expectations, extra work, memories of previous holidays, and long-standing relationship strains that have not been successfully addressed. Your family's greatest strengths and its most painful vulnerabilities are generally in the air at holiday time. And what happens during a holiday becomes part of your family's indelible store of memories, easily tapped year after year.

For all of these reasons, we recommend that holiday celebrations *not* be the time and place that you choose to raise hot topics with your family or disclose potentially upsetting news. To do so runs the risk of provoking family cutoffs or freezing family relationships that need to be flexible in order to deal with difference and change. The Christmas dinner table is decidedly not the place to announce a pending divorce, a decision to move three thousand miles away, a surprising career change, or a relationship that your family will have trouble accepting.

"TOM AND I ARE GETTING A DIVORCE"

Angela MacDougal arrived at her parents' home for the family's annual Easter dinner without her husband, Tom. When she entered, she told her parents that Tom was working and wouldn't be coming for dinner.

Angela and Tom were married four years earlier in an elaborate Catholic wedding. Unbeknownst to any family members, they had been having severe marital problems for the past two years. Both came from families where there was no history of divorce, and religious proscriptions against divorce were strong.

The Easter celebration was an important ritual in Angela's family, going all the way back to her childhood. The family always gathered for sunrise services and remained together for the entire day, culminating in a special dinner. The family's holiday ritual style was fairly rigid and obligatory, and deviations from it were treated angrily by Angela's father.

That year, Angela had called and said she and Tom couldn't make the service but would be along later in the day. Tom had, in fact, moved out several weeks earlier, but Angela had been too afraid to tell her family.

She felt particularly intimidated by her father, who had disapproved of her decision to marry Tom, and who, she felt certain, would not support her now. "My father always told us, 'You made your own bed, so sleep in it,' and he and my mother often fought over choices my brothers and I made in our lives." She implored Tom to join her at her family's for Easter, but he refused.

When Angela arrived without Tom, the tension was palpable. Angela's mother asked many questions, and her father criticized her for not insisting that he give up his work on this important day. When her father put her down, her mother came to her defense, reenacting an old familiar pattern. Finally, when all were gathered at the dinner table, and her father again remarked about Tom's absence, Angela blurted out, "Tom and I are getting a divorce!"

Everyone at the table erupted. Angela's father was shouting at her, blaming her for not being able to keep her husband happy. Her mother began to yell at her father. One of her brothers stormed out of the room, yelling at Angela, "You've broken Dad's heart!" No one thought to offer her any support. Easter dinner disintegrated. Angela left, feeling both ashamed and very alone.

Following this painful Easter holiday, Angela's father refused to talk to her. He ordered her mother not to have anything to do with her, and for many months her mother obeyed this order, and then began to see Angela secretly. This outcome further rigidified the old family pattern, with Angela caught between her parents in a painful triangle. The following Easter came and went without Angela present for the celebration.

In our experience as family therapists, what happened in Angela's family happens in many families to a greater or lesser degree when upsetting information emerges, especially in an unplanned way, during holiday celebration rituals. While Angela's family and especially her father would have had difficulty accepting her divorce under any circumstances, the revelation during Easter dinner made resolving the issue that much more difficult. Instead of slowly and planfully telling family members individually in a way that would have gathered enough support to then tell her father, Angela's unplanned announcement had the effect of unleashing all that was most dysfunctional in her family. Rather than being able to integrate this painfully sharp change in the family's sense of itself as a family where "no one gets divorced," the family's memory and identity became fixated on "the Easter when Angela broke Dad's heart."

If you are facing an important change in your life that you want your family to know about, or deciding to disclose a long-held secret to members of your family, or wanting to change family rules regarding taboos, lengthy preparation is required. Trying to talk to several people at once who are gathered for a holiday leaves you vulnerable to all of the relational cross currents and anxieties in your family that may have little to do with your specific issue, but which get activated by the hint of difference and change. We are *not* recommending year after year of pretense at holiday celebrations, since this breeds alienation and distance. We are, however, recommending that you choose regular time, not holiday ritual time, to share news that your family may initially resist. There is nothing to be gained by the freezing of relationships that so often occurs when holiday rituals fuse with fear and anger.

Communities and Holidays

Communities often set the tone for holidays. When Janine was growing up in the 1950s, teachers in her elementary school centered much of the school curriculum on major holidays, including religious ones. In the weeks before Veterans' Day the children learned about different wars; at Thanksgiving they made turkeys out of pine cones and studied the Pilgrims. They studied nothing about Native Americans even though some of the children in the school *were* Native Americans. At Christmas, they learned all kinds of Christian songs that were sung at an all-school concert while different children dressed up as Mary and Joseph. No one blinked an eye at Easter when they made Easter baskets, and cut out chicks and rabbits to put in the window. No Jewish holidays were ever mentioned, although there were Jewish children in the school. The message they were learning as children was that there was one dominant tradition in the outside calendar of holidays, rather than multiple cultural and religious traditions.

This same issue was dramatically highlighted in December 1990 when Kyle and Mayra Suhas took their three children to the White House. For years the White House has been opened and decorated for the public in December. It was Christmas, and only Christmas, that was being celebrated throughout all the rooms, down the long corridors, and outside in the gardens. There were Christmas trees and gingerbread houses and crèches and Christmas songs being sung. Nowhere was there a menorah, or a dreidel, or the Kwanza candelabrum with its seven holders for the seven days of Kwanza. Nothing there represented Diwali, or some of the unique aspects of the Eastern Orthodox Church, or symbolized the winter solstice. Recognition of the cultural diversity of holidays that occur in this country was missing altogether. Yet here was a rich opportunity to make a national statement in front of millions of people that the diversity of our cultures and peoples is a unique and central part of our country.

TOWARD A MULTICULTURAL OUTSIDE CALENDAR

Other communities have wrestled with their relationship to the outside calendar in different ways. At the University of Massachusetts, a calendar is sent to all people on campus each year that lists the major Muslim, Hindu, Confucian, Baha'i, Sikh, Buddhist, and Jewish holidays along with the Christian ones. Days off at the university adhere to a fairly traditional outside calendar. But on this more expansive calendar, all members of the faculty are directed to give permission for classes to be missed and reschedule exams on days that conflict with religious observances.

Many schools have stopped organizing curricula around the traditional outside calendar holidays and have chosen a wider variety of cultures to honor. Parents and community members come in and share what happens on Children's Day in Japan, or in celebrations of Buddha's birth. In December, a school might choose a broad-based theme such as the "Gift of Giving" that makes space for a wide number of ways to think about the different holidays that are celebrated during these shortest days of the year. A local library used to ask parents and children to make ornaments for a Christmas tree that they put up each year. Recognizing that this was honoring a primarily Christian tradition, they decided to no longer put up a tree in the library. Instead they had a party for families to make decorations inspired from various books that they had read, including a book display of writings on all different kinds of winter celebrations. These were used to make mobiles and chains to decorate the library in the winter holiday season.

Another town organized a cultures-and-community celebration for

December. There were different music groups, foods, and crafts tables. People made God's eyes, danced to salsa bands, decorated gingerbread cookies, cracked open a piñata with tiny gifts from around the world, ate chicken in peanut sauce and nian gao (sticky rice cake). Contrast this to your local mall where the centerpiece from the day after Thanksgiving to Christmas Day is probably Santa Claus, a gigantic Christmas tree, and red and green decorations everywhere, with piped-in Christmas carols.

Communities need to be aware that the public symbols they choose to display on holidays send many messages to the community. What are the holiday symbols that are found in your community? What do they communicate about our society? What holidays are promoted in stores, community centers, newspapers, television, and schools? What messages are families receiving in the community about the outside calendar? How do you see your children or your friend's children incorporating these messages?

Families can all use the shared purpose and vision that can emerge when they feel that they have outside support for their various traditions. Families should not be left alone to make meaning. If you think that your community has a narrow outside calendar there are a number of things you can do. You can ask schools to diversify what they honor. You can mention to store owners that you would like to see more than a Christmas tree in the store. Write letters to the newspaper, to malls, to the White House. Ask in stores for cards that represent more holidays and different kinds of families. Where you work, ask coworkers about what holidays they celebrate. Bring in food to share from your background, and ask them to do the same.

Reworking Holidays Little by Little

Holidays are different than daily rituals and family traditions such as birthdays and anniversaries. Since they involve the larger community more, they often include a wider circle of people; meanings that are supported by the media, religious groups, and other institutions; and cultural and societal history. There are more levels to integrate and link in order to create vibrant, memorable holidays. Here is a grid, Revitalizing Holidays, to help you think about the range of things that have been discussed in this chapter and apply them to one of your own

Reflecting On Your Holidays

	SIGNIFICANT—be sure to include; enhances meaning-making	HOLLOW MEANING OR PRESSURE—detracts from the holiday	THE UNSPOKEN—that needs to be talked over	SMALL CHANGES—to try to make this year
Family heritage—include ethnic, religious, cultural symbols, and symbolic actions				
Unique shifts in the family—migrations, loss, trauma, intermarriage, entrance and exit of members				
Media messages—from TV, magazines, radio, video, movies, computer games				
Larger culture—decorating, gatherings, music, protected time and space, common symbols and symbolic actions				

holidays. Pick one holiday and fill this chart out for it. Ask your family members to do likewise. Use the charts to initiate a family discussion of holiday celebrations.

In the next chapter, we will look at the last type of rituals, ones that carry us through the life cycle. Because life-cycle rituals are often more public events, you may find yourself experiencing similar pressures from the larger culture, as you do with holidays, about how they should be done. They are also quite different from holidays because they usually happen only once. They do not offer as many possibilities as the other three types of rituals to rework them. Careful planning of life-cycle rituals may be even more important than for daily rituals, family traditions, and holidays, so that they truly reflect your evolving beliefs and values.

Life-Cycle Rituals

LIVING LIFE'S CHANGES

WHEN KERRIE POST AND ALAN GOLDENBERG decided to get married, they also decided that they would elope. "We'll just go to City Hall and then tell everyone afterwards. It's not what I had dreamed about, but it's just too hard to make a wedding," Kerrie said.

Kerrie and Alan are a 1990s couple. Kerrie is Presbyterian and Alan is Jewish. Each of their families initially objected to their getting married, but have gradually accepted their decision. Each family, however, wants the wedding ceremony to reflect its own religious identity.

Complicating matters further is the fact that Kerrie's parents are divorced and still angry with each other. Kerrie was raised by her stepfather from age five. She considers him to be her "psychological" father. "If I had a wedding, who would walk me down the aisle?" she wondered. "My mother doesn't even want my father to be invited! It really is easier just to elope."

The Essence of Life-Cycle Rituals

Those rituals studied and described by anthropologists are primarily life-cycle rituals, ones that *make* and *mark* major transitions through life. Historically and across all cultures, these are the rituals of birth, adolescence, marriage, and death. The profound and often precarious changes inherent in these transitions are made safe and manageable through rituals that connect us to our past, our cultural and religious roots, our potential future, and our common humanity. Life-cycle rituals are often imbued with a sense of the sacred and with an element of the mysterious.

All human beings throughout the world and throughout time are born and die. All experience emerging sexuality. And most make sustained adult relationships to form new family units and new generations. Such changes are enormously complicated. They *simultaneously* involve beginnings and endings. These changes often require holding and expressing both pain and joy. They may shape and give voice to profoundly conflicting beliefs about our personal existence and our relationships. It is little wonder that every culture has created rituals to celebrate and guide our way through these life-cycle passages.[1]

Life-cycle rituals enable change at multiple levels of our existence. For instance, an individual's life status is changed by going through a ceremony that transforms a child into an adolescent, or an adolescent into a young adult. A single adult is transformed into a married adult through a wedding ritual. This one life-cycle ritual holds and expresses the profound changes of loss of children in their primary allegiance to their parents, creation of a new couple and family, and the formation of in-law relationships. Naming ceremonies for babies simultaneously celebrate new life, designate new roles of parents, grandparents, and godparents, and generally welcome a child into a religious, ethnic, or spiritual community. Funerals mark the loss of a person, celebrate that person's existence on earth, and begin the process of mourning and healing that ultimately allows the living to go on with their lives. When we prepare and participate in life-cycle rituals, our sense of self and our entire network of relationships in our family, extended family, and community undergo change.

Life-cycle rituals use familiar symbols and symbolic actions in order to ease what would otherwise be unfamiliar changes. Thus choosing and exchanging rings in a wedding ceremony is a familiar part of our consciousness, even if we've never been married before. The symbol of a ring and the symbolic action of placing a ring on the finger of one's beloved connects us to committed relationships across time and place. The symbolic action of baptizing infants joins Christian parents with millions of others around the world who share a belief in washing away original sin and providing sacred rebirth. Flowers often adorn coffins, symbolizing ongoing life even in the face of death.[2] The familiar symbolic action of burying a coffin links us to the cycle of life and death throughout the ages. Since life-cycle changes generally occur only once in a person's life, rituals that are deeply embedded in history and in a given culture provide a map for personally uncharted territory.

SACRED TIME AND PLACE IN LIFE-CYCLE RITUALS

In many life-cycle rituals, time and place are not simply special as in most rituals but are often sacred. Many of our life-cycle rituals are held in churches, synagogues, temples, mosques, or on other consecrated ground, such as a cemetery. Often, just entering such places brings us in touch with life-cycle rituals through the ages. Even when religious sites are not chosen for life-cycle rituals, people generally take great care in selecting a place that conveys meaning, such as a particular home or park or woods.

Different cultures and religions observe unique time requirements for various life-cycle rituals. In many Christian denominations, babies are baptized early in infancy; Mormons give their infants "the Father's Blessing" but wait until the child is eight years old for baptism; Greek Orthodox babies are baptized and given a symbolic First Communion and then take part in a special ceremony when they are five years old, using candles from the original baptism that have been saved for this ceremony. Jewish families circumcise their baby boys eight days after birth, and Orthodox Jews mark the passage from baby to little boy with a ritual haircut at age three.[3] While the exact particulars of these time requirements certainly differ, they share the notion that time needs to be marked in a special way to welcome infants and children into a family, a religion, or a community.

Time is also highlighted in many life-cycle rituals by three distinct stages. In the first stage, special preparations are made for the ritual. During this preparation stage, individuals, families, and the whole community are readying for many changes. All of the arrangements that are made during this phase, such as selecting a place to hold the ritual, inviting people, choosing clothing, or deciding on food, serve as a signal that life-cycle change is under way. In more traditional cultures, a person may be sent away or separated from the larger community during this phase. In our own culture, separating a bride and not allowing her to be seen on her wedding day until she comes down the aisle is an example of this use of time. Time here may be used to pass on new knowledge, as in adolescent rites of passage. As you think about life-cycle rituals in your own life, think over how the preparation phase affected the actual changes that occurred in individuals and in relationships. If you are anticipating a life-cycle ritual, think about ways to use the preparation phase to initiate the changes that will occur in the ritual. For instance, part of the preparation phase before a retirement party might include changing a room in your home that the soon-to-be-retired person will use for new activities. This announces in action that life will be different soon.

The second stage is the actual ritual event, when people experience themselves in new actions and roles, such as a bride and groom at a wedding, or parents and godparents at a christening. During this phase, ceremonies take place that transform us from one role in life to another. For instance, a child becomes a responsible member of a religious community during a confirmation or a Bar Mitzvah ceremony. During the ritual event, time becomes a boundary marker, as we move from regular time to special ritual time. Such time boundaries in our life-cycle rituals provide a sense of safety, enabling us to express deep and heartfelt emotions.

Finally, in the third stage, participants in the ritual return to regular life.[4] A period of time after a life-cycle ritual is usually spent reflecting on the event. In our culture, this is often a time to look at photographs or videos and to tell stories about the actual ritual. These activities anchor the changes that have occurred during the life-cycle ritual.

The worldwide wisdom regarding time in life-cycle rituals is particularly clear in funeral rituals. Time periods for intense mourning, when the regular activities of life cease temporarily, are often prescribed, such as the seven days of sitting Shiva in Judaism. In Jamaican culture, a period of nine days is required, punctuated by the ritual called Nine Nights, including a celebratory wake focusing on storytelling about the deceased. Christ's feeding fish to the multitudes is symbolized during a large shared community meal of fried fish.[5] These various time requirements for immediate mourning rituals share a sense of the approximate time we require as human beings to cope with the *initial* shock of a death and provide ways to give support to the grieving. Time appears again as a factor in healing the profound life-cycle change of death and loss with rituals held one year following a death, such as a Catholic anniversary Mass, or the placing of a headstone in Judaism, symbolizing the official end of the religiously prescribed mourning period. All of these rituals use time in ways that offer the living a glimpse of the cycle of life and death that touches us all.

Life-Cycle Rituals in Changing Times

While traditional cultures still mark birth, adolescence, marriage, and death with known and accepted rituals, we see something quite different when we look at our own multicultural society with its varying family forms. The sustenance and creation of meaningful rituals to celebrate and make safe all of the individual and relationship shifts attendant to life-cycle transitions has lagged behind the swift pace of social and cultural changes.

Alan and Kerrie's decision to "skip the wedding" reflects many of the dilemmas attached to our life-cycle rituals as we enter the twenty-first century. Several issues regarding life-cycle rituals can be seen in Kerrie and Alan's story. For instance, does the usual wedding ritual that exists in the culture actually fit their circumstances? What happens to their personal and interpersonal need for meaningful rituals if they were to omit having a wedding? And finally, what can they do to deal with the lack of familiar and accepted rituals for newly formed or newly addressed life-cycle changes?

The traditional wedding ritual doesn't fit this couple's circumstances. Like an increasing number of couples today, Alan and Kerrie come from differing religious and ethnic backgrounds. A Presbyterian wedding ceremony or a Jewish wedding ceremony, which would have fit for their respective parents' marriages, will not do. Since the couple were deeply spiritual, a wedding at City Hall really wouldn't do either.

Kerrie's parents' angry divorce, her mother's remarriage, and her close relationship with her stepfather all required new elements in whatever wedding ritual was to be created.

While Alan and Kerrie at first thought they would elope, they began to realize that all of the difficult relationship issues that faced them as they contemplated a wedding would still exist. They wisely concluded that simply skipping this critically important life-cycle ritual would not erase these issues, and might, in fact, force them underground. They decided that it would be better for their married life to start to tackle some of these issues, rather than to pretend they didn't exist. By making this decision, Alan and Kerrie avoided beginning their new life with a minimized ritual style that would have affected subsequent rituals and relationships.

They began by finding a minister and a rabbi who would perform an interfaith ceremony. They met several times with the clergy who counseled them to find out from each of their families what symbols and words would be important in their ceremony. This opened a very important dialogue at many levels. Each spoke first to their own parents. Having these talks made them more aware of religious meanings and beliefs in their parents' and grandparents' lives. This led to a deeper discussion between Alan and Kerrie about being an intermarried couple and how they were going to work out their differences. Through hearing what was important to their parents, each learned more about the other's heritage. While not religiously observant themselves, neither one wanted to convert. They agreed to work to respect their differences. They acknowledged that they could not yet figure out how they would raise their children, but promised to go into counseling later if this became an issue they could not resolve on their own. Of most importance, they agreed never to use their children in battles over religion. While they could not fully anticipate what they might later think and feel, Alan and Kerrie were setting up a situation where the subject of their religious differences would be open rather than hidden.

Kerrie went to see her grandmother, who still objected to their marriage. She calmly described the process she and Alan were going through. She let her grandmother know that she would respect her decision, but she hoped her grandmother would come to their wedding. She ended this talk by asking her grandmother if she could wear a piece of her jewelry for the ceremony. While still not agreeing to attend, her grandmother quietly left the room and returned with a pin, given to her by her mother, that she had worn on her own wedding day. As she silently handed this pin to Kerrie, she symbolically expressed her ongoing love, even if she could not give her approval to their intermarriage. By giving Kerrie a pin that had come down the generations, and was worn by women in the family at their weddings, she also symbolically acknowledged that Kerrie would soon be a married woman, one who would maintain connections to her family-of-origin.

While Alan and Kerrie were working on the religious issue, Kerrie began to work on the relationship with her own father. With the coaching of a family therapist, Kerrie spoke separately to each of her parents and told them how important it was to her that they find a way to transcend their bitterness during her wedding. She also decided to walk down the aisle alone, concluding that being "given away" was not a symbolic action that really fit for her.

She and Alan planned a portion of their ceremony in which they would thank each of their parents, including her father and stepfather, for the various roles each had played in bringing them to this point in their lives. They decided to conclude this brief symbolic action, which honored each parent and simultaneously affirmed the new family form that Kerrie came from, by asking for their abiding support in the future.

The relationship work that Kerrie and Alan did took them seven months. "It was the most worthwhile seven months of my life so far," Kerrie said. "We had a real wedding, one that spoke to who we are and who our families are. I can't help but think that we're starting out stronger having done it this way."

As you think about your life-cycle rituals, you will want to consider whether the ritual that exists for this transition fits your situation. It makes little sense to go through the motions of an obligatory ritual that does not express your particular life circumstances. Most often, the ritual you create will contain many elements that are common to that particular life-cycle transition as it exists in the culture, and some new aspects that express your unique conditions.

For example, the wedding ceremony for a remarried couple needs to contain elements that are similar to a first marriage, such as vows between the couple and community witnessing, but it also needs to include different parts that speak to the realities of remarriage. If a couple who are planning to remarry have children from previous marriages, then the ceremony needs to affirm this complicated set of new relationships. When Sophia Gentry, a widow, married Gordon Becker, who was divorced, they each had two children from their prior marriages. In their ceremony, Sophia promised Gordon's children that she would always respect them as children who have two families, and Gordon promised Sophia's children that he would always help them to honor the memory of their father. In offering these brief vows to their children, following their own vows to each other, they marked and began the complex transition to becoming a remarried family.

As described earlier, when Evan's daughter, Jennifer, turned thirteen, having a Bat Mitzvah as a rite of passage was not possible due to her learning handicaps. Rather than omit a rite-of-passage ritual from her life altogether, the family waited until she was nineteen to create a ritual that truly marked her coming of age.

When Sherry and Bruce Callahan had their first baby, they planned a christening ritual that was exactly like all such rituals, with the addition of one aspect. Their baby had been conceived through artificial insemination with donor sperm. They decided well before their baby's birth that they did not want the artificial insemination to be a secret that part of their family knew and others did not know. They also wanted to be able to speak about this easily with their child when the time came, and not let it become a taboo subject. Following the actual christening, Bruce spoke briefly, thanking their anonymous donor for helping them have the precious gift of their baby. "I was so scared to say those words, but when I did, any shame I had previously felt just lifted," Bruce said.

As you look ahead to future life-cycle rituals, you will want to ask yourself how this particular transition is usually marked in your family and in your ethnic and religious group. Begin to compare the meanings expressed in this ritual with what your particular situation requires:

• What symbols and symbolic actions are generally used to make and mark this life-cycle passage?

• Do these symbols and symbolic actions fit your circumstances? If not, what symbols and symbolic actions would better express your unique situation?

• What might you need to subtract from or add to this ritual so that it genuinely reflects yours and your family's needs?

• Does the time chosen for this ritual fit your circumstances? Do you want to select a special time that coincides with an anniversary of a prior change, or conversely, do you want to deliberately avoid connecting this ritual with other important times?

• Does the place chosen for this ritual fit your circumstances? For instance, if you are religious or spiritual, then a house of worship may be the appropriate place. Or there may be special reasons to hold the ritual at your home or another place that holds meaning to you.

• What relationship issues need attention in order for this life-cycle ritual to feel authentic?

Celebration and Healing in Life-Cycle Rituals

Life-cycle rituals tap all of the ways that rituals can work for us— relating, changing, healing, believing, and celebrating. Changing our life status and expressing our beliefs are often the most obvious aspects of these rituals. How they provoke shifts in our relationships is usually only obvious to us long after the ritual, unless, like Alan and Kerrie, we deliberately work on relationships in advance of the ritual event. Most subtle is how these rituals can work to promote healing in the midst of celebration. Often such healing occurs with spontaneous symbolic actions that emerge during a life-cycle ritual. Judy Davis tells about a Bar Mitzvah during which a father handed his son a prayer shawl and prayer book that had belonged to the boy's grandfather, who was no longer living. These religious items had been in the family for five generations. While handing down these important religious and family symbols had been planned, the father's words were unplanned. Before the entire congregation, he told his son what he believed the grandfather would have wanted for him, saying, "Live your life to the fullest! Do what you think is right! What my father gave me above all else was a feeling that I was always loved, that I was always good—and if I could give you anything it would be that."[6] In handing down these symbols and voicing these words, the memory of a grandfather was honored, as were previous generations, and healing merged with celebration in one powerful moment.

Since life-cycle rituals tend to put us in touch with the profound circle of life and death, it is not surprising that healing moments emerge spontaneously during these celebrations. You can also plan a life-cycle ritual to include healing aspects. This may be especially important to consider if a prior loss is preventing a needed life-cycle passage.

"JOANIE HAS A COMMENCEMENT"

Joanie and Jeralynn Thompson were identical twins who had a close and loving relationship. They went away to the same college together and planned to graduate together. During their junior year, Jeralynn developed leukemia and died within the year. When Jeralynn was ill, she talked with Joanie and told her how important it was that Joanie continue college and graduate. Joanie went back to school after her sister's funeral, but she found it impossible to study. At the urging of friends, she took a year off in order to be with her family and begin to deal with the terrible loss of her sister. The year turned into two years and two years into three. Finally, her family began to insist that she go back to college. When she returned to school, she finished all of her courses, but remained unable to do her senior thesis. She was unable to graduate that June. "I don't know how I can graduate without Jeralynn. It'll mean that she's really gone," she told her mother. As her mother began to understand just what was stopping Joanie from finishing, she began to talk with her about how they might honor Jeralynn's life and still celebrate Joanie entering adulthood with her college graduation. She developed her plan with Joanie, who then finished her thesis in time to graduate the following December.

They planned a special ceremony to be held two nights before Joanie's graduation. They invited extended family and close friends, asking them to bring symbols of Jeralynn and to speak about her openly. During a very moving ceremony, many people spoke about what they thought Jeralynn would have wished for Joanie. One aunt made a video that had no people in it, but portrayed places that the two sisters had both loved. At the end she told Joanie, "These places still belong to you." Joanie's father brought photographs of several pets that the twins had raised, and carefully explained what contributions Jeralynn had made to these animals and what things Joanie had given them that were different. In a five-minute talk, he highlighted the strengths and gifts of each young woman, and gave Joanie permission to be her own person. People grieved the loss of Jeralynn openly and fully and then embraced Joanie for finishing school and going on in life.

Several months later, settled in a new job as a teacher, Joanie talked about this ceremony and her graduation. "They all helped me to graduate. If we hadn't had our memorial first, I know all I would have been wondering about on graduation day was what my family was feeling about Jeralynn's death. Instead all of it was out in the open. We could be sad together and then we could be happy together on my graduation day. They call graduation a commencement, an ending that's really a beginning, and that's what mine was. I miss my sister terribly—I'll always miss her. My family and friends helped me take the next step in my life, and Jeralynn's spirit was right there with me."

If a particular loss seems to be preventing you or your family from moving forward and making appropriate life-cycle rituals, you may want to think about ways to make a special memorial either prior to or as a short part of the ritual. Since rituals can hold dual realities and simultaneously express contradictions of joy and pain, you can place healing in the midst of a life-cycle celebration. Think about what symbols and brief words might enable such healing. Often something as simple as a toast offered with your belief about what a deceased family member or friend would have hoped for this life-cycle passage can bring solace and greater authenticity to a life-cycle ritual.

When Life-Cycle Rituals Go "Off Track"

"OUR WEDDING WAS THE PITS!"

When Mary and Frank McAllister came for couples' therapy, they had already been separated four times. They could not seem to get together and they could not seem to get apart. Their fourteen-year marriage had been marked by periods of intense conflict alternating with quiet but largely distant times. "It's never been right between us, not from the very start," Mary said. Their therapist decided to find out about their wedding, the life-cycle ritual that marked "the very start."

"Our wedding was the pits!" Frank remarked. They went on to

explain that Mary had been pregnant and that her father simply demanded that they get married. "The priest said we had to turn around to the congregation to say our vows, and there were his parents and my parents staring up at us—I felt so ashamed. I just hated it."

Their first life-cycle ritual as a couple, their wedding, came about in a context of shame and intimidation. When their baby was born with cerebral palsy, they decided not to have a christening ceremony. "I just couldn't go back into that church for another one of those gatherings— I felt sure our families thought we got what we deserved," Mary said. Here, an obligatory wedding ritual led to an interrupted ritual style, and the McAllisters set off on a life with little joy and much turmoil.

Life-cycle rituals can go "off track" for many different reasons. The true purpose of the ritual may be distorted by shame, as it was for the McAllisters. The person or the relationship for whom the ritual is intended may get lost in a flurry of elaborate preparations. The ritual may be overshadowed or intruded upon by a traumatic event that occurs close in time to the important life-cycle passage. Already troubled family relationships may overwhelm the ritual. Or the ritual may be unbalanced, reflecting the needs and desires of only one part of the family.

Since life-cycle rituals work to change our sense of ourselves and to transform our central relationships, there can be lasting and profound effects when these rituals go awry. Many families date major relationship cutoffs and painfully unresolved conflicts from interactions during life-cycle rituals. When a life-cycle ritual is recalled with pain and disappointment, subsequent rituals, such as birthdays, anniversaries, or holidays, are often interrupted or minimized.

"GRANDPA DIED ON GINA'S GRADUATION DAY"
Gina Torini was the first person in her family to finish high school. Her entire extended family had migrated to the United States from Italy twenty years earlier. As her graduation day approached, there was much excitement. Everyone seemed to sense that this graduation was both for Gina and for the whole family, as it marked their success in their new country. Her parents planned an elaborate party to mark this rite of passage for their daughter and for themselves.

Two days before the graduation ceremony, Gina's grandfather had a massive heart attack. He died the morning of the graduation. All of the festivities were, of course, canceled. Many months later, Gina went over to the school alone and picked up her diploma. Her graduation was never mentioned again in the family.

Gina's story is not unusual. A severe illness or death immediately preceding or immediately following an important life-cycle ritual will frequently derail the important meanings of such a transition. Gina's graduation was lost in the family's grief and shock and was never recovered. Rather than moving on in life and going to college as had been planned, Gina remained at home. If your own family or a given member of your family appears to be stuck and not moving forward in time, you may want to review previous life-cycle rituals to discover if a particular ritual went off track. Think about what ways this might have influenced your family's development.

Redoing a Life-Cycle Ritual That Has Gone "Off Track"

If you determine that one of your central life-cycle rituals has gone "off track," you may want to think about making the ritual over. This may involve a new wedding ceremony, a confirmation, a Bar Mitzvah, or a graduation later in life, or a memorial service many years after an unmourned death. Redoing life-cycle rituals can provide renewal in relationships and heal long-standing pain and anguish.

"Brett Buries His Father"

Brett Atkins was eleven years old when his father died of cancer. His mother and grandparents decided he was too young to go to the funeral, and he was left with neighbors while the ceremony took place. After the burial everyone returned home. "There was lots of food. It seemed like a party. People were sitting around talking about my father. I was just sure he would walk in any minute, and I became angrier and angrier when he didn't."

Following this confusing event, Brett began to build his life around his father. He took all of his father's pictures out of the family album and put them up in his room. Gradually, his room seemed to turn into a shrine to his father. Teachers complained to his mother that he wrote all of his school papers idealizing his father. His mother tried to talk to him about what was happening, but Brett refused to talk.

When Brett was eighteen, he took down all of his father's pictures. At first, his mother was relieved, but he soon began to get into trouble. Finally, just before he should have graduated, he was arrested for bringing marijuana to school. Not surprising, Brett got into difficulties just before the first major life-cycle ritual to occur without his father. At this point, Brett's mother decided to seek a family therapist.

During the therapy, the subject of Brett's father, his death, his funeral, and Brett's actions after the funeral were explored. The therapist counseled Brett to begin to find out more about his father by talking to various family members. At first, his mother was upset by this, but she began to see her son calming down and functioning well for the first time in many years. Brett began to learn that his father was a real human being, with many good qualities and some foibles, as well. After Brett gathered a lot of material about his father, the therapist coached him to make a new funeral, one that he could attend. Brett talked to his mother and explained what he wanted to do. He chose to hold this ceremony on the anniversary of his father's original funeral, the one he had not been allowed to attend. He talked to the family's minister, who had officiated at his father's original funeral, and asked for his help. With his mother's support, he talked to family members and asked them to please come to a memorial service for his father.

At the ceremony, Brett read a letter he had written to his father. In the letter, he detailed many of the things he had learned about his father from talking to relatives, both the good and the not so good. He spoke of his father with caring and humor, relating incidents he had recently learned about. He ended his letter, "I miss you. I remember the summer you taught me to ride a bike. Now I can drive a car. I wish you were here to see me do it. I remember when we went camping and I got lost and you found me. I got lost again after you died. I have to let you go now and find myself. I'll always love you." Following the service, Brett and his mother went out to the cemetery for the first time. After redoing this crucial life-cycle ritual that Brett had missed earlier, he returned to school and graduated.

Redoing life-cycle rituals most often requires a period of work on the relationships and aspects of your life that have become frozen since the ritual went "off track." There is no point in making a second wedding ceremony that only repeats the difficulties of the first wedding. If relationship cutoffs have ensued from a life-cycle ritual, you will need to do careful work to open and reestablish relationships. While redoing the life-cycle ritual may be your ultimate goal, the road to this point needs to be carefully walked. Life-cycle rituals are not simply discrete events. They are part of an ongoing process of self and relationship transition and change occurring before, during, and following the actual ritual.

Take some time to review the major life-cycle rituals that have affected your life:

• Did the ritual live up to most of your expectations, or was it disappointing to you in some significant way? Has this disappointment lasted far beyond the ritual?

• Was relationship development enhanced by the ritual, or did any relationships become frozen or cut off?

• Can you speak about the ritual, or has it become a taboo subject?

• Is there a life-cycle ritual that you would like to do over? Try to imagine all of the details of how it might be different this time. What relationships and issues will you need to address in order to create a meaningful ritual?

• Is there a part of a life-cycle ritual you would like to redo? For instance, you may want to redo your wedding vows without making a whole new wedding.

When Life-Cycle Rituals Are Trivialized

Life-cycle rituals have the capacity to bring us in touch with the sacred and mysterious aspects of human existence—birth, growth, sexuality, love, and death. At the same time, like all rituals they are embedded in and reflect current social and cultural values. Perhaps more than any other category of ritual, when we look at our life-cycle rituals, we look into a mirror reflecting what is most important to us as a community.

In the 1980s, many life-cycle rituals such as weddings or adolescent rites of passage like Bar Mitzvah, confirmation, or high school graduation became trivialized by an overemphasis on material display. Popular articles on weddings went on for pages about expensive gowns, food, caterers, and wedding bands, while omitting any reference to the essential meanings about commitment and the profound changes in family relationships that a wedding actually symbolizes. In our work as family therapists, we have seen well-to-do families go into debt for a wedding, and poor families struggle to gather the three or four hundred dollars or more needed to meet all of the expenses connected with a high school graduation. When financial costs overwhelm the intended meanings of a life-cycle ritual, something has gone very wrong with our ritual life at a cultural level.

Changes in our own values may not be adequately reflected in a life-cycle ritual, leaving us feeling empty. For instance, ties to established religion are less intense for many people, making religious funeral rituals less familiar and less meaningful. The funeral ritual, whose purpose is to celebrate a life now gone and offer comfort and begin healing for the living, may not do so. Cathryn Morehouse spoke poignantly to us about her father's funeral: "The minister didn't really know Daddy. He talked a little bit to each of us and then wrote his eulogy, which sounded so canned. I was so disturbed by his words that I didn't experience any sense of comfort."

Life-cycle rituals may also be separated from their spiritual, emotional, and developmental power when they become attached to industries that overwhelm our personal choices. When Bar Mitzvahs become "theme parties" run by consultants, and funeral visitation is done by driving up to a video screen to view a dead body, then we need to stop and ask ourselves what we really want to be expressing in our life-cycle rituals.

If you find yourself more caught up in the "show" than in the substance of an important life-cycle ritual, it may be that this serves as a distraction from difficult internal or relationship issues raised by the impending ritual. For instance, when Sally Masterson was getting married, her parents were in the midst of a bitter divorce. Rather than deal directly with the many issues storming through the family, Sally and her mother got busy planning an incredibly elaborate wedding that ended up costing Sally's father $50,000. Determined to be seen as generous by his daughter, Sally's father took each suggestion by her mother and made it even more costly. The gowns and flowers and food were visually exquisite, but everyone felt the enormous but unspoken tension. Years later, Sally remarked, "My parents tried to do the right thing. Unfortunately, my wedding got caught in the conflict between them. I think it was especially hard for any of us to think about commitment at a time when my parents' long marriage was disintegrating. It was quite a show, but it didn't belong to me and my husband."

If you are anticipating a particular life-cycle ritual, you may want to spend some time focusing on the values you and your family would like this ritual to express.

• Whose values are these?

• Where do they come from? Deep inside yourself? Your family? Your ethnic or religious group?

• What pressure are you experiencing to make this ritual conform to commercial values?

• In what ways might family relationship struggles overwhelm the values you want this ritual to express?

When No Life-Cycle Rituals Exist for an Important Transition: Creating New Life-Cycle Rituals

There are many crucial life-cycle transitions for which there are no familiar and accepted rituals in our culture. In your own life or in the lives of those close to you, you may have experienced such changes. Life-cycle changes that often go unmarked include divorce, the end of a nonmarried relationship, adoption, forming a committed homosexual relationship, leaving home (especially the leaving home of a handicapped young adult not previously expected to leave), pregnancy loss, and menopause. There may be other central changes in your own life for which there were no rituals to ease the transition. Or you may be anticipating such a transition. Since life-cycle rituals enable us to begin to rework our sense of self and our relationships as required by life's changes, the lack of such rituals can make change more difficult.

Fortunately, we live in a time when many people have begun to think about creating new rituals for previously unmarked and uncelebrated life-cycle changes. Knowledge about creating life-cycle rituals no longer belongs only to religious institutions. Social movements and support groups have recognized the importance of developing new life-cycle rituals, such as gay weddings, menopause celebrations, or ceremonies to mark the loss of a pregnancy. Individuals and couples have developed their own divorce rituals in order to mark the end of a marriage and to invite comfort from friends and family.

"THE HOUSE-COOLING PARTY"

When Candice Meyers's husband, Brent, suddenly left her for another woman, she was devastated. They had been married for six years, and had recently been talking about having a baby. Unbeknownst to Candice, her husband had actually been thinking about separating for over a year. After leaving, he moved swiftly to get a divorce.

When her husband left, Candice withdrew from all of her friends and family. She became more and more isolated and stopped participating in any family rituals. Realizing how depressed she was becoming, she decided to seek some therapy. During her meetings with Evan, Candice began to explore the many losses connected to her divorce—her husband, a hoped-for baby, and all of her previously rich relationships with friends and family.

Candice felt ashamed that she had been left by her husband, and stopped inviting anyone to her home. Having people over and hosting them by herself seemed to underscore her abandonment. This was in marked contrast to her earlier life with Brent, when her home had been the center of activity for her large extended family and friends. She called her house "her loneliness and her memories" and she decided to begin the difficult process of change demanded by her divorce by buying some new furniture.

As she decorated her home with changes that reflected her tastes rather than her former husband's, Candice realized that she was still having difficulty even imagining having people over. "I feel like a strange sort of prisoner in my own house. But I'm not locked in—other people are locked out."

Evan began to set the groundwork for a life-cycle ritual that would mark Candice's divorce and ease her passage into her new life as a single woman. Since Candice felt she had "locked people out," she and her therapist agreed that a new lock on the front door would be a necessary symbol to express many changes. Candice agreed to buy a new lock and to sit with this lock for one hour each day for a week, asking herself, "What would it take to put this new lock on my door—a lock that I could open to family and friends?"

As Candice pondered this question, she experienced many emotions. At first, she felt very sad, remembering all the earlier good times with her husband and their family and friends. After a few days, however, she became very angry at the way Brent had treated her. This was the first time she realized just how betrayed and angry she felt. Following this sense of anger, she began to reclaim her own life. She decided to make a special ritual that she called a "house-cooling party." The purpose of this ritual was to announce her new life and her new availability to family and friends. She said, "People usually have house-warming parties when they move to a new home. I'm moving to a new period of my life. I'd like to mark my divorce with a bit of humor and have a 'house-cooling' party." She designed an invitation that read: "Please come to my house-cooling party. Please do bring gifts appropriate for the lovely home of a single woman—I need to replace the 'his and her' stuff!" Just before the party, she hired a locksmith to put the new lock on her front door.[7]

Life-cycle rituals for newly formed or newly acknowledged life-cycle transitions use many of the elements that are common to more familiar rituals, including symbols and symbolic action, gathering a community of witnesses to give public support to the life-cycle passage, and drawing up documents or certificates that mark the particular change. In this way, new life-cycle rituals can connect us to the universality of change in human life. The specific symbols and symbolic actions selected for newly created rituals may express the uniqueness or difference in this particular life-cycle transition. Thus Candice used a new lock to symbolize that she was solely in charge of her life now. The "house-cooling" party was a symbolic action to announce her divorce and ask for support. Her preparation for the ritual, both through therapy and through sitting each day with the lock, resembled the preparation connected with all major life-cycle rituals. The invitation that she creatively crafted became the "document" to announce her divorce. Friends and family gathered to witness and celebrate her transition, just as they would for any life-cycle ritual.

LEAVING HOME: AN OFTEN UNMARKED LIFE-CYCLE PASSAGE

One of the most critical changes in any family occurs when a child leaves home. When your child is ready to leave, you need to figure out how to give "permission" to go. All of the established relationships in your family will undergo change. Parents who were very close to a child in ways that minimized couple time may need to reexamine their relationship with each other. Single parents who relied on a child may need to call upon new resources. And parent and child both are challenged to develop an adult-to-adult relationship with each other.[8]

Like many life-cycle passages, a child leaving home is an event that carries deeply mixed feelings, including a sense of joy and accomplishment, fear regarding what lies ahead, sadness over the loss of relationships in their present form, and curious anticipation over what life will look like next. Many families find that the period before a child leaves is fraught with conflict and arguments. Leaving mad seems to feel easier than leaving sad. In our experience as family therapists, however, when young people leave home in anger, the leaving transition takes longer to work out, and may be marked by many repeated comings and goings. Issues belonging to one's family-of-origin then get carried into subsequent relationships. Creating a leaving-home ritual, whose symbols and symbolic actions speak to the many contradictory issues, can ease this passage for everyone in the family.

The life-cycle passage of leaving home may be even more difficult when the leaving is unanticipated, such as when a handicapped young adult leaves home who was never expected to do so, or when a younger child leaves home in a custody shift.

"THE GIVING OF GIFTS: A LEAVING-HOME RITUAL"

Karen Berry, twenty-two, was a mentally handicapped young woman who lived at home with her parents and her twenty-year-old brother, Andrew. When Karen was born, her parents were determined to raise her and never to place her in an institution. They could not imagine that she would be able to leave home and live in the community. When Karen was an adolescent, however, community group homes began to be established. Still, the Berrys were skeptical and simply assumed Karen would remain with them.

When Karen became a teenager, her parents grew worried that she would be exploited sexually. Andrew became her protector. He gave up many of his own interests in order to escort her to events from her special school. Any thought of going away to college disappeared for him.

When she turned twenty, Karen's school began pressuring the Berrys to let her live in a group home. Each time the parents seemed close to agreeing, however, fighting broke out at home between them and Karen, convincing them that she was not ready to leave.

When the parents consulted Evan about their dilemma, it seemed clear that the family was just on the verge of Karen leaving home, but seemed to get stuck in ways that prevented her actual leaving. The parents agreed that Karen should move to the group home. They liked the home and the staff, but they were unable to choose a date for her to go.

Evan talked to them about all of the issues involved when any child leaves home. She raised with them the idea of making a leaving-home ritual for Karen, in order to mark this important passage and to ease everyone's way.

The parents and Andrew were asked to prepare gifts for Karen to take to her new home. These gifts were not to be bought in a store, but rather were to be something that belonged to them that they believed would help Karen on her way. Karen was asked to prepare gifts for her mother, her father, and Andrew, consisting of items that belonged to her that she thought should remain with them when she moved out.

During a two-week period, the family prepared their gifts secretly. In these two weeks, all arguments stopped, and the parents and Karen agreed on a date for her to move to the group home, which they had not been able to do before. As in all life-cycle rituals, this preparation period served as a signal for the changes that were coming.

Then the family held their gift-giving and receiving ritual. Mr. Berry handed the first gift to Karen. It was an odd-shaped package, which turned out to be his favorite frying pan. The family had a weekly Sunday breakfast ritual during which Mr. Berry cooked pancakes. When Karen was learning cooking skills in school, she had wanted to use his frying pan, but her father had been afraid she would ruin it. He gave her the frying pan and said he would teach her to make the pancakes for the people in her new home. With this one gift, he acknowledged her development, her readiness for the next phase in her life, and the changes that would need to occur in the family's old weekly ritual.

Mrs. Berry gave Karen two small boxes. The first contained a partly used bottle of perfume. The second held a pair of pearl earrings. Karen had not been allowed to wear perfume or jewelry. As a teen, she used to sneak into her mother's room and use her perfume, only to be scolded when she appeared at the supper table doused in fragrance. "I think you're old enough for these now," her mother said. "These earrings belonged to my mother. She gave them to me when I left home and now I'm giving them to you." Her gift affirmed Karen as an emerging young woman, and connected three generations of women in their family. Karen cried softly and thanked her mother.

Andrew's gift shifted the mood profoundly. He gave Karen a box of birdseed. With Karen's moving out, Andrew had quickly made plans to go away to college. He had a pet parakeet that would need care, and he had secured permission from the group home for Karen to bring the bird. This gift symbolized new responsibility for Karen, since all through their growing up, only Andrew had been expected to care for the family's pets. Mrs. Berry breathed a sigh of relief that the parakeet was leaving home, too.

Following Karen's receipt of her gifts, she began to hand out the ones she had prepared. She gave her mother her very favorite stuffed bear, which she had slept with since childhood. "I can't sleep with this in my new home—please keep it for me." This gift spoke of her own knowledge that she was growing up, and that she knew what would be appropriate in her new setting. She handed her father a photograph that had been taken of her at a visit to the group home, portraying her at a table with four young men. "These are my new friends," she explained. This gift directly confronted the family's fears of her moving away from their protection. Finally, she handed Andrew her clock radio, a prized possession that had been an earlier Christmas gift. She looked at her brother and said, "Don't be late for school!" She chose a gift that symbolized the many changes the family was facing.

Following this very moving leaving-home ritual, in which family members spoke volumes to each other through their gifts, Karen moved into the group home and Andrew left for college. Like most young adults who leave home, they visited their parents on holidays and special occasions.[9]

You can use variations of the "giving of gifts" ritual in your own family when any child is leaving. We have seen families who are in the midst of bitter custody changes alter the entire meaning of the leaving through this ritual. Some families have created leaving-home rituals that use an album as the central gift, detailing the young person's life and leaving a section blank to be filled in with future life experiences. Still other families have written special leaving-home documents to mark this passage. The Gable family prepared a "certificate of leaving home" for their son, Joseph, detailing all of his accomplishments as a young adult and declaring him to be "ready for life in the outside world." They framed this document and Joseph hung it in his first apartment. Permission to go and acknowledgments of deep ongoing connections are expressed in these rituals that require family members to reflect carefully on their symbols in order to express what relationships have meant in the past and will mean in the future.

If you are currently experiencing or anticipating major changes in your life for which there are no familiar and accepted life-cycle rituals, or if you feel that an important change in the past went unmarked and is still unresolved, you may want to think about creating a new ritual:

- What is the change you are experiencing or anticipating? (It may be that this change occurred quite a while ago, like a miscarriage, but had no ritual to help you to deal with the loss.)

- What aspects of yourself and of your relationships will be touched by this transition?

- How would you most like to mark this transition?

- What are the necessary symbols and symbolic actions?

- Who are the people you would like to gather to witness this life-cycle transition?

- What would you put into a document or a certificate to mark this change?

Life-cycle rituals ease our passage through life. They shape our relationships, help to heal our losses, express our deepest beliefs, and celebrate our existence. They announce change and create change. The power of life-cycle rituals belongs to all of us. You and your family can make life-cycle rituals that are rich with meaning. As you plan, be sure to leave some aspects of the ritual open and unplanned, since this is where rituals' magic will emerge—unanticipated relationship connections, a new sense of self, brief memorials to heal losses during celebrations, and expressions of deeply held values.

12

Keeping Your Rituals Alive

WHERE TO GO FROM HERE

AS YOU HAVE READ through this book, you have no doubt remembered many rituals from your childhood and reflected on the rituals in your adult life. Perhaps your memories of rituals were rich and satisfying; perhaps some were tinged with sadness, anger, or regret; and perhaps some were frustrating as you recalled the same old rituals that everyone in the family truly wished would change. Whether you have thought about holiday celebrations from when you were younger or last night's family dinner, likely you have also been considering how you would like your ritual life to be now and in the future.

How Not to Become the Ritual "Boss"—
Engaging Others

If, on the one hand, you are excited about revitalizing old rituals or creating totally new ones, and on the other, you have read this book without the participation of your family or friendship network doing so, you run the risk of becoming the ritual "boss." You'll know if this is happening if you find that *all* of the ideas about rituals come from you and you remain more invested in the planning and outcome of rituals than anyone else. To avoid this burdensome and thankless role, you will need to share your interest in ways that invite participation from your spouse, your children, extended family, and friends.

THE TURKEY BELONGS TO ME

Every year after New Year's, Cora Mathison collapsed in exhaustion. The holidays were over and she needed January to recoup. As Cora talked about the period from Thanksgiving to New Year's, it was little wonder that she required a period of recovery. Refusing her family's help, she put on dinners for thirty or more people for Thanksgiving, Christmas Eve, and Christmas, and on New Year's she always made a huge open house for all of their neighbors.

Cora came from a family where there were no holiday celebrations, no birthday parties, no rituals. Even daily dinners were "catch as catch can." Her parents had been continually and bitterly angry with each other throughout her childhood, and finally divorced when she was fifteen. "They couldn't even take time out from their fights to make Christmas for us kids—I was determined that it would be different when I had my own family," Cora said. And different it was! Cora went to the other extreme, creating elaborate holidays, lavish birthday parties, and uniquely memorable anniversaries. One year when her mother-in-law offered to make the Christmas turkey, Cora found herself snapping, "The turkey belongs to me!" Then she began to cry. When she began to reflect on what she had said and all of the pain and anger she felt in saying it, Cora started to realize that something was quite amiss. "I wanted to control all of the rituals—it was like I couldn't trust anyone else to even have a finger in any of it. I was too afraid that if I didn't do all of it, the rituals would disappear and I'd be living my childhood all over again."

Cora sat her husband and children down and told them the story of her own childhood, something they had never heard in detail before. She told them what it was like to watch other children have birthday parties and never have one. She told them about the year her mother made a meatloaf for Thanksgiving, "not because we couldn't afford a turkey, but just to get back at my father." And she told them that she was exhausted, and that all of their rituals had become sadly dissatisfying to her.

She then heard for the first time what the holidays and family traditions had become to her husband and children. "I've been wishing we'd stop all of this, simplify it, but I haven't known how to tell you," her husband said. "It's gotten so out of hand—more and more each year, but it all seemed so important to you." Cora's children let her know that they wanted some of their ideas considered, especially for their birthdays. They all told her there were many things they would like to do to participate in making *family* rituals, not what her son called "Mom's rituals." The family began to embark on whole new ways of creating their rituals. When the following Thanksgiving came, they talked over who would do what. They pared down their guest list to their immediate family and in-laws. They decided they wanted to go to Manhattan in the morning to see the annual Macy's parade, which then became a whole new part of their celebration. Three weeks before Thanksgiving, Cora phoned her mother-in-law and asked her to make the turkey.

While Cora had become the ritual "boss" in her family due to the anguishing experiences in her childhood, it's all too easy to slip into this role if you are the one who knows more about rituals, or who shows more of an interest than other family members. If you come from a family where only one person was in charge of family rituals, this role will seem familiar to you, and all too easy to assume. In Cora's family, it took a crisis to begin to change this pattern. You can work on this *before* there is a crisis and before you become exhausted and resentful.

Keep in mind that there will always be differing levels of eagerness and participation to reflect, create, and enter into family rituals. Conversations about rituals should be done with a spirit of exploration and willingness to hear everyone's point of view. Part of being flexible in your ritual style involves making room for people who might have less enthusiasm than you.

Looking at Rituals—a True "Photo Opportunity"

A nonthreatening way to engage other people in a discussion about rituals is to bring out some photographs or videos of previous rituals, and open a conversation about what people remember, what each one liked about this occasion, what was satisfying, what was enriching. As people begin to recall positive parts of the experience, it becomes safer to begin to talk about what might have been dissatisfying or uncomfortable. If you have been the sole ritual maker, it may be difficult for you to hear complaints—try to listen with a spirit of openness. If you want to avoid becoming the ritual "boss," you will need to guard against taking responsibility for all of the changes people may be saying that they want. Spend some time asking each family member or close friend what he or she might be willing to do to make the next ritual more satisfying. Remember that small changes are more likely to be effective. As people gain a sense of their own successful participation in ritual making, they will want to do more.

If some of your ritual photographs are action-oriented and not simply portraits, you will have an opportunity to see your family making their rituals. If you look at twelve years of Christmas photos and always see Mother serving, Father carving, children decorating the tree, and Uncle Jim asleep in front of the TV, you will all likely get some thoughts about what might be different and who can make that difference happen.

TELLING AND HEARING RITUAL STORIES
Taking some time to tell stories about previous rituals is another way to draw people into a process of ritual reflection, and ultimately broader participation. The Luggard family has an annual gathering on New Year's Day during which each family member tells a story of a favorite ritual from the year gone by and what made it so good. This storytelling leads naturally to a discussion of what they want to preserve and what they want to change. The Scalas tell stories of previous birthdays as part of their birthday celebrations, and thereby connect family members with a sense of shared rituals.

Gerald Golden felt that his family had fallen away from having meaningful rituals. Many family members had moved away and they seldom gathered anymore. He decided to collect brief stories on audiotape of past rituals from his parents and grandparents. He made copies of these tapes and sent them to his siblings and cousins. Three months later, his cousin, Jonathan, called to suggest that they organize a family reunion. Gerry had actually thought about a reunion earlier, but he didn't think others would be interested and he didn't want to organize it all by himself. His ritual story tapes had sparked an interest in many members of the family, and the reunion became a much easier event to create.

When Sara Ogden felt that too much of her family's ritual life had fallen on her to create and maintain, she organized "funniest moments in our family's history of birthdays, anniversaries, holidays, vacations, and other momentous occasions," and asked her husband and four children to make skits about their rituals. In her own skit, she made fun of herself rushing around making sure the ritual was "just right." Her children parodied the annual "night before vacation family fight." George, her husband, playing both himself and his wife in a series of quick costume changes, perfectly captured her enthusiasm and his cynical approach to family rituals, a pattern that had escalated through the years. These skits led to an open discussion of their differences and the first examination of George's childhood experiences with very painful rituals in an alcoholic family. The entrenched pattern of Sara as the "ritual maker, ritual cheerleader, and ritual boss" and George as the "reluctant guest" began to shift.

Jacqueline LaBray used a creative approach to stories in order to move out of an overly central role in all of her family's rituals. At the close of yet another Mother's Day during which she had been responsible for a celebration of her own mother, her mother-in-law, her grandmother, and *herself*, she asked her husband and two children to each tell a brief story about next year's Mother's Day and what it would be like. A bit puzzled, they each recited a similar story, describing the same kind of Mother's Day they always had. When it was Jacqueline's turn, she told them the story of her next "Mother's Day" and proceeded to describe a day in which she made a special breakfast only for her own mother, while her husband took his mother out for lunch, and came home in time to help his children make a special surprise dinner for her. Her family got the message of this future fantasy. You may want to try this with other rituals in order to discover what various family members might imagine for a future ritual. This can lead easily to a discussion of what is going well and what people might like to experiment with changing.

Revitalizing Your Rituals—One Ritual at a Time

Now that you have read about four types of rituals (daily rituals, traditions, holidays, and life-cycle rituals), five ways that rituals work (relating, changing, healing, believing, and celebrating), six ritual styles (minimized, interrupted, rigid, obligatory, imbalanced, and flexible), and all of the ways to use symbols, symbolic action, time, and place to make rituals, you may be thinking that you need to set about reshaping *all* of your rituals, complete with massive lists and charts. Or you may be considering adding lots of new rituals. Or you may be feeling that there is so much to do regarding rituals that it's all too overwhelming. Rather than moving in any of these directions, we want to propose that you go slowly to revitalize your rituals. Remember that the aim is not to have lots and lots of rituals, but to have meaningful ones. If you choose just one ritual and experiment with ways to make it rich and satisfying for yourself and those close to you, many roads for other rituals in your life will open.

SELECTING ONE TYPE OF RITUAL FOR ATTENTION

A good way to begin renewing your rituals is to think about the four types of rituals. As you do this, you will likely discover that one category—for instance, daily rituals—attracts more of your attention and interest than the others. It may be that one of the four types of rituals is more uniformly dissatisfying or disappointing. Or a particular type of ritual, such as a holiday celebration, may be occurring in the near future. Perhaps an important life-cycle ritual is six months away and occupies much of your thought.

As you focus on one of the four types of rituals, you can refine your attention further by selecting one ritual within a category. Thus, within the broader category of daily rituals, you may decide that saying "hello" and "good-bye" needs some attention between you and your partner, or that all of your family traditions feel satisfying except for vacations.

As you consider all of the rituals in your life, you may decide that what you most want to experiment with is a ritual that is missing. Many busy families who don't have time to eat together most of the week decide to try a weekend dinner or brunch. Through this they often rediscover what families one or two generations ago found to be so meaningful about Sunday dinners, or they find some brand new ways to be together. Abe and Vera Connelly realized that they had given their wedding anniversary short shrift over the years because they had married on Christmas Eve and were always too overwhelmed with Christmas. They couldn't figure out how to mark their anniversaries without upsetting many established Christmas Eve traditions that included their children and extended family. They decided to experiment with moving this missing ritual to the first Sunday after Christmas and to make a private celebration that included revisiting the local community college campus where they first met.

RITUAL STYLES REVISITED

As you reflect on the rituals in your life, likely you will find that your ritual style differs for the four different types of ritual. You may, for example, find that your daily rituals and immediate family traditions are quite flexible, while your holiday rituals have become imbalanced due to extended family pressures. Or you may be quite satisfied with the flexibility in your daily rituals, traditions, and holiday celebrations, but life-cycle rituals, involving the in-gathering of many relatives, have become totally interrupted due to family conflicts and cutoffs.

In deciding how to address your ritual style, you may decide that one particular type of ritual may hold more possibilities for you or your family for addressing some of the larger issues connected to ritual style. For instance, you might decide that changing an imbalanced ritual style will be best worked on through holiday rituals that reflect only your partner's way of doing things. Or you may feel that your daily rituals have become too haphazard and interrupted by the demands of work and school.

You can use the ritual style chart below to determine where you want to put your attention. Jot some notes in the boxes about how you see your own and your family's ritual style across the four types of rituals. Ask for other family members' input and compare their responses with yours. Has your evening meal become so minimized that family mem-

Ritual Styles Revisited

RITUAL STYLE

RITUAL TYPE	MINIMIZED	INTERRUPTED	RIGID	OBLIGATORY	IMBALANCED	FLEXIBLE
Daily 1. Hello and good-bye 2. Bedtime 3. Meals 4. Once a week						
Traditions 1. Birthdays 2. Anniversaries 3. Vacations 4. Reunions 5. Seasonal 6. Other						
Holiday Celebrations 1. Religious 2. Religious and secular 3. Secular						
Life Cycle 1. Birth of children 2. Adolescent rites of passage 3. Weddings 4. Funerals, memorials 5. New life-cycle events						

bers have no opportunity to connect each day? Have holidays been interrupted by a death in the family? Since ritual style so often reflects important dimensions of your family's history and current relationships, working on just one ritual can have positive reverberating effects in other parts of your life. Questions and conversation regarding ritual style and the four types of rituals can help you decide where to begin.

RITUALS' PURPOSES REVISITED

You can also select one ritual category for attention through a careful consideration of how you want rituals to work for you. Would relationships in your life be improved by a different kind of nightly dinner? Would the impending change in your parents' lives be eased by marking your father's retirement with a special ritual? Might healing be evoked in a broken friendship by working together on a ritual of reconciliation? Can you imagine a more satisfying way to express your beliefs to your children in a bedtime ritual? Is celebration of some key aspect of your family's life best expressed in a family reunion?

You can use the ritual purposes chart below to ask yourself what purposes are being served in the four types of rituals in your life. Remember, too, that any one ritual can be quite efficient in carrying out multiple purposes, including ones you hadn't even considered. A bedtime ritual can enable warm relating between a father and his children, while also being a time to express and share beliefs, and a time to acknowledge changes in a youngster's growing competencies. A Passover Seder can celebrate freedom, bring extended family and friends together, honor changes in participants from one year to the next, express religious beliefs, and heal losses through moments of remembering those who have died. As you work with this chart, write down some notes in the boxes about how your rituals are working for you now and how you would like them to work in the future. Ask for ideas from other family members and friends. You may find that there is a particular ritual for which you would like to develop a purpose that seems missing. For instance, you may discover that your Christmas ritual enables people to express their deeply held religious beliefs, but that individuals remain too distant and unknown to one another. You can begin to think about and talk over ways to enable more genuine relating to occur next Christmas. Or you may find that as you plan for a baby-welcoming ritual, you want to include

Ritual Purposes Revisited

RITUAL PURPOSE

RITUAL TYPE	RELATING	CHANGING	HEALING	BELIEVING	CELEBRATING
Daily 1. Hello and good-bye 2. Bedtime 3. Meals 4. Once a week					
Traditions 1. Birthdays 2. Anniversaries 3. Vacations 4. Reunions 5. Seasonal 6. Other					
Holiday Celebrations 1. Religious 2. Religious and secular 3. Secular					
Life Cycle 1. Birth of children 2. Adolescent rites of passage 3. Weddings 4. Funerals, memorials 5. New life-cycle events					

a brief moment to honor a relative who is ill and cannot attend, thereby using rituals' capacity to make relationship connections. Reflecting on rituals' purposes and the four types of rituals can guide where you would like to start.

THINKING ABOUT LIFE-CYCLE STAGES

Once you have decided to focus on a particular ritual, you need to consider your own and your family's life-cycle stage and how this might affect any given ritual.[1] As you have discovered in reading this book, rituals look and feel different if you are newly married and trying to figure out whose family you will spend Easter with, or if you are recently divorced and coping with custody and visitation issues that affect daily rituals, birthday parties, vacations, and holiday celebrations. Ritual making and participating are quite distinct if you are a single adult who lives far away from any family and you are trying to create a friendship network to make rituals, or if you are a remarried family trying both to honor the past and create a new present set of relationships across all of your rituals.

Life-cycle issues directly affect participation in rituals. When your family has adolescents, there may be a period of time when these teenagers are less involved with family rituals. Or they may begin to create new boundaries for your family, bringing home boyfriends and girlfriends to participate in what were formerly "family only" rituals. If you have aging parents, your rituals will naturally begin to change in ways that include where the ritual is held and who prepares it. You may also decide as parents and other relatives grow older that it's time to deliberately include storytelling or interviewing them about their lives as part of your rituals.

Very few individuals or families fall neatly into a given life-cycle stage. Your own family may simultaneously be dealing with divorce, teenagers, and aging parents, any one of which can profoundly affect your rituals. When these or other life-cycle stages occur all at once, your ritual life may feel a bit chaotic at first. What is important to remember is that rituals can also provide an anchor, a steadying point for you and those close to you when you are experiencing intense change. As Mitch Wilder, a recent single parent of two teenage daughters, remarked, "That weekly Sunday night dinner, which we hold week in and week out with my daughters and my dad, gives us all a sense of connection despite the changes. My dad is getting old and when he's not up to going out, we take the dinner to his apartment. My kids work after school, and they go out with their friends much of the weekend, but Sunday night is sacred."

When Rituals Hold Painful Memories

As you've worked with this book, you may have come in touch with very painful memories of childhood and family rituals. Because rituals do enable a sense of continuity over time, they may all too easily connect us with anguished parts of our past. If you come from a family that was fractured by alcoholism, drug addiction, or abuse, you may recall birthday parties that were canceled, Thanksgivings that were ruined, or nightly dinners that were filled with violence. Intense marital conflict, parent-child relationship turmoil, or angry cutoffs with extended family may have overwhelmed or eroded family rituals. Since rituals often stand out for us as condensed dramas of what went on in our families, these memories can intrude even as you are embarking on a whole new ritual path for yourself. We have talked to people who have abandoned nearly all rituals in their adult lives because the memories evoked by current rituals are simply too painful. If you begin to revitalize your rituals and you find that very difficult material from your own family-of-origin is evoked, you may want to consult with a therapist, or if you are already in therapy, talk some of this over with your therapist. You may want to open a conversation about rituals in a self-help group, where you will likely find many friends who struggle with painful ritual memories. In a safe environment, even highly anxiety-provoking memories of past rituals can become a resource of your own growth.

When you are deciding where to go from here with the rituals in your life and you have unhappy recollections of earlier rituals, don't select the most difficult ritual as a place to begin. If family vacations in your own childhood were filled with furious arguments, you will likely do better to start with a ritual that is less loaded. If your extended family left in silent hurt during Christmas three years ago, don't try to repair relationships by inviting everyone over for Christmas. Give yourself all of the time that you need to reflect on earlier rituals, and to let those who participate in rituals with you know when particular rituals evoke painful memories. Use regular time, not ritual time, to do the slow work of relationship reconciliation.

Remember, too, that rituals have the capacity to hold and express contradictions. As you work and play to make a different kind of birthday celebration, for instance, than you were able to have as a child, you may want to include a moment that deliberately helps you to reflect on what was in the past and move into the present. When Karen Gorlin found that Thanksgiving, Christmas, and other holidays were especially difficult to create because her own mother had been an alcoholic who drank to excess at every celebration, she began to add a small, private piece to her rituals. Before her family sits down for holiday dinners, she goes to her own favorite place in the house by herself. For just fifteen minutes, she takes out an empty Scotch bottle and reflects on what these rituals had been like for her as a child. When the fifteen minutes are up, she puts the bottle away and is able to fully enter into her current ritual life. "Over the many years that I've done this, the meanings of that Scotch bottle have changed," Karen said. "At first, it contained my anger, and seemed to stop me from totally nonsensical fights with my husband and children that used to happen at holidays. Later, it seemed to hold my sorrow that things were the way they were when I was a kid. Recently, I've noticed that when I sit down for my fifteen minutes, I'm flooded with wanting to understand what was behind my mother's pain."

Hearing Everyone's Voice

The best resource for creating meaningful rituals is, of course, each person's own experience of any given ritual. Tapping that experience can help you begin to alter unsatisfying rituals and make the difference between rituals that are guided by only one person and rituals that feel "owned" by all.

One good way to be sure that everyone has a voice in how rituals are shaped and reshaped is to ask all participants soon after a ritual is over to write down the three best aspects and the three worst aspects of that ritual experience.[2] The three best can be parts of the ritual that you absolutely want to preserve and repeat, or they might be something that can never happen again, but whose memory you deeply cherish and want to maintain. The three worst are those parts of the ritual that really need to change and that you hope you will never experience again. Writing your responses down shortly after the ritual allows for the immediacy and intensity surrounding the ritual to stay alive, while reducing needless conflict. The views of each person, from the smallest child to the oldest adult, are respected as valid. If this is an annual ritual, put these comments away in a box without discussing them. The symbolism of everyone writing the most heartfelt opinions about a given ritual and then placing these aside for a while announces in action that everyone is involved and that it's okay to take some time before talking together about what should happen next. Six or eight weeks before that particular ritual rolls around again, take these written responses out and read them aloud together. Some of what people wrote in this "postritual" ritual may no longer seem important. Or angry moments may have become humorous with the passage of time. Those items that remain important can form the basis of planning the ritual this time. As you talk together, you will discover what each person wants to maintain and continue, what may need some changing to more closely express changing realities, and what should disappear. If you do this for a few years, your rituals will become closer and closer to what everyone truly wants.

If you want to examine a daily or weekly ritual, you may want to collect "best" and "worst" responses for several days or weeks in a row, and agree upon a time when you will look at them together. Don't be too surprised if you discover that the "worst" on one day, such as eating in front of the television when you really want to talk with your spouse, turns out to be the "best" on a day when you're just too frazzled from work to have a conversation. Seeing these differences will help you refine daily rituals so that they truly fit your life circumstances.

Certain rituals in our lives can be satisfying for many years, and then can start to feel rigid or obligatory. Often this is because we haven't paid enough attention to the developmental changes in all three generations. We may keep telling ourselves that "this is a wonderful ritual" because once it was. Using the "postritual" ritual or your own variation of it can help keep you current about everyone's needs. Sometimes one seemingly small complaint, like the year Seth Allenby, fifteen, wrote that the worst thing about Easter was having to sit at the children's table where he had sat all of his life, can speak volumes about what is happening in the family. "Hearing what Seth had to say, and making a seat for him at the adult table this Easter, told me there were lots of changes going on in my family. My firstborn was growing up, and the others weren't far behind," said Marsha, Seth's mother. "My husband and I were entering a different phase of our marriage and hardest of all, my parents were getting old. As long as Seth sat at that children's table, I didn't have to think about all of this, even though it was happening right under my nose."

You may discover that one person's "best" is another person's "worst." For instance, Sal Morano adored the large Italian Christmas Eve gathering at his parents' home. His wife of two years, Christina O'Connor, never felt comfortable at these celebrations—they were simply too unfamiliar to her, as she came from a family where Christmas Eve meant going to Midnight Mass and then going to sleep. Sal's family felt overwhelming to her, but she just felt too shy to raise the issue. The opportunity to write down their responses about Christmas opened the way for them to talk about their differences. When they got stuck in their own point of view, they reversed roles. "I began to see that my family really hadn't done enough to make Christina feel welcome," Sal said, "and I began to think about some things I could do to change that, including not running off to be with my brothers the minute we entered the house, and telling my father that there would be no more jokes about the Irish!" "I saw how important this gathering was to him, and we began to talk about how we could change Christmas Day itself to reflect more of what I needed in the holiday, including a bit more focus on the spiritual part of the holiday," Christina remarked. Their ritual became less imbalanced and more flexible. If your "best" is someone else's "worst," try to come to the discussion with a spirit of openness. Remember that meaningful rituals are most often not the same for each participant, and that to try to make them so is to court a rigid ritual style. Aim to develop rituals that contain at least some of the elements that each person finds satisfying.

Rituals: The Larger Picture

The rituals in our lives contribute to our changing sense of ourselves over time, while also connecting us to the generations who came before us. They are a bridge capable of linking our history, our present lives, and what we most hope for our children, our grandchildren, and our great-grandchildren. They can provide an opening into ways of being and beliefs that both affirm our own and are totally different from our own.

Your present ritual life is no doubt both similar to and quite different from that of your parents and grandparents. The adult ritual lives of today's children and grandchildren will both resemble ours and be brand-new. Take a moment to imagine a ritual in your or your family's life in the future. You may want to think about a year from now, or five years, or twenty-five years. What subtle changes do you think will have occurred? What major changes? And what will look quite the same as now? Are there symbols and actions that you hope will be handed down and continued? How will this happen? Who will do this?

You may want to think about your family and your culture's ritual life a hundred years from now, a time when human beings will still be making rituals. As perhaps no other aspect of life can do, it is our rituals that simultaneously connect us with what is universal in human experience, while allowing our own unique personhood, family, ethnic group, and culture to emerge. We wish you meaning, connection with those you love and care for, and safe passage in all of your rituals.

Authors' Note

We hope this book has been meaningful to you. Our own interest in rituals never seems to end. We would be delighted to hear how you use this book, and what rituals you shape or reshape. Please write us.

EVAN IMBER-BLACK, PH.D.
Department of Psychiatry
Albert Einstein College of Medicine
Bronx Municipal Hospital Center
Pelham Parkway South and Eastchester Road
Nurses Residence Building—Room 4N17
Bronx, NY 10461

JANINE ROBERTS, ED.D.
School, Consulting and Counseling Psychology Program
University of Massachusetts
460 Hills South
Amherst, MA 01003

Notes

CHAPTER 1

1. More than thirteen percent of all children under the age of eighteen are living in step-families. One-third of all children born in the 1980s may live with a step-parent before they are eighteen.

By the year 2030, elders (age sixty-five and over) will be about 21 percent of the total population in the United States. In 1960, they were 9.3 percent. Women continue to live on the average seven to eight years longer than men. (*Newsweek*, Winter/Spring 1990 special issue on The 21st Century Family, pp. 24, 63.)

2. Tad Tuleja, *Curious Customs: The Stories Behind 296 Popular American Rituals* (New York: Harmony Books, 1987).

CHAPTER 2

1. *New York Times*, July 15, 1991, p. B2.

2. For a moving discussion of rituals to heal and aid in the recovery from political terror, see Cecilia Kohen's chapter, "Political Traumas, Oppression and Rituals," in E. Imber-Black, J. Roberts, and R. Whiting, eds., *Rituals in Families and Family Therapy* (New York: W. W. Norton & Co., 1988).

3. You can contact the Clothesline Project at the Cape Cod Women's Agenda, P.O. Box 822, Brewster, MA 02631.

4. *Ms.*, July/August 1991, p. 95.

5. E. Imber-Black, "Ritual Themes in Families and Family Therapy," in E. Imber-Black, J. Roberts, and R. Whiting, eds., *Rituals in Families and Family Therapy* (New York: W. W. Norton & Co., 1988).

6. *Ibid.*

7. M. Selvini-Palazzoli, L. Boscolo, G. Cecchin, and G. Prata, "A Ritualized Prescription in Family Therapy: Odd Days and Even Days," *Journal of Family Counseling*, 4 (3) 1978, pp. 3–9. This article describes an innovative intervention for therapy, especially useful when children are receiving conflicting and competing messages from parents.

8. T. Tuleja, *Curious Customs: The Stories Behind 296 Popular American Rituals* (New York: Harmony Books, 1987).

9. We thank our colleague Richard Whiting for this creative ritual.

CHAPTER 4

1. Judith Davis, "Mazel Tov: The Bar Mitzvah as a Multigenerational Ritual of Change and Continuity," in E. Imber-Black, J. Roberts, and R. Whiting, eds., *Rituals in Families and Family Therapy* (New York: W. W. Norton & Co., 1988), pp. 177–208.

2. The chuppah was originally a chamber reserved for the bride. Later, when weddings were held out of doors, the chuppah demarcated a special place from the rest of the marketplace. See Richard Siegel, Michael Strassfeld, and Sharon Strassfeld, eds., *The Jewish Catalogue*, Volume 1 (Philadelphia: Jewish Publication Society of America, 1973). Thanks are given to Ariel B. Imber for his helpful comments on the symbolism of the chuppah.

3. Jo Robinson and Jean Coppock Staeheli, *Unplug the Christmas Machine: How to Have the Christmas You've Always Wanted* (New York: Quill, 1982), p. 39.

4. "Middletown" is the town of Muncie, Indiana. Family life has been studied closely there since the 1920s. See T. Caplow, H. Bahr, B. A. Chadwick, R. Hill, and M. H. Williamson, *Middletown Families: Fifty Years of Change and Continuity* (Minneapolis: University of Minnesota Press, 1982), p. 230.

5. Robert L. Selman and Lynn H. Schultz, *Making a Friend in Youth: Developmental Theory and Pair Therapy* (Chicago: The University of Chicago Press, 1990).

6. Sheila Alson, "Only My Favorite Mommy," in Nan B. Maglin and Nancy Schneidewind, eds., *Women and Stepfamilies: Voices of Anger and Love* (Philadelphia: Temple University Press, 1989), p. 104.

7. Peter Steinglass, with Linda A. Bennett, Steven J. Wollin, and David Reiss, *The Alcoholic Family* (New York: Basic Books, 1987), pp. 221, 243.

8. L. A. Bennett, S. J. Wolin, D. Reiss, M. Teitelbaum, "Couples at Risk for Transmission of Alcoholism: Protective Influences," *Family Process*, 26 (1987), pp. 111–29.

9. Maymie R. Krythe, *All About Christmas* (New York: Harper & Brothers, 1954).

10. Jo Robinson, and Jean Coppock Staeheli, *Unplug the Christmas Machine: How to Have the Christmas You've Always Wanted* (New York: Quill, 1982), p. 39.

11. Tad Tuleja, *Curious Customs: The Stories Behind 296 Popular American Rituals* (New York: Harmony Books, 1987).

12. Many thanks to our colleague Dr. Richard Whiting, who first developed a form of this grid.

CHAPTER 5

1. E. Imber-Black, "Idiosyncratic Life Cycle Transitions and Therapeutic Rituals," in E. A. Carter and M. McGoldrick, eds., *The Changing Family Life Cycle: A Framework for Family Therapy* (New York: Gardner Press, 1988).

2. For a moving and beautiful pictorial view with explanations of symbols and symbolic action in rituals around the world, see David Cohen, *The Circle of Life: Rituals from the Human Family Album* (San Francisco: HarperCollins, 1991).

CHAPTER 6

1. J. Roberts, "Rituals and Trainees," in E. Imber-Black, J. Roberts, and R. Whiting, eds., *Rituals in Families and Family Therapy* (New York: W. W. Norton & Co., 1988), p. 397.

2. M. Whiteside, "Ritual Performance in Early Remarriage," in E. Imber-Black, J. Roberts, and R. Whiting, eds., *Rituals in Families and Family Therapy* (New York: W. W. Norton & Co, 1988). This chapter is an intriguing piece of research. Mary Whiteside made repeated visits to several newly remarried families in order to detail the ways that rituals work to integrate disparate family backgrounds.

3. S. Lieberman, *Let's Celebrate: Creating New Family Traditions* (New York: The Putnam Publishing Group, 1984). This book contains many creative ritual ideas for families, organized in what the author calls a "recipe book" for families "everywhere struggling to maintain some very old-fashioned values in the context of newfangled life-styles" (p. 18).

CHAPTER 7

1. T. Tuleja, *Curious Customs: The Stories Behind 296 Popular American Rituals* (New York: Harmony Books, 1987), p. 26.

2. Linda Rannells Lewis, *Birthdays* (Boston: Little, Brown & Co., 1976).

3. Theodore C. Humphrey and T. Lin, *We Gather Together: Food and Festival in American Life* (Ann Arbor: University of Michigan Press, 1988), p. 22.

4. S. J. Zeitlin, A. J. Kotlin, and H. Cutting-Baker, eds., *A Celebration of American Family Folklore: Tales and Traditions from the Smithsonian Family Folklore Collection* (New York: Pantheon Books, 1982), pp. 178–79.

5. Letty Cottin Pogrebin, "Celebration Friendship: Ceremonies for a 'Relationship Without Rules,'" *Ms.*, December 1986, pp. 48–51, 77–78.

6. For ideas on how to make a half-birthday party, see the June 1989 issue of *Highlights for Children*. Suggestions include sending half an invitation in the mail one day and the other half the next day, as well as games to play in "halves." The half-birthday party is treated like an unbirthday party.

7. S. J. Zeitlin, A. J. Kotlin, and H. Cutting-Baker, eds., *A Celebration of*

American Family Folklore: Tales and Traditions from the Smithsonian Family Folklore Collection (New York: Pantheon Books, 1982), p. 179.

8. Doug Whynott, *Contact Magazine* (Amherst, Massachusetts), Spring 1989, pp. 38–39.

9. S. J. Zeitlin, A. J. Kotlin, and H. Cutting-Baker, eds., *A Celebration of American Family Folklore: Tales and Traditions from the Smithsonian Family Folklore Collection* (New York: Pantheon Books, 1982), p. 180.

10. *To Celebrate: Reshaping Holidays and Rites of Passage* (Ellenwood, Georgia: Alternatives Press, 1987), p. 210.

CHAPTER 8

1. *To Celebrate: Reshaping Holidays and Rites of Passage* (Ellenwood, Georgia: Alternatives Press, 1987), p. 200.

2. David Feinstein and Peg E. Mayo, *Rituals for Living and Dying* (New York: HarperCollins, 1990), pp. 169–171.

3. Laura Markowitz, "Homosexuality: Are We Still in the Dark?" *The Family Therapy Networker*, January/February 1991, pp. 27–35.

CHAPTER 9

1. Mary Whiteside, "Creation of Family Identity Through Ritual Performance in Early Remarriage, in E. Imber-Black, J. Roberts, and R. Whiting, eds., *Rituals in Families and Family Therapy* (New York: W. W. Norton & Co., 1988), p. 276.

2. S. J. Zeitlin, A. J. Kotlin, and H. Cutting-Baker, eds., *A Celebration of American Family Folklore: Tales and Traditions from the Smithsonian Family Folklore Collection* (New York: Pantheon Books, 1982), pp. 180–81.

3. For excellent tips on how to gather oral history, see the last chapter in S. J. Zeitlin, A. J. Kotlin, and H. Cutting-Baker, eds., *A Celebration of American Family Folklore: Tales and Traditions from the Smithsonian Family Folklore Collection* (New York: Pantheon Books, 1982).

4. "A Reunion of Recipes" (*Better Homes and Gardens* pamphlet, 1988). Free from *Better Homes and Gardens*.

5. Dorothy Spruill Redford, with Michael D'Orso, *Somerset Homecoming: Recovering a Lost Heritage* (New York: Doubleday, 1988), p. 236.

6. S. J. Zeitlin, A. J. Kotlin, and Cutting-Baker, eds., *A Celebration of American Family Folklore: Tales and Traditions from the Smithsonian Family Folklore Collection* (New York: Pantheon Books, 1982), p. 172.

7. Byrd Baylor, *I'm in Charge of Celebrations* (New York: Charles Scribner's Sons, 1986).

CHAPTER 10

1. *Boston Globe Magazine*, November 1990.

2. Jack Larkin, *The Reshaping of Everyday Life, 1790–1840* (New York: Harper & Row, 1988), p. 271.

3. Edna Barth, *Holly, Reindeer and Colored Lights* (New York: Clarion Books, 1971), pp. 18–19.

4. See Susan Mumm's book *Rituals for a New Age: Alternative Weddings, Funerals, Holidays, etc.* (Ann Arbor, Michigan: Quantum Leap Publishing and Distributing, 1987) for a good synopsis of the history of Labor Day.

5. For a more complete list of secular holidays, see Alice van Straalen's *The Book of Holidays Around the World* (New York: E. P. Dutton, 1986). Another good inexpensive resource is the calendar put out by UNICEF each year. It lists all the national holidays of the member countries of the UN, as well as the most significant holidays of the world's major religions. Each calendar also has descriptions of some of the holidays as well as further resources. Write to UNICEF House, 3 UN Plaza, New York, NY 10017.

6. *To Celebrate: Reshaping Holidays and Rites of Passage* (Ellenwood, Georgia: Alternatives Press, 1987).

CHAPTER 11

1. See D. Cohen, *The Circle of Life: Rituals from the Human Family Album* (San Francisco: HarperCollins, 1991). This beautiful volume contains photographs of life-cycle rituals taken from cultures around the world. The common elements of life-cycle rituals are made visually apparent.

2. *Ibid.*, p. 223. The section on funeral rituals provides evidence that flowers have been put on graves of loved ones for at least thirty thousand years.

3. *Ibid.* See particularly the section on "initiation and adolescence" for descriptions of many rituals in traditional cultures that utilize a period of seclusion prior to the ritual event.

4. A. Van Gennep, *The Rites of Passage* (Chicago: University of Chicago Press, 1960). Anthropologist Van Gennep originally described these three times phases as *separation*, the time when special preparations are made and new knowledge is passed on; *liminal* or *transitional*, referring to the ritual event itself when changes are being enacted; and *reaggregation* or *reintegration*, when people return to their community in their new status.

5. Thanks are expressed to Lascelles Black for his description of this Jamaican funeral ritual.

6. See J. Davis, "Mazel Tov: The Bar Mitzvah as a Multigenerational Ritual of Change and Continuity," in E. Imber-Black, J. Roberts, and R. Whiting, eds., *Rituals in Families and Family Therapy* (New York: W. W. Norton & Co.,

1988) for a description of four very different families experiencing Bar Mitzvah and the changes this ritual provided for the child, the family, and the community.

7. E. Imber-Black, "Normative and Therapeutic Rituals in Couples' Therapy," in E. Imber-Black, J. Roberts, and R. Whiting, eds., *Rituals in Families and Family Therapy* (New York: W. W. Norton & Co., 1988).

8. See P. G. McCullough and S. K. Rutenberg, "Launching Children and Moving On," in B. Carter & M. McGoldrick, eds., *The Changing Family Life Cycle: A Framework for Family Therapy* (Boston: Allyn & Bacon, 1988) for a full description of the individual and relationship challenges involved when a young adult leaves home.

9. E. Imber-Black, "Idiosyncratic Life Cycle Transitions and Therapeutic Rituals," in B. Carter and M. McGoldrick, eds., *The Changing Family Life Cycle: A Framework for Family Therapy* (Boston: Allyn & Bacon, 1988).

CHAPTER 12

1. For a clear and complete discussion of the family life cycle, including social class variations, see B. Carter and M. McGoldrick, eds., *The Changing Family Life Cycle: A Framework for Family Therapy* (Boston: Allyn & Bacon, 1988).

2. Our thanks to Gina O'Connell Higgens, Ed.D., for sharing her family's Christmas ritual evaluation tool, from which these ideas have been adapted.

Suggested Reading

Applebaum, Diana Karter. *Thanksgiving: An American Holiday, an American History*. New York: Facts on File Publications, 1985.

Cohen, David, and David Van Biema. *The Circle of Life: Rituals from the Human Family Album*. San Francisco: HarperCollins, 1991.

Cunningham, Nancy Brady. *Feeding the Spirit: How to Create Your Own Rites, Festivals and Celebrations*. San Jose, Calif.: Resource Publications, 1988.

Feinstein, David, and Peg E. Mayo. *Rituals for Living and Dying*. New York: HarperCollins, 1990.

Humphrey, Theodore C., and T. Lin. *We Gather Together: Food and Festival in American Life*. Ann Arbor: University of Michigan Press, 1988.

Imber-Black, Evan, Janine Roberts, and Richard Whiting, eds. *Rituals in Families and Family Therapy*. New York: W. W. Norton, 1988.

Krythe, Maymie R. *All About American Holidays*. New York: Harper & Row, 1962.

Milinaire, Caterine. *Celebrations from Birth to Death and from New Year's to Christmas*. New York: Harmony Books, 1981.

Mumm, Susan M. *Rituals for a New Age: Alternative Weddings, Funerals, Holidays, etc.* Ann Arbor, Mich.: Quantum Leap Publishing & Distributing, 1987.

Robinson, J., and Jean Coppock Staeheli. *Unplug the Christmas Machine: A Complete Guide to Putting Love and Joy Back into the Season*. New York: William Morrow & Co., 1991.

Shenk, Sara Wenger. *Why Not Celebrate!* Intercourse, Pennsylvania: Good Books, 1987.

Siegel, R., M. Strassfeld, and S. Strassfeld, eds. *The Jewish Catalogue*, Vol. 1. Philadelphia: Jewish Publication Society of America, 1973.

To Celebrate: Reshaping Holidays and Rites of Passage. Ellenwood, Georgia: Alternatives Press, 1987.

Tuleja, Tad. *Curious Customs: The Stories Behind 296 Popular American Rituals*. New York: Harmony Books, 1987.

van Straalen, Alice. *The Book of Holidays Around the World*. New York: E. P. Dutton, 1986.

Weiser, Francis X. *The Christmas Book*. New York: Harcourt, Brace, 1952.

_____. *The Easter Book*. New York: Harcourt, Brace, 1954.

Zeitlin, Steven J., Amy J. Kotkin, and Holly Cutting Baker. *A Celebration of American Family Folklore: Tales and Traditions from the Smithsonian Collection*. New York: Pantheon Books, 1982.

Index